CAESAR

THE CIVIL WARS

LCL 39

CAESAR

THE CIVIL WARS

WITH AN ENGLISH TRANSLATION BY

A. G. PESKETT

HARVARD UNIVERSITY PRESS
CAMBRIDGE, MASSACHUSETTS
LONDON, ENGLAND

First published 1914
Reprinted 1921, 1928, 1938, 1951, 1957, 1961, 1966, 1979, 1990,
1996

ISBN 0-674-99043-9

Printed in Great Britain by St Edmundsbury Press Ltd,
Bury St Edmunds, Suffolk, on acid-free paper.
Bound by Hunter & Foulis Ltd, Edinburgh, Scotland.

CONTENTS

INTRODUCTION

THE history of the years 49 and 48 B.C., the period covered by this book, centres round two striking personalities—Gaius Julius Caesar and Gnaeus Pompeius. Caesar, associated with Pompeius and Crassus in the powerful Triumvirate of 60, had further increased his influence and popularity by his vigorous administration of the Consulship in 59. In this year the *lex Vatinia* conferred on him for five years from March 1, 59, the governorship of Gallia Cisalpina and Illyricum, to which the Senate subsequently added Gallia Narbonensis. This office was renewed in 55 by the *lex Trebonia* for another five years, from March 54 to March 49. During this period he subjugated Gaul by a series of brilliant campaigns, the details of which are familiar to all readers of the *Gallic War*. At the conclusion of this war keen observers began to recognize that the Roman world possessed a man of military capacity equal to that of Pompeius, and of personal qualities that outshone those of his rival. His daring exploits, his profuse liberality, his attractive humanity, and the extraordinary versatility of his genius, in which he may be compared with the first Napoleon, made him subsequently the most striking figure in the world of his day. Pompeius, his son-in-law, was a great and successful soldier who, having subdued the Far East, crushed the power of the pirates, and quelled a

vii

INTRODUCTION

dangerous revolt in Spain, undoubtedly aspired to the supremacy once held by Sulla. He had been three times Consul—on the third occasion, in 52, for some months without a colleague—yet, notwithstanding his apparent power, he seems to have had no firm hold on the mass of his countrymen; his stiff formality stirred no enthusiasm, his political vacillation made him generally mistrusted. Between two such men, each at the head of a veteran army, one the popular democratic leader, the other, nominally at any rate, the champion of the senatorial order and of all who upheld the constitutional republic, an open rupture was inevitable. The severance came slowly. In 54 Pompeius lost his wife Julia, Caesar's daughter; and in 53 M. Crassus, who, as one of the Triumvirate, had also served as a connecting link, was killed in battle with the Parthians. Pompeius, as sole Consul in 52, had a unique opportunity of consolidating his position and arming himself against his great rival by various measures passed in his own interests. He posed as the defender of the republic and the restorer of social order. He obtained a prolongation of his administration in Spain for another five years, by which he secured the continued control of a powerful army. The divergence of aim and policy was further accentuated by the acrimonious discussions that began in 52 about Caesar's candidature for the Consulship of 48, and the difficulty of adjusting the conflicting claims of provincial governorship and personal canvass at Rome. Caesar's provincial administration terminated strictly on March 1, 49, but he wished to be allowed to retain his proconsular command till the commencement of his Consulship and the arrival of his successor in January 48, knowing that if he appeared in Rome as a private person

he would be liable to impeachment. We need not enter now into the merits of this dispute, which involved legal technicalities and was hotly debated by the constitutional lawyers on each side. It is sufficient to say that towards the end of 50 matters reached a deadlock. Caesar, who had entered Cisalpine Gaul to watch events, sent overtures to Rome with the desire, if we may believe his statements, of promoting a peaceable settlement; but, finding his efforts unavailing, he sent an ultimatum to the Senate on January 1, 49, by the hands of G. Curio, whose adherence he had bought for an immense sum of money, offering to disband his army if Pompeius would do the same. The Pompeian party in the Senate strongly resisted this proposal, and a vote was passed that Caesar should disband his army by a fixed date. The tribunes, M. Antonius and Q. Cassius, interposed their veto, which led to considerable disorder. At last, after a prolonged debate, the Senate passed the summary decree, adopted only in times of supreme peril, that all magistrates should take measures to protect the state from harm. This decree, by removing all constitutional checks, was equivalent to a proclamation of martial law. The tribunes fled to Caesar at Ravenna, and he at once crossed the Rubicon. The great war had now begun. The three books of the *Bellum Civile* narrate the fortunes of the war from its outbreak to the decisive battle of Pharsalus in June 48, with a brief sketch of the subsequent events leading up to the Alexandrian war.

The narrative may be regarded as in the main trustworthy, though it is evidently intended by Caesar to justify his political action in the eyes of his countrymen, and sometimes he appears to mis-

state the political situation or understate a military reverse. Caesar's style is singularly clear, simple, and restrained, enlivened now and then by a touch of vivacity, emotion, or sarcasm. Perhaps its most prominent characteristic is his constant use of the present tense, due, I suppose, to his vivid realization of the scenes that he describes. He sees as it were the past event unfolding itself before his eyes. This peculiarity, though not generally acceptable in English, I have thought fit to preserve to some extent in my translation.

Like all ancient historians, Caesar omits much that we should be glad to know. It probably never occurred to him that in future ages his campaigns would be closely investigated by students, military and civilian, who would be distracted by the paucity of chronological and topographical information that he vouchsafes. One wishes he could have known that eighteen centuries and a half after his death the greatest conqueror in the history of the world, as ruler of the Gaul that he had subdued, would compile a *Précis des guerres de Jules César,* and that a later Emperor of the French would organize, and himself contribute to, an elaborate *Histoire de Jules César,* to be completed at a later date by a distinguished soldier and scholar, Baron Stoffel.

The perplexities of the modern editor are increased by the defects of the MSS. In two or three places whole passages have been lost, and in many others the readings are so various and uncertain that one cannot be sure of the proper interpretation. The manuscripts date mostly from the tenth, eleventh, and twelfth centuries. They fall roughly into three groups, which may be represented by the following scheme, in which **X** represents the arche-

type, and α, β, γ, δ, ε certain supposed links in the series.

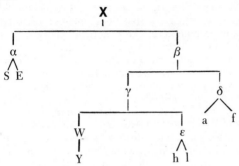

In this scheme

    S = Laurentianus Ashburnhamiensis.
    E = Lovaniensis.
    W = Mediceus Laurentianus I.
    Y = Mediceus Laurentianus II.
    h = Ursinianus.
    l = Riccardianus.
    a = Thuaneus.
    f = Vindobonensis.

The *editio princeps* was published in Rome in 1469.
I have noted variations of reading here and there and sundry plausible corrections, restricting myself mainly to such as seemed of interest or importance. It may be worth mentioning that the *tabula coniecturarum* in Heinrich Meusel's great lexicon occupies, for the *Bellum Civile* alone, about fifty-six two-columned pages.
Anything in the way of commentary on the sub-

INTRODUCTION

ject-matter is excluded by the scope of the Loeb Library, and I have only added a few explanatory notes here and there, though there is scarcely a chapter in the book that does not give occasion for lengthy comment in the sphere of political or military history, antiquities, and topography. My own Pitt Press edition of the Third Book (1900) contains one hundred pages of notes, few of which, I think, are wholly superfluous. The reader, if he wishes for a thorough understanding of Caesar's narrative, should have for reference some comprehensive history of Rome, such as Mommsen, Drumann, Ferrero, or Heitland; a good recent manual of antiquities, especially the *Companion to Latin Studies;* and above all the great work of Baron Stoffel, *Guerre civile de J. César* (2 vols.), with its admirable atlas, from which I have taken some maps and plans for this edition. For the constitutional questions involved in Caesar's candidature for the Consulship the student should consult Mommsen, *Die Rechtsfrage zwischen Caesar und dem Senat*, and Nissen, *Uber den Ausbruch des Bürgerkrieges*, to mention only two among the numerous books, pamphlets, or articles in periodicals, British or foreign, dealing with the constitutional history of the period. The best recent edition of the *Civil War* that I am acquainted with is that of F. Kraner and F. Hofmann, revised by H. Meusel (1906), in the Weidmann Series.

BIBLIOGRAPHICAL NOTE (1990)

Editions:

César, La guerre civile, texte établi et traduit par Pierre Fabre, 2 vols, Paris 1936

C.Iuli Caesaris Commentarii (Teubner vol. 2): A. Klotz, Leipzig 1957[2]

Commentary:

F. Kraner, F. Hofmann, H. Meusel, and H. Oppermann, Berlin 1959

Other:

F. E. Adcock, *Caesar as Man of Letters*, Cambridge 1956

K. Barwick, *Caesars Bellum Civile: Tendenz, Abfassungszeit und Stil*, Leipzig 1951

Virginia Brown, *The Textual Transmission of Caesar's Civil War*, Leiden 1972

Matthias Gelzer, *Caesar: Politician and Statesman* (Eng. translation of the 1960[6] German edition), Oxford: Blackwell and Cambridge: Harvard University Press 1968

BOOK I

LIBER I

1 LITTERIS Caesaris consulibus redditis aegre ab his impetratum est summa tribunorum plebis contentione, ut in senatu recitarentur; ut vero ex litteris ad senatum referretur, impetrari non potuit. Referunt consules de re publica.[1] Incitat L. Lentulus consul senatum rei publicae se non defuturum pollicetur, si audacter ac fortiter sententias dicere velint; sin Caesarem respiciant atque eius gratiam sequantur, ut superioribus fecerint temporibus, se sibi consilium capturum neque senatus auctoritati obtemperaturum: habere se quoque ad Caesaris gratiam atque amicitiam receptum. In eandem sententiam loquitur Scipio: Pompeio esse in animo reipublicae non deesse, si senatus sequatur; si cunctetur atque agat lenius, nequiquam eius auxilium, si postea velit, senatum imploraturum.

2 Haec Scipionis oratio, quod senatus in urbe habebatur Pompeiusque aderat, ex ipsius ore Pompei mitti videbatur. Dixerat aliquis leniorem sententiam, ut primo M. Marcellus, ingressus in eam orationem, non oportere ante de ea re ad senatum

---

[1] MSS. add in civitate: H. Schiller incitat.

2

BOOK I

WHEN Caesar's dispatch had been handed to the 1
consuls, the tribunes, with difficulty and after much
wrangling, gained their permission for it to be read
in the senate, but they could not obtain consent for
a motion to be brought before the senate on the
subject of the dispatch. The consuls bring forward
a motion on the state of public affairs. The consul
L. Lentulus puts pressure on the senate, and promises that he will not fail the republic if the
senators are willing to express their opinions with
boldness and resolution; but if they pay regard to
Caesar and try to win favour with him as they have
done on previous occasions, he says that he will
consider his own interests and will not obey their
authority. "I too," said he, "can shelter myself
under the favour and friendship of Caesar." Scipio
expresses himself in similar terms—that Pompeius is
inclined not to desert the republic if the senate
follows him; but if it delays and acts remissly, it
will in vain solicit his aid should it wish to do so
in the future.

This speech of Scipio appeared to come from the 2
mouth of Pompeius himself, since the senate was
meeting in the city and Pompeius was close at hand.
Some had expressed less rigorous views, such as
M. Marcellus, who at first embarked on a speech to
the effect that the question ought not to be referred to

3

referri, quam delectus tota Italia habiti et exercitus conscripti essent, quo praesidio tuto et libere[1] senatus, quae vellet, decernere auderet; ut M. Calidius, qui censebat, ut Pompeius in suas provincias proficisceretur, ne qua esset armorum causa: timere Caesarem ereptis ab eo duabus legionibus, ne ad eius periculum reservare et retinere eas ad urbem Pompeius videretur; ut M. Rufus, qui sententiam Calidii paucis fere mutatis rebus sequebatur. Hi omnes convicio L. Lentuli consulis correpti exagitabantur. Lentulus sententiam Calidii pronuntiaturum se omnino negavit. Marcellus perterritus conviciis a sua sententia discessit. Sic vocibus consulis, terrore praesentis exercitus, minis amicorum Pompei plerique compulsi inviti et coacti Scipionis sententiam sequuntur: uti ante certam diem Caesar exercitum dimittat; si non faciat, eum adversus rem publicam facturum videri. Intercedit M. Antonius, Q. Cassius, tribuni plebis. Refertur confestim de intercessione tribunorum. Dicuntur sententiae graves; ut quisque acerbissime crudelissimeque dixit, ita quam maxime ab inimicis Caesaris collaudatur.

3   Misso ad vesperum senatu omnes, qui sunt eius ordinis, a Pompeio evocantur. Laudat promptos Pompeius atque in posterum confirmat, segniores castigat atque incitat. Multi undique ex veteribus Pompei exercitibus spe praemiorum atque ordinum

[1] *Meusel* tutus libere.

4

the senate till levies had been held throughout Italy and armies enrolled under whose protection the senate might venture to make such decrees as it wished safely and freely; such, too, as M. Calidius, who expressed the opinion that Pompeius should go to his own provinces in order that there might be no motive for hostilities: Caesar, he said, was afraid lest it should be thought that Pompeius, having extorted two legions from him, was holding them back and retaining them near Rome with a view to imperilling him; such also as M. Rufus, who with a few modifications followed the opinion of Calidius. All these speakers were assailed with vehement invective by the consul L. Lentulus. He absolutely refused to put the motion of Calidius, and Marcellus, alarmed by the invectives, abandoned his proposal. Thus most of the senators, compelled by the language of the consul, intimidated by the presence of the army and by the threats of the friends of Pompeius, against their will and yielding to pressure, adopt the proposal of Scipio that Caesar should disband his army before a fixed date, and that, if he failed to do so, he should be considered to be meditating treason against the republic. The tribunes M. Antonius and Q. Cassius intervene. The question of their intervention is immediately brought before the senate. Opinions of weighty import are expressed, and the more harsh and cruel the speech the more it is applauded by the personal enemies of Caesar.

When the senate was dismissed in the evening all 3 the members of the order are summoned out of the city by Pompeius. He praises the zealous and encourages them for the future; the sluggish he reproves and stimulates. Everywhere a number of reserves from the old armies of Pompeius are called

evocantur, multi ex duabus legionibus, quae sunt
traditae a Caesare, arcessuntur. Completur urbs et
ipsum comitium tribunis, centurionibus, evocatis.
Omnes amici consulum, necessarii Pompei atque
eorum, qui veteres inimicitias cum Caesare gerebant,
in senatum coguntur; quorum vocibus et concursu
terrentur infirmiores, dubii confirmantur, plerisque
vero libere decernendi potestas eripitur. Pollicetur
L. Piso censor sese iturum ad Caesarem, item L.
Roscius praetor, qui de his rebus eum doceant: sex
dies ad eam rem conficiendam spatii postulant.
Dicuntur etiam ab nonnullis sententiae, ut legati
ad Caesarem mittantur, qui voluntatem senatus ei
proponant.

4 Omnibus his resistitur, omnibusque oratio consulis, Scipionis, Catonis opponitur. Catonem veteres inimicitiae Caesaris incitant et dolor repulsae.
Lentulus aeris alieni magnitudine et spe exercitus
ac provinciarum et regum appellandorum largitioni-
bus movetur, seque alterum fore Sullam inter suos
gloriatur, ad quem summa imperii redeat. Scipionem
eadem spes provinciae atque exercituum impellit,
quos se pro necessitudine partiturum cum Pompeio
arbitratur, simul iudiciorum metus, adulatio atque
ostentatio sui et potentium,[1] qui in re publica iudi-
ciisque tum plurimum pollebant. Ipse Pompeius,
ab inimicis Caesaris incitatus et quod neminem

[1] *The text of this passage is probably corrupt.*

out to serve by the prospect of prizes and promotion; many are summoned from the two legions handed over by Caesar. The city and the comitium[1] itself are filled with tribunes, centurions, reserves. All the friends of the consuls, all the adherents of Pompeius and of those whose enmity to Caesar was of long standing, are compelled to attend the senate. By their clamorous throngs the weaker are terrified and the wavering are confirmed, while the majority are robbed of the privilege of free decision. The censor L. Piso promises to go to Caesar, also the praetor L. Roscius, to inform him of these matters. They demand a period of six days for the execution of their purpose. Some express the opinion that envoys should be sent to Caesar to set before him the feelings of the senate.

All these speakers encounter opposition and are 4 confronted with speeches from the consul, from Scipio, and from Cato. Cato is goaded on by his old quarrels with Caesar and vexation at his defeat.[2] Lentulus is moved by the greatness of his debts, by the prospect of a military command and a province, and by the lavish bribes of rulers claiming the title of king, and boasts among his friends that he will prove a second Sulla to whom shall fall the supreme command. Scipio is stimulated by the same hope of a province and of armies, which he thinks that kinship will entitle him to share with Pompeius; also by the dread of the law courts, by the flattery of certain powerful men who had then great influence in public affairs and in the law courts, and by his own and their ostentatious character. Pompeius, urged on by Caesar's enemies and by his desire that no one should

---

[1] A part of the forum adjacent to the Senate House.
[2] When he stood for the consulship in 51.

dignitate secum exaequari volebat, totum se ab eius amicitia averterat et cum communibus inimicis in gratiam redierat, quorum ipse maximam partem illo affinitatis tempore iniunxerat Caesari; simul infamia duarum legionum permotus, quas ab itinere Asiae Syriaeque ad suam potentiam dominatumque converterat, rem ad arma deduci studebat.

5   His de causis aguntur omnia raptim atque turbate. Nec docendi Caesaris propinquis eius spatium datur, nec tribunis plebis sui periculi deprecandi neque etiam extremi iuris intercessione retinendi, quod L. Sulla reliquerat, facultas tribuitur, sed de sua salute septimo die cogitare coguntur, quod illi turbulentissimi superioribus temporibus tribuni plebis octavo denique mense suarum actionum respicere ac timere consuerant.[1] Decurritur ad illud extremum atque ultimum senatusconsultum, quo nisi paene in ipso urbis incendio atque in desperatione omnium salutis sceleratorum audacia numquam ante descensum est: dent operam consules, praetores, tribuni plebis quique pro consulibus sint ad urbem, ne quid res publica detrimenti capiat. Haec senatusconsulto perscribuntur a. d. VII. Id. Ian. Itaque v primis diebus, quibus haberi senatus potuit, qua ex die consulatum iniit Lentulus, biduo excepto comitiali

----

[1] *The text of this sentence and of the next is faulty, and cannot be restored with certainty.*

8

be on the same level of authority with himself, had completely withdrawn himself from Caesar's friendship and become reconciled with their common enemies, most of whom he had himself imposed upon Caesar at the time of their connexion by marriage.[1] Stirred, too, by the discredit attaching to his diversion of two legions from their route by Asia and Syria and his appropriation of them for his own power and supremacy, he was eager that the issue should be brought to the arbitrament of war.

For these reasons everything is done in hurry and 5 confusion. Caesar's friends are allowed no time to inform him, nor are the tribunes given any opportunity of protesting against the peril that threatened them, nor even of retaining, by the exercise of their veto, the most fundamental of their rights, which L. Sulla had left them, but within the limit of seven days they are compelled to take measures for their own safety, whereas the most turbulent of the tribunes in earlier times had been wont to regard with apprehension the conclusion of at least eight months of administration. Recourse is had to that extreme and ultimate decree of the senate which had never previously been resorted to except when the city was at the point of destruction and all despaired of safety through the audacity of malefactors: "The consuls, the praetors, the tribunes, and all the proconsulars who are near the city shall take measures that the state incur no harm." These resolutions are recorded by decree of the senate on January 7. So on the first five days on which a meeting of the senate could be held after the date on which Lentulus entered on his consulship, except two election days, decrees of

[1] Julia, daughter of Caesar and wife of Pompeius, died in 54.

et de imperio Caesaris et de amplissimis viris, tribunis plebis, gravissime acerbissimeque decernitur. Profugiunt statim ex urbe tribuni plebis seseque ad Caesarem conferunt. Is eo tempore erat Ravennae exspectabatque suis lenissimis postulatis responsa, si qua hominum aequitate res ad otium deduci posset.

6 Proximis diebus habetur extra urbem senatus. Pompeius eadem illa, quae per Scipionem ostenderat, agit; senatus virtutem constantiamque collaudat; copias suas exponit; legiones habere sese paratas x; praeterea cognitum compertumque sibi, alieno esse animo in Caesarem milites neque eis posse persuaderi, uti eum defendant aut sequantur. Statim de reliquis rebus ad senatum refertur: tota Italia delectus habeatur; Faustus Sulla propere in Mauritaniam mittatur; pecunia uti ex aerario Pompeio detur. Refertur etiam de rege Iuba, ut socius sit atque amicus; Marcellus vero passurum se in praesentia negat. De Fausto impedit Philippus, tribunus plebis. De reliquis rebus senatusconsulta perscribuntur. Provinciae privatis decernuntur duae consulares, reliquae praetoriae. Scipioni obvenit Syria, L. Domitio Gallia; Philippus et Cotta privato consilio praetereuntur, neque eorum sortes deiciuntur. In reliquas provincias praetores mittuntur. Neque exspectant, quod superioribus annis acciderat, ut de eorum imperio ad populum feratur, paludatique

10

the severest and harshest character are passed affecting
Caesar's imperial command and those highly important
officials, the tribunes of the people. The tribunes at
once flee from the city and betake themselves to Caesar.
He was at that time at Ravenna and was awaiting a
reply to his very lenient demands, in the hope that
by some sense of equity a peaceable conclusion might
be reached.

On the following days the senate meets outside 6
the city. Pompeius carries out the policy which he
had indicated by the mouth of Scipio. He commends
the manly consistency of the senate, and sets forth
the strength of his forces, showing that he has ten
legions ready to hand, and, moreover, that he had
ascertained for certain that the troops were ill-
disposed to Caesar and could not be persuaded to
defend or follow him. Other matters are at once
referred to the senate—that a levy should be held
throughout Italy, that Faustus Sulla should be
at once sent into Mauritania, and that a grant of
money should be made to Pompeius from the
treasury. A motion is also proposed that King
Juba should be styled Ally and Friend. But Marcellus refuses to allow this for the present. The
tribune Philippus vetoes the motion about Faustus.
On the other matters decrees of the senate are recorded in writing. The provinces, two consular, the
rest praetorian, are decreed to private persons.
Syria falls to Scipio, Gallia to L. Domitius; Philippus
and Cotta are passed over by private arrangement,
nor are their lots cast into the urn. To the rest of
the provinces praetors are sent. Nor do they wait,
as had been the habit in previous years, for a motion
to be brought before the people about their imperial
command; but, wearing the scarlet military cloak, they

11

votis nuncupatis exeunt. Consules, quod ante id
tempus accidit numquam, ex urbe proficiscuntur,
lictoresque habent in urbe et Capitolio privati contra
omnia vetustatis exempla. Tota Italia delectus ha-
bentur, arma imperantur; pecuniae a municipiis
exiguntur, e fanis tolluntur: omnia divina huma-
naque iura permiscentur.

7　　Quibus rebus cognitis Caesar apud milites con-
tionatur. Omnium temporum iniurias inimicorum
in se commemorat; a quibus deductum ac deprava-
tum Pompeium queritur invidia atque obtrectatione
laudis suae, cuius ipse honori et dignitati semper
faverit adiutorque fuerit. Novum in re publica intro-
ductum exemplum queritur, ut tribunicia intercessio
armis notaretur atque opprimeretur, quae superioribus annis armis esset restituta.[1] Sullam nudata
omnibus rebus tribunicia potestate tamen interces-
sionem liberam reliquisse. Pompeium, qui amissa
restituisse videatur, dona etiam, quae ante habuerint,
ademisse. Quotienscumque sit decretum, darent
operam magistratus, ne quid res publica detrimenti
caperet (qua voce et quo senatusconsulto populus
Romanus ad arma sit vocatus), factum in perniciosis
legibus, in vi tribunicia, in secessione populi templis
locisque editioribus occupatis: atque haec superioris

---

[1] *The clause* quae . . . restituta *should perhaps be omitted as
difficult to reconcile with the context.*

leave Rome after offering the usual vows. The consuls quit the city, a thing which had never previously happened, and private persons have lictors in the city and the Capitol,[1] contrary to all the precedents of the past. Levies are held throughout Italy, arms are requisitioned, sums of money are exacted from the municipal towns and carried off from the temples, and all divine and human rights are thrown into confusion.

When this was known Caesar addresses his troops. 7 He relates all the wrongs that his enemies had ever done him, and complains that Pompeius had been led astray and corrupted by them through jealousy and a desire to detract from his credit, though he had himself always supported and aided his honour and dignity. He complains that a new precedent had been introduced into the state whereby the right of tribunicial intervention, which in earlier years had been restored by arms, was now being branded with ignominy and crushed by arms. Sulla, he said, though stripping the tribunicial power of everything, had nevertheless left its right of intervention free, while Pompeius, who had the credit of having restored the privileges that were lost, had taken away even those that they had before. There had been no instance of the decree that the magistrates should take measures to prevent the state from suffering harm (the declaration and decision of the senate by which the Roman people are called to arms) except in the case of pernicious laws, tribunicial violence, a popular secession, or the seizure of temples and elevated positions: and he explains that these precedents of a former age had been

[1] Private persons not holding military command could not have lictors in the city.

aetatis exempla expiata Saturnini atque Gracchorum casibus docet; quarum rerum illo tempore nihil factum, ne cogitatum quidem. Hortatur, cuius imperatoris ductu VIIII annis rem publicam felicissime gesserint plurimaque proelia secunda fecerint, omnem Galliam Germaniamque pacaverint, ut eius existimationem dignitatemque ab inimicis defendant. Conclamant legionis XIII, quae aderat, milites—hanc enim initio tumultus evocaverat, reliquae nondum convenerant—sese paratos esse imperatoris sui tribunorumque plebis iniurias defendere.

8   Cognita militum voluntate Ariminum cum ea legione proficiscitur ibique tribunos plebis, qui ad eum profugerant, convenit; reliquas legiones ex hibernis evocat et subsequi iubet. Eo L. Caesar adulescens venit, cuius pater Caesaris erat legatus. Is reliquo sermone confecto, cuius rei causa venerat, habere se a Pompeio ad eum privati officii mandata demonstrat: velle Pompeium se Caesari purgatum, ne ea, quae rei publicae causa egerit, in suam contumeliam vertat. Semper se rei publicae commoda privatis necessitudinibus habuisse potiora. Caesarem quoque pro sua dignitate debere et studium et iracundiam suam rei publicae dimittere neque adeo graviter irasci inimicis, ut, cum illis nocere se speret, rei publicae noceat. Pauca eiusdem generis addit cum excusatione Pompei coniuncta. Eadem fere atque

14

expiated by the downfall of Saturninus and of the Gracchi. No event of this kind had occurred at the time in question or had even been thought of. He exhorts them to defend from his enemies the reputation and dignity of the commander under whose guidance they have administered the state with unfailing good fortune for nine years, fought many successful battles, and pacified the whole of Gaul and Germany. Thereupon the men of the Thirteenth Legion, which was present (he had called this out at the beginning of the disorder; the rest had not yet come together), exclaim that they are ready to repel the wrongs of their commander and of the tribunes.

Having thus learnt the disposition of the soldiery, 8 he sets out for Ariminum with that legion, and there meets the tribunes who had fled to him. The rest of the legions he summons from their winter quarters and orders them to follow him. Thither comes the young L. Caesar whose father was one of Caesar's legates. When their first greetings were over he explains—and this was the real reason of his coming—that he has a message from Pompeius to give him regarding a personal matter. He says that Pompeius wishes to be cleared of reproach in the eyes of Caesar, who should not construe as an affront to himself what he had done for the sake of the state. He had always placed the interests of the republic before private claims. Caesar, too, considering his high position, should give up for the benefit of the state his partisan zeal and passion, nor be so bitterly angry with his enemies as to injure the commonwealth in the hope that he is injuring them. He adds a few other remarks of this kind, at the same time making excuses for Pompeius. The praetor Roscius lays substantially the same proposals before

eisdem verbis[1] praetor Roscius agit cum Caesare sibique Pompeium commemorasse demonstrat.

9   Quae res etsi nihil ad levandas iniurias pertinere videbantur, tamen idoneos nactus homines, per quos ea, quae vellet, ad eum perferrentur, petit ab utroque, quoniam Pompei mandata ad se detulerint, ne graventur sua quoque ad eum postulata deferre, si parvo labore magnas controversias tollere atque omnem Italiam metu liberare possint. Sibi semper primam rei publicae fuisse dignitatem vitaque potiorem. Doluisse se, quod populi Romani beneficium sibi per contumeliam ab inimicis extorqueretur, ereptoque semenstri imperio in urbem retraheretur, cuius absentis rationem haberi proximis comitiis populus iussisset. Tamen hanc iacturam honoris sui rei publicae causa aequo animo tulisse: cum litteras ad senatum miserit, ut omnes ab exercitibus discederent, ne id quidem impetravisse. Tota Italia delectus haberi, retineri legiones ii, quae ab se simulatione Parthici belli sint abductae, civitatem esse in armis. Quonam haec omnia nisi ad suam perniciem pertinere? Sed tamen ad omnia se descendere paratum atque omnia pati rei publicae causa. Proficiscatur Pompeius in suas provincias, ipsi exercitus dimittant, discedant in Italia omnes ab armis, metus e civitate

[1] verbis *Clarke: MSS.* rebus. *Perhaps* eisdem de rebus.

Caesar, and in the same language, and makes it clear that he received them from Pompeius.

Though these proceedings seemed to have no 9
effect in lessening the sense of wrong, nevertheless now that he had found suitable persons to convey his wishes to Pompeius he makes a request of each of them that, as they had brought him the messages of Pompeius, they should not object to convey his demands in reply, in the hope that by a little trouble they might be able to put an end to serious disputes and free the whole of Italy from alarm. "As for myself," he said, "I have always reckoned the dignity of the republic of first importance and preferable to life. I was indignant that a benefit conferred on me by the Roman people was being insolently wrested from me by my enemies, [1] and that, robbed of my six months' command, I was being dragged back to the city, when the people had directed that I should be allowed to be a candidate in absence at the next election. Nevertheless, for the sake of the state I have borne with equanimity this infringement of my prerogative; when I sent a dispatch to the senate proposing that all should give up arms I failed to obtain even this request. Levies are being held throughout Italy, two legions which had been filched from me under the pretence of a Parthian war are being held back, the state is in arms. To what does all this tend but to my own ruin? Still I am prepared to resort to anything, to submit to anything, for the sake of the commonwealth. Let Pompeius go to his own provinces, let us disband our armies, let everyone in Italy lay down his arms, let

[1] If Caesar were recalled in July to stand for the consulship, he would lose the last six months of his proconsular command in Gaul.

tollatur, libera comitia atque omnis res publica senatui populoque Romano permittatur. Haec quo facilius certisque condicionibus fiant et iureiurando sanciantur, aut ipse propius accedat aut se patiatur accedere: fore, uti per colloquia omnes controversiae componantur.

10 Acceptis mandatis Roscius cum L. Caesare Capuam pervenit ibique consules Pompeiumque invenit; postulata Caesaris renuntiat. Illi deliberata re respondent scriptaque ad eum mandata per eos remittunt; quorum haec erat summa: Caesar in Galliam reverteretur, Arimino excederet, exercitus dimitteret; quae si fecisset, Pompeium in Hispanias iturum. Interea, quoad fides esset data Caesarem facturum, quae polliceretur, non intermissuros consules Pompeiumque delectus.

11 Erat iniqua condicio postulare, ut Caesar Arimino excederet atque in provinciam reverteretur, ipsum et provincias et legiones alienas tenere; exercitum Caesaris velle dimitti, delectus habere; polliceri se in provinciam iturum neque, ante quem diem iturus sit, definire, ut, si peracto consulatu Caesar profectus esset, nulla tamen mendacii religione obstrictus videretur; tempus vero colloquio non dare neque accessurum polliceri magnam pacis desperationem afferebat. Itaque ab Arimino M. Antonium cum cohortibus v Arretium mittit; ipse Arimini cum duabus subsistit ibique delectum habere instituit; Pisaurum, Fanum, Anconam singulis cohortibus occupat.

18

fear be banished from the state, let free elections and the whole control of the republic be handed over to the senate and the Roman people. That this may be done more easily and on definite terms and be ratified by an oath, let Pompeius himself come nearer or allow me to approach him. In this way a conference will settle all disputes."

Having received his instructions, Roscius arrives at Capua with L. Caesar, and there finds the consuls and Pompeius, and delivers Caesar's demands. After deliberation they reply and send him back by their hands written instructions, the main purport of which was that Caesar should return to Gaul, quit Ariminum and disband his forces; if he did this, Pompeius would go to the Spanish provinces. Meanwhile, until a pledge was given that Caesar would carry out his promise, the consuls and Pompeius would not interrupt their levies.

It was an unfair bargain to demand that Caesar should quit Ariminum and return to his province while he himself retained his provinces and legions that were not his own: to wish that Caesar's army should be disbanded while he himself continued his levies: to promise that he would go to his province and not to fix a limit of time for his departure, so that if he had not gone when Caesar's consulship was over he would nevertheless be held guiltless of breaking his word: finally, his refusal to give an opportunity for a conference and to promise that he would approach Caesar tended to produce a profound despair of peace. And so he sends M. Antonius with five cohorts from Ariminum to Arretium, and himself stops at Ariminum with two cohorts and arranges to hold a levy there; he occupies Pisaurum, Fanum, and Ancona, each with one cohort.

10

11

CAESAR

12   Interea certior factus Iguvium Thermum praetorem
cohortibus v tenere, oppidum munire, omniumque esse
Iguvinorum optimam erga se voluntatem, Curionem
cum tribus cohortibus, quas Pisauri et Arimini habebat, mittit. Cuius adventu cognito diffisus municipii
voluntati Thermus cohortes ex urbe reducit et profugit. Milites in itinere ab eo discedunt ac domum
revertuntur. Curio summa omnium voluntate Iguvium recipit. Quibus rebus cognitis confisus municipiorum voluntatibus Caesar cohortes legionis XIII
ex praesidiis deducit Auximumque proficiscitur; quod
oppidum Attius cohortibus[1] introductis tenebat delectumque toto Piceno circummissis senatoribus
habebat.

13   Adventu Caesaris cognito decuriones Auximi ad
Attium Varum frequentes conveniunt; docent sui
iudicii rem non esse; neque se neque reliquos mu-
nicipes pati posse C. Caesarem imperatorem, bene
de re publica meritum, tantis rebus gestis oppido
moenibusque prohiberi; proinde habeat rationem
posteritatis et periculi sui. Quorum oratione permotus Varus praesidium, quod introduxerat, ex
oppido educit ac profugit. Hunc ex primo ordine
pauci Caesaris consecuti milites consistere coëgerunt.
Commisso proelio deseritur a suis Varus; nonnulla
pars militum domum discedit; reliqui ad Caesarem
perveniunt, atque una cum eis deprensus L. Pupius,
primi pili centurio, adducitur, qui hunc eundem
ordinem in exercitu Cn. Pompei antea duxerat. At

---

[1] cohortibus *MSS.: cohortibus tribus Paul, perhaps rightly.*

Meanwhile, having been told that the praetor 12
Thermus was holding Iguvium with five cohorts and
fortifying the town, and that all the inhabitants of
Iguvium were extremely well disposed towards himself, he sends Curio thither with the three cohorts
which he had at Pisaurum and Ariminum. Learning of
his approach, Thermus, mistrusting the goodwill of the
community, withdraws his cohorts from the town and
flies. His troops desert him on the way and return
home. Curio with the utmost goodwill of everyone recovers Iguvium. Hearing of this, Caesar, relying on the goodwill of the townsfolk, removes the
cohorts of the Thirteenth Legion from the garrisons
and proceeds to Auximum. This town Attius was
holding with cohorts that he had introduced into
it, and, sending round senators, was levying troops
throughout Picenum.

Learning of Caesar's approach, the decurions of 13
Auximum throng to meet Attius Varus and explain
that they are not free to act at their discretion; that
neither they nor the rest of their fellow-townsmen
can endure that G. Caesar, holding imperial command,
having deserved so well of the state and after per-
forming such exploits, should be prevented from entering the walls of the town: so let Varus have regard to
the future and his own peril. Stirred by their words,
he withdraws from the town the garrison that he had
brought in and takes to flight. A few of Caesar's
men of the first century followed him and compelled
him to halt. An engagement is fought and Varus is
deserted by his followers; some of his men retire to
their homes, the rest make their way to Caesar; and
among them L. Pupius, a centurion of the first
company who had previously held the same rank in
the army of Gn. Pompeius, is arrested with them and

Caesar milites Attianos collaudat, Pupium dimittit, Auximatibus agit gratias seque eorum facti memorem fore pollicetur.

14 Quibus rebus Romam nuntiatis tantus repente terror invasit, ut, cum Lentulus consul ad aperiendum aerarium venisset ad pecuniam Pompeio ex senatusconsulto proferendam, protinus aperto[1] sanctiore aerario ex urbe profugeret. Caesar enim adventare iam iamque et adesse eius equites falso nuntiabantur. Hunc Marcellus collega et plerique magistratus consecuti sunt. Cn. Pompeius pridie eius diei ex urbe profectus iter ad legiones habebat, quas a Caesare acceptas in Apulia hibernorum causa disposuerat. Delectus circa urbem intermittuntur; nihil citra Capuam tutum esse omnibus videtur. Capuae primum se confirmant et colligunt delectumque colonorum, qui lege Iulia Capuam deducti erant, habere instituunt; gladiatoresque, quos ibi Caesar in ludo habebat, ad forum productos Lentulus spe libertatis confirmat atque his equos attribuit et se sequi iussit; quos postea monitus ab suis, quod ea res omnium iudicio reprehendebatur, circum familiares conventus Campani custodiae causa distribuit.

15 Auximo Caesar progressus omnem agrum Picenum percurrit. Cunctae earum regionum praefecturae

---

[1] aperto *MSS.*: non aperto *KII after Rubenius.*

brought before him. Caesar, however, commends the men of Attius' detachment, sends Pupius away, and thanks the inhabitants of Auximum, promising to remember their action.

When these events were announced at Rome such 14 consternation seized at once on the inhabitants that when the consul Lentulus had come to open the treasury for the purpose of providing a sum of money for Pompeius in accordance with a decree of the senate, as soon as ever he had opened the inner treasury he fled from the city; for news was falsely brought that Caesar was on the very point of arriving and that his cavalry had already come. Lentulus was followed by his colleague Marcellus and by most of the magistrates. Gn. Pompeius had left the city the day before and was on his way to the legions which he had taken from Caesar and distributed in winter quarters in Apulia. The levying of troops round the city is broken off; no one thinks there is any safety this side of Capua. It was at Capua that they first rally with renewed courage and begin to raise a levy among the colonists who had been planted there under the Julian law, while Lentulus brings the gladiators, whom Caesar kept in a training school there, into the forum and encourages them by the prospect of liberty, gives them horses, and orders them to follow him; but afterwards, on the admonition of his followers, because such a proceeding was censured by the general judgment, he distributes them for safe keeping among his friends in the burgess-body[1] at Capua.

Caesar, starting from Auximum, traverses the whole 15 of the Picene territory. All the prefectures of those

[1] The Roman citizens inhabiting a provincial district formed a kind of close corporation called *conventus*.

libentissimis animis eum recipiunt exercitumque eius omnibus rebus iuvant. Etiam Cingulo, quod oppidum Labienus constituerat suaque pecunia exaedificaverat, ad eum legati veniunt quaeque imperaverit se cupidissime facturos pollicentur. Milites imperat: mittunt. Interea legio XII Caesarem consequitur. Cum his duabus Asculum Picenum proficiscitur. Id oppidum Lentulus Spinther X cohortibus tenebat; qui Caesaris adventu cognito profugit ex oppido cohortesque secum abducere conatus magna parte militum deseritur. Relictus in itinere cum paucis incidit in Vibullium Rufum missum a Pompeio in agrum Picenum confirmandorum hominum causa. A quo factus Vibullius certior, quae res in Piceno gererentur, milites ab eo accipit, ipsum dimittit. Item ex finitimis regionibus quas potest contrahit cohortes ex delectibus Pompeianis; in his Camerino fugientem Lucilium Hirrum cum sex cohortibus, quas ibi in praesidio habuerat, excipit; quibus coactis XIII efficit. Cum his ad Domitium Ahenobarbum Corfinium magnis itineribus pervenit Caesaremque adesse cum legionibus duabus nuntiat. Domitius per se circiter XX cohortes Alba, ex Marsis et Pelignis, finitimis ab regionibus coëgerat.

16   Recepto Firmo expulsoque Lentulo Caesar conquiri milites, qui ab eo discesserant, delectumque instituti iubet; ipse unum diem ibi rei frumentariae causa moratus Corfinium contendit. Eo cum venisset,

parts receive him with the utmost gladness and assist his army with supplies of every kind. Even from Cingulum, a town which Labienus had founded and built at his own expense, envoys come to him and promise to do his bidding with the utmost eagerness. He requisitions soldiers; they send them. Meanwhile the Twelfth Legion overtakes Caesar. With these two legions he goes to Asculum in Picenum. Lentulus Spinther, who was holding that town with ten cohorts, as soon as he hears of Caesar's approach, flies from the town, and while endeavouring to take his cohorts away with him is deserted by a great part of his men. Abandoned on the march with a few followers, he falls in with Vibullius Rufus, who had been sent by Pompeius into the Picene district to confirm the loyalty of the inabitants. Vibullius, on learning from him of what was going on in Picenum, takes over his soldiers and lets him go free. He also collects from the neighbouring districts what cohorts he can from the Pompeian levies; among them he captures Lucilius Hirrus, flying from Camerinum with six cohorts which he had there in garrison. By gathering all these together he makes up thirteen cohorts. With them he makes his way by forced marches to Domitius Ahenobarbus at Corfinium and reports the arrival of Caesar with two legions. Domitius by himself had collected and brought from Alba about twenty cohorts, consisting of Marsi and Peligni, drawn from the neighbouring districts.

On the recovery of Firmum and the expulsion of 16 Lentulus, Caesar gives orders that the men who had deserted Lentulus should be sought for and a levy instituted. He stays there himself one day for foraging purposes and then hastens to Corfinium. On

cohortes v praemissae a Domitio ex oppido pontem fluminis interrumpebant, qui erat ab oppido milia passuum circiter III. Ibi cum antecursoribus Caesaris proelio commisso celeriter Domitiani a ponte repulsi se in oppidum receperunt. Caesar legionibus transductis ad oppidum constitit iuxtaque murum castra posuit.

17 Re cognita Domitius ad Pompeium in Apuliam peritos regionum magno proposito praemio cum litteris mittit, qui petant atque orent, ut sibi subveniat: Caesarem duobus exercitibus et locorum angustiis facile intercludi posse frumentoque prohiberi. Quod nisi fecerit, se cohortesque amplius XXX magnumque numerum senatorum atque equitum Romanorum in periculum esse venturum. Interim suos cohortatus tormenta in muris disponit certasque cuique partes ad custodiam urbis attribuit; militibus in contione agros ex suis possessionibus pollicetur, quaterna in singulos iugera et pro rata parte centurionibus evocatisque.

18 Interim Caesari nuntiatur Sulmonenses, quod oppidum a Corfinio VII milium intervallo abest, cupere ea facere, quae vallet, sed a Q. Lucretio senatore et Attio Peligno prohiberi, qui id oppidum VII cohortium praesidio tenebant. Mittit eo M. Antonium cum legionis XIII cohortibus v. Sulmonenses, simulatque signa nostra viderunt, portas aperuerunt universique, et oppidani et milites, obviam gratulantes Antonio exierunt. Lucretius et Attius de muro se

26

his arrival there five cohorts dispatched from the town by Domitius were breaking down the bridge over the river, distant about three miles from the town. A conflict taking place there with Caesar's skirmishers, the Domitian troops were quickly driven from the bridge and withdrew into the town. Caesar, leading his troops across, halted outside the town and pitched camp close to the wall.

Learning what had occurred, Domitius offers a 17 large reward to some men acquainted with the district, and sends them with dispatches to Pompeius in Apulia to beg and beseech him to come to his assistance, pointing out that Caesar could easily be cut off by two armies operating in the narrow passes and so be prevented from foraging. If Pompeius does not do this, Domitius says that he himself and more than thirty cohorts and a great number of senators and Roman knights will be imperilled. Meanwhile, having exhorted his men, he places engines on the walls and assigns each man a definite duty for the protection of the town. In a speech he promises the troops lands out of his own possessions, four acres apiece, and in like proportion to the centurions and reserves.

Meanwhile word is brought to Caesar that the 18 inhabitants of Sulmo, a town seven miles distant from Corfinium, are ready to carry out his wishes, but are prevented by the senator Q. Lucretius and by Attius the Pelignian, who were in occupation of the town with a garrison of seven cohorts. He sends M. Antonius thither with five cohorts of the Thirteenth Legion. The people of Sulmo as soon as they saw our standards opened the gates and sallied forth in a body, townsmen and soldiers, to meet and congratulate Antonius. Lucretius and Attius flung

deiecerunt. Attius ad Antonium deductus petit, u
ad Caesarem mitteretur. Antonius cum cohortibu
et Attio eodem die, quo profectus erat, revertitu
Caesar eas cohortes cum exercitu suo coniunxit At
tiumque incolumem dimisit. Caesar primis diebu
castra magnis operibus munire et ex finitimis muni
cipiis frumentum comportare reliquasque copias ex
spectare instituit. Eo triduo legio VIII ad eum ven
cohortesque ex novis Galliae delectibus XXII equi
tesque ab rege Norico circiter CCC. Quorum advent
altera castra ad alteram oppidi partem ponit; h
castris Curionem praefecit. Reliquis diebus oppidu
vallo castellisque circummunire instituit. Cuius operi
maxima parte effecta eodem fere tempore missi
Pompeio revertuntur.

19   Litteris perlectis Domitius dissimulans in consili
pronuntiat Pompeium celeriter subsidio venturun
hortaturque eos, ne animo deficiant quaeque usu
ad defendendum oppidum sint parent. Ipse arcan
cum paucis familiaribus suis colloquitur consiliumqu
fugae capere[1] constituit. Cum vultus Domitii cun
oratione non consentiret atque omnia trepidantiu
timidiusque ageret, quam superioribus diebus con
suesset, multumque cum suis consiliandi causa secret
praeter consuetudinem colloqueretur, concilia con
ventusque hominum fugeret, res diutius tegi dis
simularique non potuit. Pompeius enim rescrip
serat: sese rem in summum periculum deducturun
non esse, neque suo consilio aut voluntate Domitiun

---

[1] *Meusel omits* capere. *The expression is faulty with or with*
out the verb.

themselves from the wall. Attius is brought to Antonius and begs to be sent to Caesar. Antonius returns with the cohorts and Attius the same day on which he started. Caesar united these cohorts with his own army and let Attius go free. He determined during the first few days to strengthen his camp with extensive works, to bring in supplies of corn from the neighbouring towns, and to wait for the rest of his forces. Three days after, the Eighth Legion joins him and twenty-two cohorts from the new levies in Gaul and about three hundred horsemen from the Noric king. On their arrival he pitches a second camp the other side of the town, and puts Curio in charge of it. On the subsequent days he set himself to surround the town with an earthwork and redoubts. The main part of this work having been carried out, about the same time the messengers sent by Pompeius return.

When the dispatch was read Domitius, concealing 19 the facts, asserts in a public meeting that Pompeius would quickly come to their aid, and exhorts them not to lose heart, but to prepare whatever was required for the defence of the town. Privately he confers with a few of his friends and determines to adopt the plan of flight. As his looks belied his words, and all his actions were marked by more haste and timidity than he had usually shown on the previous days, while, contrary to his custom, he conversed much in secret with his own friends by way of taking counsel, and shunned general deliberations and gatherings, concealment and dissimulation were no longer possible. For Pompeius had sent back word that he would not utterly imperil the whole situation, and that it was not by his advice or consent that Domitius had betaken himself into the

29

se in oppidum Corfinium contulisse; proinde, si qu
fuisset facultas, ad se cum omnibus copiis veniret
Id ne fieri posset, obsidione atque oppidi circum
munitione fiebat.

20   Divulgato Domitii consilio milites, qui eran
Corfinii, prima vesperi secessionem faciunt atqu
ita inter se per tribunos militum centurionesqu
atque honestissimos sui generis colloquuntur: ob
sideri se a Caesare, opera munitionesque prope ess
perfectas; ducem suum Domitium, cuius spe atqu
fiducia permanserint, proiectis omnibus fugae con
silium capere: debere se suae salutis rationem haber
Ab his primo Marsi dissentire incipiunt eamque oppic
partem, quae munitissima videretur, occupant, tan
taque inter eos dissensio exsistit, ut manum conserer
atque armis dimicare conentur; post paulo tame
internuntiis ultro citroque missis quae ignorabant, d
L. Domitii fuga, cognoscunt. Itaque omnes un
consilio Domitium productum in publicum circum
sistunt et custodiunt legatosque ex suo numero a
Caesarem mittunt: sese paratos esse portas aperir
quaeque imperaverit facere et L. Domitium vivun
eius potestati tradere.

21   Quibus rebus cognitis Caesar, etsi magni interess
arbitrabatur quam primum oppido potiri cohortesqu
ad se in castra traducere, ne qua aut largitionibu
aut animi confirmatione aut falsis nuntiis con
mutatio fieret voluntatis, quod saepe in bello parv

30

town of Corfinium, and bade him therefore come to him with all his forces if there should be any opportunity of doing so. This, however, was being rendered impossible by the blockade and investment of the town.

When the intentions of Domitius had been di- 20 vulged, the troops who were at Corfinium draw apart in the early evening and hold a conference among themselves by means of the military tribunes, centurions, and the most respectable men of their own class. They say that they are being invested by Caesar; that his siege works and fortifications are almost completed; that their leader Domitius, in confidence and reliance on whom they have remained steadfast, has abandoned them all and is meditating flight; that they are bound to consider their own safety. The Marsi at first disagree with them and occupy that part of the town which seemed the most strongly fortified; and so great a dissension arises among them that they attempt to engage in hostilities and to fight out the issue, but soon after, messengers having been sent to and fro, they learn the facts, of which they were unaware, about the proposed flight of L. Domitius. And so all unanimously surround Domitius, who had been brought out before them, and guard him, and send envoys out of their number to Caesar, saying that they are ready to open the gates, to do his bidding, and to give up L. Domitius alive into his hands.

When these things were known, although Caesar 21 thought it of great importance to get possession of the town at once and to transfer the cohorts to his own camp, lest any change of feeling should be effected by lavish gifts or by a strengthening of their courage or by false news, since, as he reflected,

momentis magni casus intercederent, tamen veritus,
ne militum introitu et nocturni temporis licentia
oppidum diriperetur, eos, qui venerant, collaudat
atque in oppidum dimittit,[1] portas murosque asser-
vari iubet. Ipse eis operibus, quae facere instituerat,
milites disponit non certis spatiis intermissis, ut erat
superiorum dierum consuetudo, sed perpetuis vigiliis
stationibusque, ut contingant inter se atque omnem
munitionem expleant; tribunos militum et praefectos
circummittit atque hortatur, non solum ab eruptionibus caveant, sed etiam singulorum hominum occultos
exitus asservent. Neque vero tam remisso ac lan-
guido animo quisquam omnium fuit, qui ea nocte
conquieverit. Tanta erat summae rerum exspectatio,
ut alius in aliam partem mente atque animo tra-
heretur, quid ipsis Corfiniensibus, quid Domitio, quid
Lentulo, quid reliquis accideret, qui quosque eventus
exciperent.

22 Quarta vigilia circiter Lentulus Spinther de muro
cum vigiliis custodibusque nostris colloquitur; velle,
si sibi fiat potestas, Caesarem convenire. Facta
potestate ex oppido mittitur, neque ab eo prius
Domitiani milites discedunt, quam in conspectum
Caesaris deducatur. Cum eo de salute sua agit, orat
atque obsecrat, ut sibi parcat, veteremque amicitiam
commemorat Caesarisque in se beneficia exponit;
quae erant maxima: quod per eum in collegium
pontificum venerat, quod provinciam Hispaniam ex

---

[1] dimittit *MSS.*: remittit *Meusel*.

great crises often occurred in war through slight influences; nevertheless, fearing lest the town should be plundered by the entry of the troops and the licence of night, he commends those who had come to him and dismisses them into the town and orders the gates and walls to be carefully guarded. He personally distributes his men over the earthworks which he had set himself to construct, not leaving fixed intervals, as had been the custom on previous days, but in an unbroken line of sentries and outposts, so that they may touch one another and fill up the whole line of investment; he sends round the tribunes and prefects, exhorting them not merely to be on their guard against sallies, but also to watch for the secret exit of individuals. And, in fact, no one among them all was so remiss and languid in spirit as to take rest that night. So keenly did they await the ultimate issue that their hearts and minds were drawn in different directions as they asked what was happening to the Corfinians themselves, what to Domitius, what to Lentulus and to the rest, and what chances were befalling each side.

About the fourth watch Lentulus Spinther confers 22 with our outposts and sentries from the wall, saying that he would like to have an interview with Caesar if the opportunity were granted him. Permission being given, he is escorted from the town, nor do the Domitian soldiers leave him till he is brought into the presence of Caesar. He pleads with him for his own safety, begs and beseeches that he will spare him, reminds him of their old-standing friendship, and sets forth the benefits that Caesar had conferred on him —and they were very great, for through his means he had been admitted to the College of the Pontifices, had held the province of Spain after his prae-

praetura habuerat, quod in petitione consulatus erat
sublevatus. Cuius orationem Caesar interpellat: se
non maleficii causa ex provincia egressum, sed uti se
a contumeliis inimicorum defenderet, ut tribunos
plebis in ea re[1] ex civitate expulsos in suam dignitatem
restitueret, ut se et populum Romanum factione paucorum oppressum in libertatem vindicaret. Cuius
oratione confirmatus Lentulus, ut in oppidum reverti
liceat, petit: quod de sua salute impetraverit, fore
etiam reliquis ad suam spem solatio; adeo esse
perterritos nonnullos, ut suae vitae durius consulere
cogantur. Facta potestate discedit.

23   Caesar, ubi luxit, omnes senatores senatorumque
liberos, tribunos militum equitesque Romanos ad se
produci iubet. Erant quinquaginta; ordinis senatorii
L. Domitius, P. Lentulus Spinther, L. Caecilius
Rufus, Sex. Quintilius Varus quaestor, L. Rubrius;
praeterea filius Domitii aliique complures adulescentes
et magnus numerus equitum Romanorum et decurio-
num, quos ex municipiis Domitius evocaverat. Hos
omnes productos a contumeliis militum conviciisque
prohibet; pauca apud eos loquitur, queritur[2] quod sibi
a parte eorum gratia relata non sit pro suis in eos maximis beneficiis; dimittit omnes incolumes. HS LX, quod
advexerat Domitius atque in publico deposuerat,
allatum ad se ab IIII viris Corfiniensibus Domitio

---

[1] in ea re *MSS.:* iniuria *Faernus, "wrongfully."*
[2] queritur *not in MSS.*

torship, and had been assisted in his candidature for the consulship. Caesar interrupts his speech, observing that he had not quitted his province with any evil intent, but to defend himself from the insults of his foes, to restore to their position the tribunes of the people who at that conjuncture had been expelled from the state, to assert the freedom of himself and the Roman people who had been oppressed by a small faction. Lentulus, encouraged by his speech, begs permission to return to the town, saying that the fact that he had gained his point about his own safety would comfort the rest in their hope for theirs; "some of them," he added, "are so terrified that they are being forced to adopt harsh measures against their own life." Receiving permission, he departs.

As soon as day dawned Caesar orders all senators 23 and their sons, military tribunes, and Roman knights to be brought before him. There were fifty of them: of the senatorial order, L Domitius, P Lentulus Spinther, L. Caecilius Rufus, Sex. Quintilius Varus the quaestor, L. Rubrius; also the son of Domitius with many other youths, and a large number of Roman knights and decurions whom Domitius had summoned from the municipal towns. All these when brought before him he protects from the clamorous insolence of the troops: he addresses them in a few words, complaining that no gratitude had been shown him on their part[1] for his signal acts of kindness, and dismisses them all unharmed. The sum of 6,000,000 sesterces which had been taken by Domitius to Corfinium and placed in the public treasury, and then handed over to him by the four magistrates of Corfinium, he restores to Domitius,

[1] Perhaps "by some of them."

reddit, ne continentior in vita hominum quam in
pecunia fuisse videatur, etsi eam pecuniam publicam
esse constabat datamque a Pompeio in stipendium.
Milites Domitianos sacramentum apud se dicere iubet
atque eo die castra movet iustumque iter conficit VII
omnino dies ad Corfinium commoratus, et per fines
Marrucinorum, Frentanorum, Larinatium in Apuliam
pervenit.

24   Pompeius his rebus cognitis, quae erant ad Corfinium gestae, Luceria proficiscitur Canusium atque
inde Brundisium. Copias undique omnes ex novis
delectibus ad se cogi iubet; servos, pastores armat
atque eis equos attribuit: ex his circiter CCC equites
conficit. L. Manlius praetor Alba cum cohortibus
sex profugit, Rutilius Lupus praetor Tarracina cum
tribus; quae procul equitatum Caesaris conspicatae,
cui praeerat Vibius Curius, relicto praetore signa ad
Curium transferunt atque ad eum transeunt. Item
reliquis itineribus nonnullae cohortes in agmen
Caesaris, aliae in equites incidunt. Reducitur ad
eum deprensus ex itinere N. Magius Cremona,
praefectus fabrum Cn. Pompei. Quem Caesar ad
eum remittit cum mandatis: quoniam ad id tempus
facultas colloquendi non fuerit, atque ipse Brundisium
sit venturus, interesse rei publicae et communis salutis
se cum Pompeio colloqui; neque vero idem profici
longo itineris spatio, cum per alios condiciones

in order that he may not be thought more self-controlled in dealing with men's lives than with their property, although there was no doubt that this money belonged to the state and had been assigned by Pompeius for military pay. The soldiers of Domitius he orders to take the oath of allegiance to himself, and on that day moves camp and completes a full day's march, having stopped at Corfinium for seven days in all, and, passing through the borders of the Marrucini, Frentani, and Larinates, arrives in Apulia.

Pompeius, learning of the events that had happened 24 at Corfinium, goes from Luceria to Canusium and thence to Brundisium. He orders that all the forces drawn from the new levies should be brought to him from every quarter; he arms the slaves and husbandmen and furnishes them with horses, making out of them about three hundred horsemen. L. Manlius the praetor flies from Alba with six cohorts, Rutilius Lupus the praetor from Tarracina with three. These, catching sight of Caesar's cavalry under the command of Vibius Curius, desert their praetor, transfer their colours to Curius, and go over to his side. So, too, on subsequent marches several cohorts fall in with Caesar's main body and others with the horse. N. Magius of Cremona, Pompeius' chief engineer, is captured on the route and brought back to Caesar, who sends him back to Pompeius with instructions to the effect that, since up to the present no opportunity of a conference has been allowed and he himself is on the way to Brundisium, it is to the interest of the state and the common welfare that he should have a conference with Pompeius; that when they are separated by long distance and terms of agreement are conveyed by others, the same results are not gained as would be

ferantur, ac si coram de omnibus condicionibus disceptetur.

25   His datis mandatis Brundisium cum legionibus VI pervenit, veteranis III et reliquis, quas ex novo delectu confecerat atque in itinere compleverat; Domitianas enim cohortes protinus a Corfinio in Siciliam miserat. Reperit consules Dyrrachium profectos cum magna parte exercitus, Pompeium remanere Brundisii cum cohortibus viginti; neque certum inveniri poterat, obtinendine Brundisii causa ibi remansisset, quo facilius omne Hadriaticum mare ex ultimis Italiae partibus regionibusque Graeciae in potestate haberet atque ex utraque parte bellum administrare posset, an inopia navium ibi restitisset, veritusque, ne ille Italiam dimittendam non existimaret, exitus administrationesque Brundisini portus impedire instituit. Quorum operum haec erat ratio. Qua fauces erant angustissimae portus, moles atque aggerem ab utraque parte litoris iaciebat, quod his locis erat vadosum mare. Longius progressus, cum agger altiore aqua contineri non posset, rates duplices quoquo versus pedum XXX e regione molis collocabat. Has quaternis ancoris ex IIII angulis destinabat, ne fluctibus moverentur. His perfectis collocatisque alias deinceps pari magnitudine rates iungebat. Has terra atque aggere integebat, ne aditus atque incursus ad defendendum impediretur. A fronte

secured if they were to discuss all the conditions face to face.

Having given these instructions, he arrives at 25 Brundisium[1] with six legions, three veteran, and the rest consisting of those which he had formed from a new levy and raised to their full complement on his march, for he had sent the Domitian cohorts straight off from Corfinium to Sicily. He finds out that the consuls had gone to Dyrrachium with a great part of the army, and that Pompeius was remaining at Brundisium with twenty cohorts, nor could it be ascertained for certain whether he had remained there for the sake of holding Brundisium, in order that he might more easily control the whole Adriatic from the extremities of Italy and the shores of Greece and so carry on war from either side, or whether he had halted there from lack of ships; and fearing lest Pompeius should think that he ought not to abandon Italy, he determined to block the exits and stop the working of the harbour of Brundisium. The following was the method of his operations. Where the mouth of the harbour was narrowest he threw out piers and a dam from the shore on each side because the sea was shallow there. As he proceeded further out, since the mole could not hold together where the water was deeper, he placed two rafts thirty feet square over against the end of the breakwater. He fastened these by four anchors, one at each of the four angles, to prevent them being shifted by the waves. When they were finished and placed in position he attached in order other rafts of a like size. These he covered with soil and a raised causeway that there might be no obstacle in the way of approach or ingress for the purpose of defence. In

[1] See plan of Brundisium.

atque ab utroque latere cratibus ac pluteis protege-
bat; in quarta quaque earum turres binorum tabula-
torum excitabat, quo commodius ab impetu navium
incendiisque defenderet.

26   Contra haec Pompeius naves magnas onerarias,
quas in portu Brundisino deprehenderat, adornabat.
Ibi turres cum ternis tabulatis erigebat easque multis
tormentis et omni genere telorum completas ad
opera Caesaris appellebat, ut rates perrumperet atque
opera disturbaret. Sic cotidie utrimque eminus
fundis, sagittis reliquisque telis pugnabatur. Atque
haec Caesar ita administrabat, ut condiciones pacis
dimittendas non existimaret; ac tametsi magnopere
admirabatur Magium, quem ad Pompeium cum mandatis miserat, ad se non remitti, atque ea res saepe
temptata etsi impetus eius consiliaque tardabat, tamen
omnibus rebus in eo perseverandum putabat. Itaque Caninium Rebilum legatum, familiarem neces
sariumque Scribonii Libonis, mittit ad eum colloquii
causa; mandat, ut Libonem de concilianda pace
hortetur; imprimis, ut ipse cum Pompeio colloqueretur, postulat; magnopere sese confidere demonstrat, si eius rei sit potestas facta, fore, ut aequis
condicionibus ab armis discedatur; cuius rei magnam partem laudis atque existimationis ad Libonem
perventuram, si illo auctore atque agente ab armis sit
discessum. Libo a colloquio Canini digressus ad Pompeium proficiscitur. Paulo post renuntiat, quod consules absint, sine illis non posse agi de compositione

front and on each side he protected them with fascines and screens; on every fourth raft he ran up towers of two stories that he might thus more conveniently defend them from an attack by ships and from fire.

To meet this Pompeius fitted out some large mer- 26 chant-ships which he had seized in the port of Brundisium. On them he erected towers of three stories each, and when they were equipped with a number of engines and weapons of every kind he brought them up close to Caesar's works so as to break through the rafts and destroy the works. Thus fighting went on every day, each side discharging slings, arrows, and other missiles. But Caesar, while carrying on these operations, did not think that nego- tiations for peace ought to be dropped; and though he was very much surprised that Magius, whom he had commissioned to carry instructions to Pompeius, was not sent back to him, and though his frequent attempts at an understanding were hindering ener- getic action and policy, yet on all accounts he thought it right to persevere therein. And so he sends to Scribonius Libo his legate Caninius Rebilus, one of Libo's intimate friends, to confer on the sub- ject. He instructs him to exhort Libo to effect a reconcilement; his chief demand is that he should himself have an interview with Pompeius. He ex- plains that if he is allowed this opportunity he has great confidence that it will result in their laying down arms on equal terms; and that a great part of the praise and credit for this achievement will fall to Libo if a cessation of hostilities should take place by his advice and efforts. Libo, quitting his interview with Caninius, goes to see Pompeius. Soon after he brings back word that, the consuls being absent, negotiations for a settlement cannot

Ita saepius rem frustra temptatam Caesar aliquando dimittendam sibi iudicat et de bello agendum.

27 Prope dimidia parte operis a Caesare effecta diebusque in ea re consumptis VIIII naves a consulibus Dyrrachio remissae, quae priorem partem exercitus eo deportaverant, Brundisium revertuntur. Pompeius sive operibus Caesaris permotus sive etiam quod ab initio Italia excedere constituerat, adventu navium profectionem parare incipit et, quo facilius impetum Caesaris tardaret, ne sub ipsa profectione milites oppidum irrumperent, portas obstruit, vicos plateasque inaedificat, fossas transversas viis praeducit atque ibi sudes stipitesque praeacutos defigit. Haec levibus cratibus terraque inaequat; aditus autem atque itinera duo, quae extra murum ad portum ferebant, maximis defixis trabibus atque eis praeacutis praesaepit. His paratis rebus milites silentio naves conscendere iubet, expeditos autem ex evocatis, sagittariis funditoribusque[1] raros in muro turribusque disponit. Hos certo signo revocare constituit, cum omnes milites naves conscendissent, atque eis expedito loco actuaria navigia relinquit.

28 Brundisini Pompeianorum militum iniuriis atque ipsius Pompei contumeliis permoti Caesaris rebus favebant. Itaque cognita Pompei profectione concursantibus illis atque in ea re occupatis vulgo ex

[1] sagittariis funditoribusque *MSS.*: sagittarios funditoresque *Meusel.*

42

be carried on without them. So Caesar decides that he must at last abandon an attempt so often made in vain and must apply himself to warfare.

When nearly half the work had been completed 27 by Caesar and nine days had been spent on it, the ships which had conveyed to Dyrrachium the first part of the army and had been sent back thence by the consuls return to Brundisium. On the arrival of the ships Pompeius, either because he was perturbed by Caesar's siege-works or else because he had originally intended to quit Italy, begins to prepare his depature, and in order to delay with greater ease any sudden attack on the part of Caesar, and prevent his troops breaking into the town at once after his departure, he blocks the gates, barricades lanes and streets, draws transverse trenches across the thoroughfares, and fixes therein stakes and blocks of wood sharpened at the ends. These he levels over with light hurdles and earth, while he shuts off the approaches and the two routes which led outside the wall to the harbour by planting in the ground huge balks of timber also sharpened to a point. Having made these preparations, he bids the soldiers embark in silence, and places light-armed men, drawn from the reserves, the archers, and the slingers, at intervals along the wall and in the towers. These he arranges to recall at a given signal when all the troops had embarked, and leaves some merchant-vessels for them in an accessible place.

The Brundisians, embittered by the wrongs inflicted 28 on them by the Pompeian soldiery and by the insults of Pompeius himself, favoured the cause of Caesar. And so when they heard of the departure of Pompeius, while his men were hurrying about occupied in the business in hand, they signalled the fact from every

tectis significabant. Per quos re cognita Caesar scalas parari militesque armari iubet, ne quam rei gerendae facultatem dimittat. Pompeius sub noctem naves solvit. Qui erant in muro custodiae causa collocati, eo signo, quod convenerat, revocantur notisque itineribus ad naves decurrunt. Milites positis scalis muros ascendunt, sed moniti a Brundisinis, ut vallum caecum fossasque caveant, subsistunt et longo itinere ab his circumducti ad portum perveniunt duasque naves cum militibus, quae ad moles Caesaris adhaeserant, scaphis lintribusque reprehendunt, reprehensas excipiunt.

29   Caesar, etsi ad spem conficiendi negotii maxime probabat coactis navibus mare transire et Pompeium sequi, priusquam ille sese transmarinis auxiliis confirmaret, tamen eius rei moram temporisque longinquitatem timebat, quod omnibus coactis navibus Pompeius praesentem facultatem insequendi sui ademerat. Relinquebatur, ut ex longinquioribus regionibus Galliae Picenique et a freto naves essent exspectandae. Id propter anni tempus longum atque impeditum videbatur. Interea veterem exercitum, duas Hispanias confirmari, quarum erat altera maximis beneficiis Pompei devincta, auxilia, equitatum parari, Galliam Italiamque temptari se absente nolebat.

44

house. Learning through them the state of affairs, Caesar orders ladders to be prepared and men to be armed, so as not to lose any opportunity of action. Pompeius weighs anchor at nightfall. The men who were placed on the wall on garrison duty are recalled by the signal agreed on and run down to the ships by familiar routes. The soldiers bring up scaling-ladders and mount the walls, but, warned by the Brundisians to beware of the blind stockade and ditches, they halt, and, taking a circuitous route, under their guidance reach the harbour, and by means of boats and punts arrest and capture two ships with troops on board which had fallen foul of Caesar's piers.

Though Caesar, in the hope of finishing the business, particularly approved the plan of collecting ships and then crossing the sea and following Pompeius before he should strengthen himself by oversea support, yet he feared the delay and length of time involved, because Pompeius by collecting all the ships had robbed him of any present opportunity of following him. It remained to wait for ships from the more distant parts of Gaul and Picenum and from the strait. [1] This, owing to the time of year, seemed a protracted and difficult task. Meanwhile he was unwilling that a veteran army and two Spanish provinces, one of which [2] was under obligation to Pompeius for very great benefits, should be confirmed in their allegiance, that auxiliary forces and cavalry should be provided, that Gaul and Italy should be tampered with, all in his absence.

[1] The Sicilian strait.
[2] The province of Hither Spain, on which Pompeius had conferred great benefits after the conclusion of the war with Sertorius in 72.

CAESAR

30   Itaque in praesentia Pompei sequendi rationem
omittit, in Hispaniam proficisci constituit: duumviris
municipiorum omnium imperat, ut naves conquirant
Brundisiumque deducendas curent. Mittit in Sardiniam cum legione una Valerium legatum, in Siciliam
Curionem pro praetore cum legionibus duabus; eundem, cum Siciliam recepisset, protinus in Africam
transducere exercitum iubet. Sardiniam obtinebat
M. Cotta, Siciliam M. Cato; Africam sorte Tubero
obtinere debebat. Caralitani, simul ad se Valerium
mitti audierunt, nondum profecto ex Italia sua sponte
Cottam ex oppido eiciunt. Ille perterritus, quod
omnem provinciam consentire intellegebat, ex Sardinia in Africam profugit. Cato in Sicilia naves
longas veteres reficiebat, novas civitatibus imperabat
Haec magno studio agebat. In Lucanis Bruttiisque
per legatos suos civium Romanorum delectus habebat
equitum peditumque certum numerum a civitatibus
Siciliae exigebat. Quibus rebus paene perfectis
adventu Curionis cognito queritur in contione sese
proiectum ac proditum a Cn. Pompeio, qui omnibus
rebus imparatissimus non necessarium bellum sus
cepisset et ab se reliquisque in senatu interrogatus
omnia sibi esse ad bellum apta ac parata confirma
visset. Haec in contione questus ex provincia
fugit.

31   Nacti vacuas ab imperiis Sardiniam Valerius, Cotta
Siciliam cum exercitibus eo perveniunt. Tubero
cum in Africam venisset, invenit in provincia cum

So far the present he gives up his plan of following 30
Pompeius and determines to go into Spain. He bids
the officials of all the municipal towns to find ships
and see that they are conveyed to Brundisium. He
sends his legate Valerius into Sardinia with one
legion and Curio as propraetor into Sicily with two,
and bids him on recovering Sicily to transport his
army forthwith to Africa. M. Cotta was in control
of Sardinia and M. Cato of Sicily; Tubero ought by
the allotment of offices to have been in command of
Africa. The people of Caralis, as soon as they heard
that Valerius was being sent to them, before he had
quitted Italy, of their own accord eject Cotta from
the town. Terror-struck, because he gathered that
the whole province was in accord with them, he flies
from Sardinia to Africa. Cato in Sicily was repairing
the old warships and requisitioning new ones from
the communities, devoting much zeal to the per-
formance of his task. Among the Lucani and Bruttii
he was raising levies of Roman citizens through his
legates, and was exacting a fixed number of cavalry
and infantry from the townships of Sicily. When
these measures were almost completed, hearing of the
approach of Curio he complains in a public meeting
that he had been flung aside and betrayed by Gn.
Pompeius, who, while utterly unprepared in every
particular, had undertaken an unnecessary war, and
when questioned by himself and the rest in the
senate had assured them that he had everything fit
and ready for war. After making these complaints
in the assembly he fled from the province.

Finding Sardinia and Sicily bereft of military 31
control, Valerius and Cotta proceed thither with their
armies. Tubero on reaching Africa finds Attius
Varus in the province in military command: he, as

47

imperio Attium Varum; qui ad Auximum, ut supra demonstravimus, amissis cohortibus protinus ex fuga in Africam pervenerat atque eam sua sponte vacuam occupaverat delectuque habito duas legiones effecerat, hominum et locorum notitia et usu eius provinciae nactus aditus ad ea conanda, quod paucis ante annis ex praetura eam provinciam obtinuerat. Hic venientem Uticam navibus Tuberonem portu atque oppido prohibet neque affectum valetudine filium exponere in terram patitur, sed sublatis ancoris excedere eo loco cogit.

32   His rebus confectis Caesar, ut reliquum tempus a labore intermitteretur, milites in proxima municipia deducit; ipse ad urbem proficiscitur. Coacto senatu iniurias inimicorum commemorat. Docet se nullum extraordinarium honorem appetisse, sed exspectato legitimo tempore consulatus eo fuisse contentum, quod omnibus civibus pateret. Latum ab x tribunis plebis contradicentibus inimicis, Catone vero acerrime repugnante et pristina consuetudine dicendi mora dies extrahente, ut sui ratio absentis haberetur, ipso consule Pompeio; qui si improbasset, cur ferri passus esset? si probasset, cur se uti populi beneficio prohibuisset? Patientiam proponit suam, cum de exer-

we have explained above, after the loss of his cohorts
at Auximum had immediately fled and gone to Africa
and had on his own account seized on the vacant
province. By raising a levy he had made up two
legions, having by his knowledge of the people
and the district and his familiarity with the province
gained an opening for engaging in such undertakings,
as he had held the province a few years previously
after his praetorship. He prevents Tubero on arrival
at Utica with his ships from approaching the port
and the town, and does not allow him to land his son
who was stricken with illness, but compels him to
weigh anchor and quit the district.

Having carried out these measures, Caesar with-   32
draws his men into the nearest towns that for the
rest of the time they might have some intermission
of toil. He himself proceeds to the city.[1] Having
called the senate together, he recounts the wrongs
done him by his personal enemies. He explains that
he had sought no extraordinary office, but, waiting for
the legitimate time of his consulship, had been content
with privileges open to all the citizens. A proposal
had been carried by the ten tribunes while Pompeius
himself was consul that he should be allowed to
compete in absence, though his enemies spoke
against it, while Cato opposed with the utmost
vehemence and after his old habit spun out the days
by obstructive speech.[2] If Pompeius disapproved,
why did he allow it to be carried? If he approved,
why did he prohibit him from taking advantage of
the people's kindness? He sets forth his own
patience when under no pressure he had made the

[1] Rome.
[2] The phrase was used of those who were excused a personal
canvass for the consulship owing to absence from Rome.

citibus dimittendis ultro postulavisset; in quo iacturam dignitatis atque honoris ipse facturus esset,
Acerbitatem inimicorum docet, qui, quod ab altero
postularent, in se recusarent atque omnia permisceri
mallent, quam imperium exercitusque dimittere.
Iniuriam in eripiendis legionibus praedicat, crudeli-
tatem et insolentiam in circumscribendis tribunis
plebis; condiciones a se latas, expetita colloquia ac
denegata commemorat. Pro quibus rebus hortatur
ac postulat, ut rem publicam suscipiant atque una
secum administrent. Sin timore defugiant, illis se
oneri non futurum et per se rem publicam adminis-
traturum. Legatos ad Pompeium de compositione
mitti oportere, neque se reformidare, quod in senatu
Pompeius paulo ante dixisset, ad quos legati mitterentur, his auctoritatem attribui timoremque eorum,
qui mitterent, significari. Tenuis atque infirmi haec
animi videri. Se vero, ut operibus anteire studuerit,
sic iustitia et aequitate velle superare.

33   Probat rem senatus de mittendis legatis: sed, qui
mitterentur, non reperiebantur, maximeque timoris
causa pro se quisque id munus legationis recusabat.
Pompeius enim discedens ab urbe in senatu dixerat
eodem se habiturum loco, qui Romae remansissent et
qui in castris Caesaris fuissent. Sic triduum dispu-
tationibus excusationibusque extrahitur. Subicitur
etiam L. Metellus, tribunus plebis, ab inimicis
Caesaris, qui hanc rem distrahat reliquasque res,
quascumque agere instituerit, impediat. Cuius cog-

request about the disbandment of the armies, a point in which he was ready to make a personal sacrifice of dignity and position. He tells them of the bitterness of his foes who refused in his case what they demanded in the other, and preferred utter confusion to the surrender of military power and armed force. He tells of their injustice in robbing him of his legions, of their cruelty and insolence in infringing the rights of the tribunes; he enumerates the terms that he had offered, the conferences asked for and refused. On these considerations he exhorts and charges them to take up the burden of state and administer it with his help; but if they shrink through fear he will not burden them, and will administer the state himself. Envoys should be sent to Pompeius to effect a settlement, nor was he afraid of the remark made by Pompeius a little before in the senate, to the effect that undue influence is attributed to those to whom envoys are sent and fear argued on the part of those that send them. Such considerations seemed to belong to a poor and weak spirit. His own wish was to be superior to others in justice and equity as he had striven to surpass them in action.

The senate approves his proposal about the 33 sending of envoys, but no one was found to be sent, each refusing for himself the duty of this embassy mainly through fear. For Pompeius when quitting the city had said in the senate that he would regard in the same light those who remained at Rome and those who were in Caesar's camp. Thus three days are spun out with discussion and excuses. Also L. Metellus, the tribune, is put up by Caesar's enemies to thwart this proposal and to hinder everything else that he proposed to do. When his design

nito consilio Caesar frustra diebus aliquot consumptis, ne reliquum tempus amittat, infectis eis, quae agere destinaverat, ab urbe proficiscitur atque in ulteriorem Galliam pervenit.

34   Quo cum venisset, cognoscit missum a Pompeio Vibullium Rufum, quem paucis ante diebus Corfinio captum ipse dimiserat; profectum item Domitium ad occupandam Massiliam navibus actuariis septem, quas Igilii et in Cosano a privatis coactas servis, libertis, colonis suis compleverat; praemissos etiam legatos Massilienses domum, nobiles adulescentes, quos ab urbe discedens Pompeius erat adhortatus, ne nova Caesaris officia veterum suorum beneficiorum in eos memoriam expellerent. Quibus mandatis acceptis Massilienses portas Caesari clauserant; Albicos, barbaros homines, qui in eorum fide antiquitus erant montesque supra Massiliam incolebant, ad se vocaverant; frumentum ex finitimis regionibus atque ex omnibus castellis in urbem convexerant; armorum officinas in urbe instituerant; muros, portas, classem reficiebant.

35   Evocat ad se Caesar Massilia xv primos; cum his agit, ne initium inferendi belli a Massiliensibus oriatur: debere eos Italiae totius auctoritatem sequi potius, quam unius hominis voluntati obtemperare. Reliqua, quae ad eorum sanandas mentes pertinere arbitrabatur, commemorat. Cuius orationem legati domum referunt atque ex auctoritate[1] haec Caesari renuntiant: intellegere se divisum esse populum

---

[1] ex auctoritate *MSS.:* ex senatus auctoritate *Menge.*

was understood, several days having been already wasted, Caesar, in order to avoid throwing away any more time, having failed to do what he had proposed, leaves the city and goes into further Gaul.

On his arrival there he learns that Vibullius Rufus, 34 whom he had captured at Corfinium and dismissed a few days before, had been dispatched by Pompeius[1]; also that Domitius had gone to seize Massilia with seven merchant-vessels which he had requisitioned from private persons at Igilium and in Cosanum, and had manned with his own slaves, freedmen, and tenants; and also that some Massilian envoys had been previously sent home, youths of noble birth, whom Pompeius when quitting the city had exhorted not to let Caesar's fresh services drive from their minds the memory of his own earlier kindnesses. Receiving these instructions, the people of Massilia had closed their gates against Caesar, and had called to their aid the Albici, a barbarian tribe, who owed allegiance to them from olden times, and inhabited the hills above Massilia; they had collected and brought into their town corn from the neighbouring districts and from all the strongholds; they had set up manufactories of arms in the town, and were engaged in repairing their walls, gates, and fleet.

Caesar summons fifteen of the chief men of Massilia. 35 He pleads with them not to let the first outbreak of hostilities come from the Massilians; they ought to follow the authority of the whole of Italy rather than be subservient to the will of one man. He leaves no point unmentioned that he thought adapted to restore their minds to sanity. The envoys report his speech, and bring back to Caesar the following authoritative reply: "We understand that the Roman people is

[1] To Spain, see 38, § 1.

Romanum in duas partes; neque sui iudicii neque suarum esse virium discernere, utra pars iustiorem habeat
causam. Principes vero esse earum partium Cn.
Pompeium et C. Caesarem patronos civitatis; quorum
alter agros Volcarum Arecomicorum et Helviorum
publice iis concesserit, alter bello victos Sallyas attri-
buerit vectigaliaque auxerit. Quare paribus eorum
beneficiis parem se quoque voluntatem tribuere debere
et neutrum eorum contra alterum iuvare aut urbe aut
portibus recipere.

36   Haec dum inter eos aguntur, Domitius navibus
Massiliam pervenit atque ab eis receptus urbi prae-
ficitur; summa ei belli administrandi permittitur.
Eius imperio classem quoquo versus dimittunt;
onerarias naves, quas ubique possunt, deprehendunt
atque in portum deducunt, parum clavis aut
materia atque armamentis instructis ad reliquas
armandas reficiendasque utuntur; frumenti quod inventum est in publicum conferunt; reliquas merces
commeatusque ad obsidionem urbis, si accidat, re-
servant. Quibus iniuriis permotus Caesar legiones
tres Massiliam adducit; turres vineasque ad oppugnationem urbis agere, naves longas Arelate numero
XII facere instituit. Quibus effectis armatisque
diebus XXX, a qua die materia caesa est, adductisque
Massiliam his D. Brutum praeficit, C. Trebonium
legatum ad oppugnationem Massiliae relinquit.

37   Dum haec parat atque administrat, C. Fabium
legatum cum legionibus III, quas Narbone circumque

divided into two parties. It is not within our discretion or our power to discriminate which side has the juster cause. The leaders of the two sides are Gn. Pompeius and G. Caesar, patrons of our state, one of whom has officially granted us the lands of the Volcae Arecomici and of the Helvii; the other, after conquering the Sallyes by armed force, has assigned them to us and increased our revenues. Wherefore it is our duty to show them equal goodwill, as their benefits are equal, and to aid neither of them against the other, nor to receive either within our city or ports."

While they are engaged on these proceedings, 36 Domitius, arriving by sea at Massilia, is received by the inhabitants and put in command of the city; the whole control of the war is placed in his hands. Under his authority they send the fleet in every direction; they seize all the merchant-ships they can find and bring them into the harbour. Those which are insufficiently provided with bolts or timber, and with tackle, they use for fitting out and repairing the rest. All the corn that they can find they collect for the general use. The rest of the merchandise and provisions they reserve for the blockade, if it should ensue. Stirred by these wrongs, Caesar conducts three legions to Massilia; he determines to bring up towers and penthouses for the siege of the city, and make twelve warships at Arelate. These having been made and equipped within thirty days from the day on which the timber was first cut down, and having been brought to Massilia, he puts D. Brutus in command of them, and leaves his legate, G. Trebonius, to conduct the siege of Massilia.

While arranging and carrying out these measures 37 he sends forward his legate, G. Fabius, into Spain

ea loca hiemandi causa disposuerat, in Hispaniam praemittit celeriterque saltus Pyrenaeos occupari iubet, qui eo tempore ab L. Afranio legato praesidiis tenebantur. Reliquas legiones, quae longius hiemabant, subsequi iubet. Fabius, ut erat imperatum, adhibita celeritate praesidium ex saltu deiecit magnisque itineribus ad exercitum Afranii contendit.

38 Adventu L. Vibullii Rufi, quem a Pompeio missum in Hispaniam demonstratum est, Afranius et Petreius et Varro, legati Pompei, quorum unus Hispaniam citeriorem tribus legionibus, alter ulteriorem a saltu Castulonensi ad Anam duabus legionibus, tertius ab Ana Vettonum agrum Lusitaniamque pari numero legionum obtinebat, officia inter se partiuntur, uti Petreius ex Lusitania per Vettones cum omnibus copiis ad Afranium proficiscatur, Varro cum eis, quas habebat, legionibus omnem ulteriorem Hispaniam tueatur. His rebus constitutis equites auxiliaque toti Lusitaniae a Petreio, Celtiberiae, Cantabris barbarisque omnibus, qui ad Oceanum pertinent, ab Afranio imperantur. Quibus coactis celeriter Petreius per Vettones ad Afranium pervenit, constituuntque communi consilio bellum ad Ilerdam propter ipsius loci opportunitatem gerere.

39 Erant, ut supra demonstratum est, legiones Afranii tres, Petreii duae, praeterea scutatae citerioris pro-

with three legions, which he had stationed at Narbo and elsewhere round that district in winter quarters, and gives orders that the Pyrenean passes, which were then held with outposts by the legate L. Afranius, should be at once seized. He orders the rest of the legions, which are wintering further off, to follow up. Fabius, in obedience to orders, acting with promptitude, drove the outpost from the pass, and hurried by forced marches to the army of Afranius.

On the arrival of L. Vibullius Rufus, who, as we 38 have shown, was sent by Pompeius into Spain, Afranius and Petreius and Varro, legates of Pompeius, of whom one held hither Spain with three legions, another further Spain from the pass of Castulo to the Anas with two legions, the third the district of the Vettones from the Anas and also Lusitania with an equal number of legions, divide their tasks in such a way that Petreius should march from Lusitania through the Vettones with all his forces to join Afranius, while Varro should protect the whole of further Spain with the legions under his command. When these arrangements were made Petreius requisitions cavalry and auxiliary troops from the whole of Lusitania, Afranius from Celtiberia, the Cantabri, and all the barbarous tribes that extend to the ocean. When they were collected Petreius quickly makes his way through the Vettones to Afranius, and with common consent they agree to wage war at Ilerda owing to the natural advantages afforded by the position.

There were, as I have explained above, three 39 legions belonging to Afranius, two to Petreius, besides about eighty cohorts, some heavy-armed[1] from the

---

[1] The *scutum* was a long heavy wooden shield; the *cetra* was a light round leather shield. The *cetrati* are frequently mentioned in the *Commentaries*.

vinciae et cetratae ulterioris Hispaniae cohortes
circiter LXXX equitumque utriusque provinciae
circiter V milia. Caesar legiones in Hispaniam
praemiserat VI, auxilia peditum V milia, equitum III
milia, quae omnibus superioribus bellis habuerat, et
parem ex Gallia numerum, quam ipse pacaverat,
nominatim ex omnibus civitatibus nobilissimo et
fortissimo quoque evocato, huc optimi generis hominum ex Aquitanis montanisque, qui Galliam provinciam attingunt, addiderat.[1] Audierat Pompeium
per Mauritaniam cum legionibus iter in Hispaniam
facere confestimque esse venturum. Simul a tribunis
militum centurionibusque mutuas pecunias sumpsit;
has exercitui distribuit. Quo facto duas res consecutus est, quod pignore animos centurionum devinxit
et largitione militum voluntates redemit.

40   Fabius finitimarum civitatum animos litteris nuntiisque temptabat. In Sicore flumine pontes effecerat
duos distantes inter se milia passuum IIII. His
pontibus pabulatum mittebat, quod ea, quae citra
flumen fuerant, superioribus diebus consumpserat.
Hoc idem fere atque eadem de causa Pompeiani
exercitus duces faciebant, crebroque inter se eques-
tribus proeliis contendebant. Huc cum cotidiana
consuetudine congressae pabulatoribus praesidio
propiore ponte legiones Fabianae duae flumen
transissent, impedimentaque et omnis equitatus se-
queretur, subito vi ventorum et aquae magnitudine
pons est interruptus et reliqua multitudo equitum

[1] *There is much uncertainty in the text of this portion of the
chapter.*

hither province, others light-armed from further Spain, and about five thousand cavalry from each province. Caesar had sent forward six legions into Spain, five thousand auxiliary infantry and three thousand cavalry which he had had with him during all his former wars, and an equal number from Gaul, which he had himself pacified, having specially called to arms all the men of conspicuous rank and bravery from every state; to these he had added men of the best class from among the Aquitani and the mountaineers who border on the province of Gaul. He had heard that Pompeius was marching at the head of his legions through Mauritania into Spain and would very soon arrive. At the same time he borrowed sums of money from the tribunes and centurions and distributed them among the soldiers. By this proceeding he gained two results: he established a lien on the loyalty of the centurions and purchased by the bounty the goodwill of the troops.

Fabius was tampering with the loyalty of the **40** neighbouring communities by letters and messengers. Over the River Sicoris he had constructed two bridges four miles apart. Over these he kept sending supplies, because during the preceding days he had exhausted all that there was this side the river. The generals of the Pompeian army were doing pretty much the same thing and for the same reason, and they were engaged in constant cavalry skirmishes. When two Fabian legions, coming together to protect the foragers according to their usual custom, had crossed the river by the nearer bridge, and the packhorses and the whole cavalry force were following them, the bridge was suddenly broken down by a storm of wind and a great rush of water, and a large force of cavalry that remained behind was cut off. When

interclusa. Quo cognito a Petreio et Afranio ex aggere atque cratibus, quae flumine ferebantur, celeriter suo ponte Afranius, quem oppido castrisque coniunctum habebat, legiones IIII equitatumque omnem traiecit duabusque Fabianis occurrit legionibus. Cuius adventu nuntiato L. Plancus, qui legionibus praeerat, necessaria re coactus locum capit superiorem diversamque aciem in duas partes constituit, ne ab equitatu circumveniri posset. Ita congressus impari numero magnos impetus legionum equitatusque sustinet. Commisso ab equitibus proelio signa legionum duarum procul ab utrisque conspiciuntur, quas C. Fabius ulteriore ponte subsidio nostris miserat suspicatus fore id, quod accidit, ut duces adversariorum occasione et beneficio fortunae ad nostros opprimendos uterentur. Quarum adventu proelium dirimitur, ac suas uterque legiones reducit in castra.

41   Eo biduo Caesar cum equitibus DCCCC, quos sibi praesidio reliquerat, in castra pervenit. Pons, qui fuerat tempestate interruptus, paene erat refectus; hunc noctu perfici iussit. Ipse cognita locorum natura ponti castrisque praesidio sex cohortes reliquit atque omnia impedimenta et postero die omnibus copiis triplici instructa acie ad Ilerdam proficiscitur et sub castris Afranii constitit et ibi paulisper sub armis moratus facit aequo loco pugnandi potestatem. Potestate facta Afranius copias educit et in

Petreius and Afranius discovered what had happened from the earth and fascines which were being carried down the river, Afranius immediately threw across four legions and all his cavalry by his own bridge with which he had joined the town and his camp, and goes to meet the two Fabian legions. On the news of his approach L. Plancus, who was in command of the legions, under the stress of necessity occupies the higher ground and draws up his lines facing in opposite directions that he might not be surrounded by cavalry. So going into action with unequal numbers, he sustains impetuous charges of the legions and cavalry. After the cavalry had engaged, the standards of two legions are seen by each side some little way off. These Fabius had sent by the further bridge to support our men, suspecting that what actually occurred would happen, namely, that the commanders on the other side would employ the opportunity which a kind chance afforded them of crushing our men. On their arrival the battle is broken off and each leader marches his legions back to camp.

Within two days Caesar reached the camp with 41 nine hundred horsemen whom he had reserved as a bodyguard for himself. The bridge which had been broken down by the storm was almost repaired: he ordered it to be finished at night. Having made himself acquainted with the character of the country, he leaves six cohorts to guard the bridge and the camp together with all his baggage, and on the following day, with his whole force drawn up in three lines, he sets out for Ilerda and halts close to the camp of Afranius, and, having waited there for a little while under arms, offers his foe an opportunity of fighting on level ground. The opportunity being thus allowed him, Afranius leads out his forces and posts them half

medio colle sub castris constituit. Caesar, ubi cognovit per Afranium stare, quo minus proelio dimicaretur, ab infimis radicibus montis intermissis circiter
passibus CCCC castra facere constituit et, ne in opere
faciundo milites repentino hostium incursu exter-
rerentur atque opere prohiberentur, vallo muniri
vetuit, quod eminere et procul videri necesse erat,
sed a fronte contra hostem pedum XV fossam fieri
iussit. Prima et secunda acies in armis, ut ab initio
constituta erat, permanebat; post has opus in occulto
a III acie fiebat. Sic omne prius est perfectum, quam
intellegeretur ab Afranio castra muniri. Sub vesperum Caesar intra hanc fossam legiones reducit
atque ibi sub armis proxima nocte conquiescit.

42   Postero die omnem exercitum intra fossam con-
tinet et, quod longius erat agger petendus, in praesentia similem rationem operis instituit singulaque
latera castrorum singulis attribuit legionibus muni-
enda fossasque ad eandem magnitudinem perfici
iubet; reliquas legiones in armis expeditas contra
hostem constituit. Afranius Petreiusque terrendi
causa atque operis impediendi copias suas ad in-
fimas montis radices producunt et proelio lacessunt,
neque idcirco Caesar opus intermittit confisus praesidio legionum trium et munitione fossae. Illi non
diu commorati nec longius ab infimo colle progressi

62

way up the slope under shelter of his camp. When Caesar learned that it was only owing to Afranius that a pitched battle was not fought he determined to pitch his camp at an interval of about four hundred paces from the lowest spurs of the mountain, and in order that his men might not be panic-stricken by a sudden onset of the foe while engaged on their task and so be prevented from working, he forbade the erection of a rampart, which could not fail to be prominent and visible from a distance, but ordered a ditch of fifteen feet width to be constructed facing the enemy. The first and second line remained under arms as they had been posted at first; behind these the work was being secretly done by the third line. So it was all completed before Afranius could become aware that the camp was being fortified. Towards evening Caesar withdraws the legions within the fosse and bivouacs there under arms the following night.

On the following day he keeps the whole army 42 within the fosse and, as material for earthworks could only be procured at a distance, he arranges a similar method of work for the present and assigns the fortifying of each side of the camp to a single legion, ordering fosses of a similar size to the first to be constructed; the rest of the legions he draws up under arms lightly equipped over against the enemy. Afranius and Petreius, with the object of causing alarm and so impeding the work, draw out their forces towards the lower spurs of the hill and harass our men. Caesar, however, does not on that account interrupt his work, trusting in the protection of the three legions and the defensive nature of the fosse. The enemy, without staying long or advancing further from the bottom of the hill, withdraw their forces

copias in castra reducunt. Tertio die Caesar vallo castra communit; reliquas cohortes, quas in superioribus castris reliquerat, impedimentaque ad se traduci iubet.

43   Erat inter oppidum Ilerdam et proximum collem, ubi castra Petreius atque Afranius habebant, planities circiter passuum CCC, atque in hoc fere medio spatio tumulus erat paulo editor; quem si occupavisset Caesar et communisset, ab oppido et ponte et commeatu omni, quem in oppidum contulerant, se interclusurum adversarios confidebat. Hoc sperans legiones III ex castris educit acieque in locis idoneis instructa unius legionis antesignanos procurrere atque eum tumulum occupare iubet. Qua re cognita celeriter quae in statione pro castris erant Afranii cohortes breviore itinere ad eundem occupandum locum mittuntur. Contenditur proelio, et quod prius in tumulum Afraniani venerant, nostri repelluntur atque aliis submissis subsidiis terga vertere seque ad signa legionum recipere coguntur.

44   Genus erat pugnae militum illorum, ut magno impetu primo procurrerent, audacter locum caperent, ordines suos non magnopere servarent, rari dispersique pugnarent; si premerentur, pedem referre et loco excedere non turpe existimarent cum Lusitanis reliquisque barbaris barbaro[1] genere quodam pugnae assuefacti; quod fere fit, quibus quisque in locis miles inveteraverit, ut multum earum regionum consuetudine moveatur. Haec tum ratio

---

[1] *The text of this passage is extremely uncertain; the MSS. omit* barbaro.

into camp. On the third day Caesar strengthens his camp with a rampart and orders the rest of the cohorts which he had left in his previous camp, and their baggage, to be brought over to him.

Between the town of Ilerda and the nearest hill 43 on which Petreius and Afranius were encamped was a plain about three hundred paces in width, and in about the middle of this space was a rather high mound. Caesar was confident that if he occupied and fortified this he would cut off his adversaries from the town and the bridge and from all the stores which they had brought into the town. In this hope he leads out of the camp three legions, and having drawn up the line in a suitable position, he orders a picked advance guard from one legion to charge and occupy the mound. This movement being quickly discovered, the cohorts of Afranius which were stationed in front of the camp are sent by a shorter route to occupy the same position. A battle is fought, and, as the Afranians had reached the mound first, our men are driven back and, fresh supports being sent up, are compelled to turn and retreat to the standards of the legions.

The method of fighting adopted by the enemy's 44 troops was to charge at first at full speed, boldly seize a position, take no particular trouble to preserve their ranks, but fight singly and in loose order; if they were hard pressed they did not consider it a disgrace to retire and quit their position, for, waging a continuous warfare against the Lusitanians and other barbarous tribes, they had become used to a barbarous kind of fighting, as it usually happens that when troops have spent a long time in any district they are greatly influenced by the methods of the country. It was this system that now threw

nostros perturbavit insuetos huius generis pugnae: circumiri enim sese ab aperto latere procurrentibus singulis arbitrabantur; ipsi autem suos ordines servare neque ab signis discedere neque sine gravi causa eum locum, quem ceperant, dimitti censuerant oportere. Itaque perturbatis antesignanis legio, quae in eo cornu constiterat, locum non tenuit atque in proximum collem sese recepit.

45 Caesar paene omni acie perterrita, quod praeter opinionem consuetudinemque acciderat, cohortatus suos legionem nonam subsidio ducit; hostem insolenter atque acriter nostros insequentem supprimit rursusque terga vertere seque ad oppidum Ilerdam recipere et sub muro consistere cogit. Sed nonae legionis milites elati studio, dum sarcire acceptum detrimentum volunt, temere insecuti longius fugientes in locum iniquum progrediuntur et sub montem, in quo erat oppidum positum Ilerda, succedunt. Hinc se recipere cum vellent, rursus illi ex loco superiore nostros premebant. Praeruptus[1] locus erat utraque ex parte derectus ac tantum in latitudinem patebat, ut tres instructae cohortes eum locum explerent, ut neque subsidia ab lateribus submitti neque equites laborantibus usui esse possent. Ab oppido autem declivis locus tenui fastigio vergebat in longitudinem passuum circiter CCCC. Hac nostris erat receptus, quod eo incitati studio inconsultius processerant; hoc pugnabatur loco, et propter angustias iniquo et

[1] *Madvig omits* praeruptus *as a marginal explanation of* derectus.

our men into confusion, unaccustomed as they were to this kind of fighting; for as the enemy kept charging singly they thought that they were being surrounded on their exposed flank. As for themselves, they had judged it right to keep their ranks and not to desert their standards nor to give up without grave cause the position they had taken. And so when the vanguard was thrown into confusion the legion posted on that wing could not stand its ground and withdrew to the nearest hill.

Finding nearly the whole of his line panic-stricken— 45 an event as unusual as it was unexpected—Caesar exhorts his men and leads the Ninth Legion to their support. He checks the foe who are pursuing our men with insolent daring, and compels them again to turn and retreat to the town of Ilerda and halt beneath the walls. But the men of the Ninth Legion, carried away by zeal in their desire to repair the loss received, rashly pursuing the flying foe too far, get into unfavourable ground and approach close under the hill on which the town of Ilerda was situated. When our men wished to retreat from this position, the enemy in turn kept pressing them hard from the higher ground. The place was precipitous with a steep descent on either side, and extended only so far in width as just to give room for three cohorts drawn up in battle array, so that supports could not be sent up on the flanks nor could cavalry be of any use if the men were in difficulties. But on the side of the town sloping ground with a slight descent stretched to the length of about four hundred paces. In this direction our men stood at bay, since, carried forward by their zeal, they had recklessly advanced thus far. The fighting took place in this spot, which was unfavourable both from its confined limits and because

quod sub ipsis radicibus montis constiterant, ut nullum frustra telum in eos mitteretur. Tamen virtute et patientia nitebantur atque omnia vulnera sustinebant. Augebatur illis copia, atque ex castris cohortes per oppidum crebro submittebantur, ut integri defessis succederent. Hoc idem Caesar facere cogebatur, ut submissis in eundem locum cohortibus defessos reciperet.

46 Hoc cum esset modo pugnatum continenter horis quinque nostrique gravius a multitudine premerentur, consumptis omnibus telis gladiis destrictis impetum adversus montem in cohortes faciunt, paucisque deiectis reliquos sese convertere cogunt. Submotis sub murum cohortibus ac nonnullam partem propter terrorem in oppidum compulsis facilis est nostris receptus datus. Equitatus autem noster ab utroque latere, etsi deiectis atque inferioribus locis constiterat, tamen summa in iugum virtute connititur atque inter duas acies perequitans commodiorem ac tutiorem nostris receptum dat. Ita vario certamine pugnatum est. Nostri in primo congressu circiter LXX ceciderunt, in his Q. Fulginius ex primo hastato legionis XIIII, qui propter eximiam virtutem ex inferioribus ordinibus in eum locum pervenerat; vulnerantur amplius DC. Ex Afranianis interficiuntur T. Caecilius, primi pili centurio, et praeter eum centuriones IIII, milites amplius CC.

47 Sed haec eius diei praefertur opinio, ut se utrique superiores discessisse existimarent: Afraniani, quod,

they had halted just under the very spurs of the mountain, so that no missile failed to reach them. Nevertheless they strove with valour and endurance and sustained every description of wound. The forces of the foe were increasing and cohorts were continually being sent up to them from the camp through the town so that the unexhausted were always taking the place of the exhausted. Caesar was obliged to adopt the same course of withdrawing the exhausted and sending up supporting cohorts to the same place.

When they had fought in this way continuously 46 for five hours, and our men were being grievously harassed by superior numbers, having spent all their missiles, they draw their swords and, breasting the hill, charge the cohorts, and after laying a few low, they force the rest to retreat. When the cohorts were thus pushed close up to the wall, and to some extent driven by terror to enter the town, an easy withdrawal was allowed our men. Our cavalry, however, on each flank, though it had been stationed on low-lying ground at the foot of the cliff, yet forces its way with the utmost valour to the ridge, and, riding between the two lines of battle, allows our men a more convenient and safer withdrawal. Thus the contest was waged with varying fortune. At the first attack about seventy of our men fell, among them Q. Fulginius, a principal centurion of the Fourteenth Legion, who by his remarkable valour had risen to that post from the lower rank of centurions, and more than six hundred are wounded. Among the Afranians, T. Caecilius, a centurion of the first company, is slain, and besides him four centurions and more than two hundred men.

But the commonly received view of the day's 47 events was that each side thought it had come off

cum esse omnium iudicio inferiores viderentur,
comminus tam diu stetissent et nostrorum impetum
sustinuissent et initio locum tumulumque tenuissent,
quae causa pugnandi fuerat, et nostros primo congressu terga vertere coëgissent; nostri autem, quod
iniquo loco atque impari congressi numero quinque
horis proelium sustinuissent, quod montem gladiis
destrictis ascendissent, quod ex loco superiore terga
vertere adversarios coëgissent atque in oppidum
compulissent. Illi eum tumulum, pro quo pugnatum
est, magnis operibus munierunt praesidiumque ibi
posuerunt.

48   Accidit etiam repentinum incommodum biduo, quo
haec gesta sunt. Tanta enim tempestas cooritur, ut
numquam illis locis maiores aquas fuisse constaret.
Tum autem ex omnibus montibus nives proluit ac
summas ripas fluminis superavit pontesque ambo,
quos C. Fabius fecerat, uno die interrupit. Quae res
magnas difficultates exercitui Caesaris attulit. Castra
enim, ut supra demonstratum est, cum essent inter
flumina duo, Sicorim et Cingam, spatio milium XXX,
neutrum horum transiri poterat, necessarioque omnes
his angustiis continebantur. Neque civitates, quae
ad Caesaris amicitiam accesserant, frumentum supportare, neque ei, qui pabulatum longius progressi
erant, interclusi fluminibus reverti neque maximi
commeatus, qui ex Italia Galliaque veniebant, in
castra pervenire poterant. Tempus erat autem
difficillimum, quo neque frumenta in hibernis erant

superior; the Afranians because, though they were generally deemed inferior, they had stood their ground so long in close combat and borne the assault of our men, and at the outset held the position and the mound which had been the object of the battle, and at the first encounter had compelled our men to retreat; our troops, on the other hand, claimed the victory because, engaging the foe on unfavourable ground and with unequal number, they had sustained the fight for five hours, had mounted the hill with drawn swords, had compelled their adversaries to retreat from a higher position, and had driven them into the town. The enemy fortified the hill, for possession of which they had fought, with great works, and placed a garrison on it.

There also happened an unforeseen disaster within 48 two days of these occurrences. A storm of such intensity springs up that it was agreed that there had never been a greater rainfall in that district. On this occasion it washed down the snow from all the mountains, overtopped the banks of the river, and in one day broke down both the bridges which G. Fabius had made. This caused serious difficulties to Caesar's army. For the camp being situated, as has been explained above, between the two rivers Sicoris and Cinga, thirty miles apart, neither of these could be crossed, and they were all necessarily confined in this narrow space. The states which had entered into friendly relations with Caesar could not supply provisions, nor could those who had travelled some distance for forage return, being cut off by the rivers, nor could the huge supplies which were on their way from Italy and Gaul reach the camp. It was, moreover, the most difficult season of the year, when there was no corn in the winter stores and the

neque multum a maturitate aberant[1]; ac civitates
exinanitae, quod Afranius paene omne frumentum
ante Caesaris adventum Ilerdam convexerat, reliqui
si quid fuerat, Caesar superioribus diebus consumpserat; pecora, quod secundum poterat esse inopiae
subsidium, propter bellum finitimae civitates longius
removerant. Qui erant pabulandi aut frumentandi
causa progressi, hos levis armaturae Lusitani peritique
earum regionum cetrati citerioris Hispaniae con-
sectabantur; quibus erat proclive tranare flumen,
quod consuetudo eorum omnium est, ut sine utribus
ad exercitum non eant.

49   At exercitus Afranii omnium rerum abundabat
copia. Multum erat frumentum provisum et con-
vectum superioribus temporibus, multum ex omni
provincia comportabatur; magna copia pabuli suppetebat. Harum omnium rerum facultates sine ullo
periculo pons Ilerdae praebebat et loca trans flumen
integra, quo omnino Caesar adire non poterat.

50   Hae permanserunt aquae dies complures. Conatus
est Caesar reficere pontes; sed nec magnitudo
fluminis permittebat, neque ad ripam dispositae
cohortes adversariorum perfici patiebantur. Quod illis
prohibere erat facile cum ipsius fluminis natura atque
aquae magnitudine, tum quod ex totis ripis in unum
atque angustum locum tela iaciebantur; atque erat
difficile eodem tempore rapidissimo flumine opera
perficere et tela vitare.

51   Nuntiatur Afranio magnos commeatus, qui iter
habebant ad Caesarem, ad flumen constitisse. Vene-

[1] *This is the reading of the MSS., but the text is open to doubt.*

crops were not far from being ripe, while the communities were exhausted because Afranius had conveyed nearly all the corn to Ilerda before Caesar's arrival, and whatever there was left Caesar had consumed during the previous days; and the cattle which could have served as a second reserve against want had been removed to a distance by the neighbouring states because of the war. The men who went out to collect fodder or corn were followed by light-armed Lusitanians and skirmishers from hither Spain acquainted with the district; and for them it was easy to swim across the rivers, it being their general custom never to join the main army without bladders.

But the army of Afranius had abundance of provisions of every kind. Much corn had been provided and collected previously, much was being brought together from every province, and there was a great supply of fodder. The bridge at Ilerda and the untouched districts across the river, which Caesar was quite unable to approach, gave opportunities for all these measures without any risk. 49

The above-mentioned floods lasted several days. Caesar made an attempt to repair the bridges, but the strength of the current did not allow it, nor did the cohorts of the enemy, distributed along the bank, suffer the work to be completed. It was easy for them to prevent it from the character of the river itself and the excessive flood, and also because from all along the banks missiles were being discharged at one narrow spot, and so it was difficult, owing to the extreme rapidity of the current, at once to carry on the work and avoid the missiles. 50

Word is brought to Afranius that the great supplies on their way to Caesar are stopped by the stream. 51

rant eo sagittarii ex Rutenis, equites ex Gallia cum multis carris magnisque impedimentis, ut fert Gallica consuetudo. Erant praeterea cuiusque generis hominum milia circiter VI cum servis liberisque; sed nullus ordo, nullum imperium certum, cum suo quisque consilio uteretur atque omnes sine timore iter facerent usi superiorum temporum atque itinerum licentia. Erant complures honesti adulescentes, senatorum filii et ordinis equestris; erant legationes civitatum; erant legati Caesaris. Hos omnes flumina continebant. Ad hos opprimendos cum omni equitatu tribusque legionibus Afranius de nocte proficiscitur imprudentesque ante missis equitibus aggreditur. Celeriter sese tamen Galli equites expediunt proeliumque committunt. Ei, dum pari certamine res geri potuit, magnum hostium numerum pauci sustinuere; sed ubi signa legionum appropinquare coeperunt, paucis amissis sese in proximos montes conferunt. Hoc pugnae tempus magnum attulit nostris ad salutem momentum; nacti enim spatium se in loca superiora receperunt. Desiderati sunt eo die sagittarii circiter CC, equites pauci, calonum atque impedimentorum non magnus numerus.

52   His tamen omnibus annona crevit; quae fere res non solum inopia praesentis, sed etiam futuri temporis timore ingravescere consuevit. Iamque ad denarios L in singulos modios annona pervenerat,

There had come thither archers from the Ruteni and horsemen from Gaul with a number of wagons and heavy baggage, after the Gallic custom. There were, moreover, about six thousand men of every class with their slaves and children, but there was no method, no fixed authority, each following his own devices, and all journeying without fear, adopting the licence of earlier days and journeys. There were a number of honourable youths, sons of senators or of the equestrian order; there were deputations from the states; there were envoys from Caesar. All these were checked by the rivers. To crush them Afranius sets forth at night with all his cavalry and three legions, and sending his horsemen on in front attacks them off their guard. Nevertheless the Gallic horsemen quickly rally and join battle. Though few, they stood their ground against a great number of the enemy, so long as an encounter on equal conditions was possible; but when the standards of the legions began to approach, after the loss of a few men, they withdraw to the nearest hills. This period of the battle was of great moment for the safety of our men, for by getting free room they withdrew to higher ground. On that day about two hundred archers were lost, a few horsemen, and a small number of camp followers and beasts of burden.

Nevertheless in all these circumstances the price of provisions rose, a difficulty which is wont to increase, not merely from the immediate dearth, but also from fear for the future. Already the price of corn had risen to fifty denarii a peck,[1] and the lack of it had

52

---

[1] The ordinary price of corn was from 3½ to 4 sesterces the peck. It was now 200 sesterces, equivalent to about thirty-five shillings.

et militum vires inopia frumenti deminuerat, atque incommoda in dies augebantur; et ita paucis diebus magna erat facta rerum commutatio ac se fortuna inclinaverat, ut nostri magna inopia necessariarum rerum conflictarentur, illi omnibus abundarent rebus superioresque haberentur. Caesar eis civitatibus, quae ad eius amicitiam accesserant, quod minor erat frumenti copia, pecus imperabat; calones ad longinquiores civitates dimittebat; ipse praesentem inopiam quibus poterat subsidiis tutabatur.

53   Haec Afranius Petreiusque et eorum amici pleniora etiam atque uberiora Romam ad suos perscribebant; multa rumor affingebat, ut paene bellum confectum videretur. Quibus litteris nuntiisque Romam perlatis magni domum concursus ad Afranium magnaeque gratulationes fiebant; multi ex Italia ad Cn. Pompeium proficiscebantur, alii, ut principes talem nuntium attulisse, alii ne eventum belli exspectasse aut ex omnibus novissimi venisse viderentur.

54   Cum in his angustiis res esset, atque omnes viae ab Afranianis militibus equitibusque obsiderentur, nec pontes perfici possent, imperat militibus Caesar, ut naves faciant, cuius generis eum superioribus annis usus Britanniae docuerat. Carinae ac prima statumina ex levi materia fiebant; reliquum corpus navium viminibus contextum coriis integebatur. Has perfectas carris iunctis devehit noctu milia passuum a

diminished the strength of the soldiery and their troubles were increasing daily. So completely had the situation been reversed in a few days, and such had been the shifting of the balance of fortune, that our men were being oppressed by a serious deficiency of necessaries, while the enemy had abundance of everything and were in an acknowledged position of superiority. The supply of corn being too small, Caesar began to requisition cattle from the states which had gone over to his side, sent sutlers to the more distant communities, and himself endeavoured by all possible resources to meet the present want.

Afranius and Petreius and their friends wrote to 53 their partisans at Rome an amplified and exaggerated account of these events. Rumour added much, so that the war seemed almost finished. When these letters and messages were conveyed to Rome great crowds thronged the house of Afranius and hearty congratulations were offered. Many set out from Italy for Gn. Pompeius, some that they might show themselves the first to bring him such news, others that they might not appear to have waited for the issue of the war and to have been the last of all to come.

As things were reduced to such a strait and all 54 the roads were blocked by the Afranian soldiers and horsemen and the bridges could not be completed, Caesar orders his men to build ships of the kind that his experience in Britain in previous years had taught him to make. The keels and the first ribs were made of light timber, the rest of the hull was wattled and covered with hides. These when finished he conveys by night on coupled wagons[1]

[1] Two wagons coupled together, one in front of the other.

castris XXII militesque his navibus flumen transportat
continentemque ripae collem improviso occupat.
Hunc celeriter, priusquam ab adversariis sentiatur,
communit. Huc legionem postea traicit atque ex
utraque parte pontem instituit, biduo perficit. Ita
commeatus et qui frumenti causa processerant tuto
ad se recipit et rem frumentariam expedire incipit.

55 Eodem die equitum magnam partem flumen
traiecit. Qui inopinantes pabulatores et sine ullo
dissipatos timore aggressi magnum numerum iumentorum atque hominum intercipiunt cohortibusque
cetratis subsidio missis scienter in duas partes sese
distribuunt, alii ut praedae praesidio sint, alii ut
venientibus resistant atque eos propellant, unamque
cohortem, quae temere ante ceteras extra aciem pro-
currerat, seclusam ab reliquis circumveniunt atque
interficiunt incolumesque cum magna praeda eodem
ponte in castra revertuntur.

56 Dum haec ad Ilerdam geruntur, Massilienses usi
L. Domitii consilio naves longas expediunt numero
XVII, quarum erant XI tectae. Multa huc minora
navigia addunt, ut ipsa multitudine nostra classis
terreatur. Magnum numerum sagittariorum, magnum
Albicorum, de quibus supra demonstratum est, im-
ponunt atque hos praemiis pollicitationibusque
incitant. Certas sibi deposcit naves Domitius atque
has colonis pastoribusque, quos secum adduxerat,
complet. Sic omnibus rebus instructa classe magna
fiducia ad nostras naves procedunt, quibus praeerat

to a distance of twenty-two miles from the camp and transports his men in them across the river and occupies unobserved the hill adjoining the bank. This he fortifies hastily before the foe should find it out. Hither he afterwards transfers a legion and sets about making a bridge from either side, finishing it in two days. Thus he recovers in safety the stores and the men who had gone out on the foraging expedition, and begins to settle the difficulties of his food supply.

On the same day he threw a great part of his 55 cavalry across the river, who, attacking the foragers when off their guard and scattered about without any fear of danger, cut off a great number of men and beasts; and when some light-armed cohorts had been sent in support of the foe they skilfully distribute themselves into two divisions, some to guard the booty, others to resist and repel aggressors; and one cohort, which had rashly advanced from the main body before the others, they cut off from the rest and surround it and put it to the sword, and return to the camp by the same bridge, unharmed, with much booty.

While this is going on at Ilerda the Massilians, 56 following the advice of L. Domitius, equip seventeen ships of war, of which eleven were decked. To these they add many smaller vessels, so that our fleet may be terrified by the mere multitude. On board they put a great number of archers and of the Albici, about whom I have explained before, and stimulate them by prizes and promises. Domitius demands special ships for himself, and mans them with farmers and herdsmen whom he had brought with him. Their fleet thus fully equipped, they advance with great confidence against our ships, of which

D. Brutus. Hae ad insulam, quae est contra Massiliam, stationes obtinebant.

57 Erat multo inferior numero navium Brutus; sed electos ex omnibus legionibus fortissimos viros, antesignanos, centuriones, Caesar ei classi attribuerat, qui sibi id muneris depoposcerant. Hi manus ferreas atque harpagones paraverant magnoque numero pilorum, tragularum reliquorumque telorum se instruxerant. Ita cognito hostium adventu suas naves ex portu educunt, cum Massiliensibus confligunt. Pugnatum est utrimque fortissime atque acerrime; neque multum Albici nostris virtute cedebant, homines asperi et montani, exercitati in armis; atque hi modo digressi a Massiliensibus recentem eorum pollicitationem animis continebant, pastoresque Domitii spe libertatis excitati sub oculis domini suam probare operam studebant.

58 Ipsi Massilienses et celeritate navium et scientia gubernatorum confisi nostros eludebant impetusque eorum excipiebant et, quoad licebat latiore uti spatio, producta longius acie circumvenire nostros aut pluribus navibus adoriri singulas aut remos transcurrentes detergere, si possent, contendebant; cum propius erat necessario ventum, ab scientia gubernatorum atque artificiis ad virtutem montanorum confugiebant. Nostri cum minus exercitatis remigibus minusque peritis gubernatoribus utebantur, qui repente ex onerariis navibus erant producti neque dum etiam vocabulis armamentorum cognitis, tum etiam tarditate et gravitate navium impediebantur;

D. Brutus was in command. These ships were stationed by the island which lies over against Massilia.

Brutus was far inferior in number of ships, but Caesar had assigned to his fleet the bravest men, front-line men and centurions, picked from all the legions, who had demanded this charge for themselves. They had prepared iron claws and grapplings and had furnished themselves with a great number of javelins, looped darts, and other weapons. So, having learnt of the arrival of the enemy, they bring their ships out of port and join battle with the Massilians. The fight was maintained with the utmost bravery and impetuosity on both sides, nor did the Albici, rough mountaineers trained in arms, fall far below our men in valour, and having lately come from the Massilians, they kept in mind their recent promises, while the herdsmen of Domitius, stimulated by the hope of liberty, were eager to display their zeal before their master's eyes.

The Massilians themselves, trusting in the speed of their ships and the skill of their pilots, eluded our men and parried their attacks, and so long as they were free to make use of a wider space they extended their line to some distance and strove to surround our men, or to attack single ships with several, or to run by them and if possible sweep off their oars. Whenever they were forced to come to close quarters, instead of the skill and devices of pilots they had recourse to the valour of mountaineers. Our men had not only to employ less well-trained rowers and less skilled pilots who had suddenly been taken out of merchant-ships, not yet knowing even the names of the various tackle, but were also retarded by the slowness and heaviness of their ships. For, having been made in a

57

58

factae enim subito ex humida materia non eundem
usum celeritatis habebant. Itaque, dum locus comminus pugnandi daretur, aequo animo singulas binis
navibus obiciebant atque iniecta manu ferrea et
retenta utraque nave diversi pugnabant atque in
hostium naves transcendebant et magno numero
Albicorum et pastorum interfecto partem navium
deprimunt, nonnullas cum hominibus capiunt, reliquas
in portum compellunt. Eo die naves Massiliensium
cum eis, quae sunt captae, [1] intereunt VIIII.

59   Hoc primum Caesari ad Ilerdam nuntiatur; simul
perfecto ponte celeriter fortuna mutatur. Illi perterriti virtute equitum minus libere, minus audacter
vagabantur, alias non longo a castris progressi spatio,
ut celerem receptum haberent, angustius pabulaban-
tur, alias longiore circuitu custodias stationesque
equitum vitabant, aut aliquo accepto detrimento aut
procul equitatu viso ex medio itinere proiectis sarcinis
fugiebant. Postremo et plures intermittere dies et
praeter consuetudinem omnium noctu constituerant
pabulari.

60   Interim Oscenses et Calagurritani, qui erant
Oscensibus contributi, mittunt ad eum legatos seseque imperata facturos pollicentur. Hos Tarraconenses
et Iacetani et Ausetani et paucis post diebus Illurgavonenses, qui flumen Hiberum attingunt, insequuntur.
Petit ab his omnibus, ut se frumento iuvent. Polli-

---

[1] cum eis quae sunt captae *MSS.*: Domitiique sunt captae VI,
Meusel after Paul. There is much difficulty about the ships.

82

hurry of unseasoned timber, they did not display the same handiness in respect of speed. And so, provided that an opportunity of fighting hand to hand were given them, with quiet courage they confronted two ships with one, and throwing aboard the iron claw and holding each ship fast, they fought on opposite sides of their vessel and so boarded the enemy's ships; and after slaying a large number of the Albici and the herdsmen they sink some of the ships, take others with their crews, and drive the rest into port. On that day nine ships of the Massilians are lost, including those that were captured.

This news is first brought to Caesar at Ilerda; at 59 once on the completion of the bridge there is a rapid change of fortune. The enemy, terror-struck by the bravery of the cavalry, now roamed with less freedom and audacity; at one time, staying their advance at no great distance from the camp, in order to ensure a speedy retreat, they foraged within narrower limits; at another, taking a wider circuit, they tried to avoid the outposts and cavalry pickets, or, on sustaining some loss or catching sight of the cavalry at a distance, they broke off their march, flung away their packs, and fled. Finally, they made up their mind to stay action for several days and, contrary to the general custom, to forage by night.

Meanwhile the inhabitants of Osca, and those of 60 Calagurris who were politically associated[1] with them, send envoys to him and promise to do his bidding. These are followed by the people of Tarraco, the Iacetani, the Ausetani, and a few days afterwards the Illurgavonenses, who border on the River Ebro. He begs all of these to assist him with corn. They

---

[1] Calagurris had been deprived of its independence and made tributary to the people of Osca.

centur atque omnibus undique conquisitis iumentis in castra deportant. Transit etiam cohors Illurgavonensis ad eum cognito civitatis consilio et signa ex statione transfert. Magna celeriter commutatio rerum. Perfecto ponte, magnis quinque civitatibus ad amicitiam adiunctis, expedita re frumentaria, exstinctis rumoribus de auxiliis legionum, quae cum Pompeio per Mauritaniam venire dicebantur, multae longinquiores civitates ab Afranio desciscunt et Caesaris amicitiam sequuntur.

61   Quibus rebus perterritis animis adversariorum Caesar, ne semper magno circuitu per pontem equitatus esset mittendus, nactus idoneum locum fossas pedum xxx in latitudinem complures facere instituit, quibus partem aliquam. Sicoris averteret vadumque in eo flumine efficeret. His paene effectis magnum in timorem Afranius Petreiusque perveniunt, ne omnino frumento pabuloque intercluderentur, quod multum Caesar equitatu valebat. Itaque constituunt illis locis excedere et in Celtiberiam bellum transferre. Huic consilio suffragabatur etiam illa res, quod ex duobus contrariis generibus, quae superiore bello cum Sertorio steterant civitates, victae nomen atque imperium absentis Pompei timebant, quae in amicitia manserant, magnis affectae beneficiis eum diligebant; Caesaris autem erat in barbaris nomen obscurius. Hic magnos equitatus magnaque auxilia exspectabant et suis locis bellum in hiemem ducere cogitabant. Hoc inito consilio toto flumine Hibero

promise to do so and, collecting all the pack-horses available, bring it into camp. A cohort of the Illurgavonenses also goes over to him on ascertaining the intention of their state and transfers its colours from its quarters. A great change of fortune rapidly follows. The bridge being completed, five important states brought over to his side, the corn supply made easy, the rumours about the auxiliaries of the legions which were said to be coming with Pompeius through Mauritania being suppressed, a number of more distant communities desert Afranius and take the side of Caesar.

When the spirits of his adversaries were cowed by 61 these events, Caesar, to prevent the need of always sending the cavalry over the bridge by a long circuitous route, found a suitable spot and decided to construct several ditches thirty feet wide, whereby he might divert some part of the Sicoris and make a ford in the river. When these were nearly completed Afranius and Petreius fall into great alarm lest they should be cut off altogether from collecting forage and fodder, as Caesar was particularly strong in cavalry. And so they determine to quit these districts and to transfer the war to Celtiberia. This design was also favoured by the fact that of the two different classes of states, those which in the earlier war had taken the side of Sertorius and had been conquered feared the name and authority of the absent Pompeius, and those which had remained loyal, having received great kindnesses, were devoted to him, while the name of Caesar was only dimly known among the barbarians. In this district they were expecting to find large reinforcements of cavalry and auxiliaries, and were proposing to prolong the war into the winter in a place of their own choosing. Having formed this plan, they order ships

naves conquiri et Octogesam adduci iubent. Id erat oppidum positum ad Hiberum miliaque passuum a castris aberat XXX. Ad eum locum fluminis navibus iunctis pontem imperant fieri legionesque duas flumen Sicorim traducunt, castraque muniunt vallo pedum XII.

62 Qua re per exploratores cognita summo labore militum Caesar continuato diem noctemque opere in flumine avertendo huc iam rem deduxerat,[1] ut equites, etsi difficulter atque aegre fiebat, possent tamen atque auderent flumen transire, pedites vero tantummodo umeris ac summo pectore exstarent et cum altitudine aquae tum etiam rapiditate fluminis ad transeundum impedirentur. Sed tamen eodem fere tempore pons in Hibero prope effectus nuntiabatur, et in Sicori vadum reperiebatur.

63 Iam vero eo magis illi maturandum iter existimabant. Itaque duabus auxiliaribus cohortibus Ilerdae praesidio relictis omnibus copiis Sicorim transeunt et cum duabus legionibus, quas superioribus diebus traduxerant, castra coniungunt. Relinquebatur Caesari nihil, nisi uti equitatu agmen adversariorum male haberet et carperet. Pons enim ipsius magnum circuitum habebat, ut multo breviore itinere illi ad Hiberum pervenire possent. Equites ab eo missi flumen transeunt et, cum de tertia vigilia Petreius atque Afranius castra movissent, repente sese ad novissimum agmen ostendunt et magna multitudine circumfusa morari atque iter impedire incipiunt.

[1] reduxerat rem *MSS*. *I transpose* rem, *thus accounting for the corruption of the correct* deduxerat.

to be sought for along the whole course of the Ebro and to be brought to Octogesa. This town was situated on the Ebro, and was thirty miles from the camp. They order a bridge to be made at this part of the river by coupling ships together and bring two legions over the Sicoris. A camp is entrenched with a rampart twelve feet high.

When this was ascertained by means of scouts, 62 Caesar, continuing day and night his task of diverting the stream by the utmost efforts of his soldiery, had so far advanced operations that the horsemen were able to cross the river, and ventured to do so, though the feat was laborious and difficult; while the foot-soldiers had only their shoulders and the upper part of their bodies above the surface, and were impeded in crossing both by the depth of the water and also by the rapidity of the current. Nevertheless about one and the same time the bridge over the Ebro was announced to be nearly finished and a ford was being found in the Sicoris.

Now, however, the enemy thought it the more 63 necessary that their march should be hastened. So, leaving two auxiliary cohorts to garrison Ilerda, they cross the Sicoris in full force and join camp with the two legions which they had led across on a previous day. The only course left for Caesar was to annoy and harass the enemy's line of march with his cavalry; for his own bridge involved a wide circuit, so that the enemy could reach the Ebro by a much shorter route. He sends horsemen who cross the river and, although Petreius and Afranius had moved camp about the third watch, suddenly show themselves in the rear of the column and begin to delay them and impede their march by pouring a great number of men around their flanks.

64   Prima luce ex superioribus locis, quae Caesaris
castris erant coniuncta, cernebatur equitatus nostri
proelio novissimos illorum premi vehementer ac non-
nunquam sustineri[1] extremum agmen atque inter-
rumpi, alias inferri signa et universarum cohortium
impetu nostros propelli, dein rursus conversos insequi. Totis vero castris milites circulari et dolere
hostem ex manibus dimitti, bellum non necessario[2]
longius duci; centuriones tribunosque militum adire
atque obsecrare, ut per eos Caesar certior fieret, ne
labori suo neu periculo parceret; paratos esse sese,
posse et audere ea transire flumen, qua traductus
esset equitatus. Quorum studio et vocibus excitatus
Caesar, etsi timebat tantae magnitudini fluminis exercitum obicere, conandum tamen atque experien-
dum iudicat. Itaque infirmiores milites ex omnibus
centuriis deligi iubet, quorum aut animus aut vires
videbantur sustinere non posse. Hos cum legione
una praesidio castris relinquit; reliquas legiones expeditas educit magnoque numero iumentorum in
flumine supra atque infra constituto traducit exercitum. Pauci ex his militibus abrepti vi fluminis ab
equitatu excipiuntur ac sublevantur; interit tamen
nemo. Traducto incolumi exercitu copias instruit
triplicemque aciem ducere incipit. Ac tantum fuit
in militibus studii, ut milium sex ad iter addito circuitu magnaque ad vadum fluminis mora interposita

[1] sustineri *Giesing:* sustinere *MSS. Perhaps Caesar wrote*
vix (*or* aegre) sustinere, "*with difficulty held their own.*"
[2] non necessario *SE: the rest omit* non.

88

At early dawn it was observed from the higher 64
ground adjacent to Caesar's camp that the enemy's
rear was being hard pressed by the attack of our
cavalry, and that sometimes the end of the column
was being held up and even being cut off from the rest,
while at other times their colours were pushed forward
and our men were driven back by a charge of the
cohorts in a body, and then again wheeled round and
pursued the foe. And now throughout the camp the
men gathered in groups, indignantly complaining that
the enemy were being let slip from their hands, and
that the war was being needlessly protracted to an
undue length. They went to the centurions and
military tribunes, and besought them to assure Caesar
that he was not to shrink from exposing them to labour
or peril. "We are ready," they said; "we can and we
dare cross the river by the way the cavalry passed
over." Caesar, urged by their zeal and their clamour,
though he feared to expose his army to such a
strength of current, nevertheless decides that he
must attempt the experiment. So he orders the
weaker men, whose spirit or strength seemed unequal to the effort, to be set aside from all the
centuries. These he leaves with one legion to guard
the camp. The rest of the legions he leads out
lightly equipped, and after placing a great number of
pack-horses in the river above and below leads across
his force. A few of these men were carried away by
the strength of the current, but were caught and supported by the horsemen; not one, however, was lost.
When his army had been led across without loss, he
draws up his forces and proceeds to lead his battle in
three lines. And there was such zeal in the soldiery
that, though a circuit of six miles was added to their
route and a long delay was interposed at the ford,

eos, qui de tertia vigilia exissent, ante horam diei
VIIII consequerentur.

65 Quos ubi Afranius procul visos cum Petreio conspexit, nova re perterritus locis superioribus constitit
aciemque instruit. Caesar in campis exercitum
reficit, ne defessum proelio obiciat; rursus conantes
progredi insequitur et moratur. Illi necessario ma-
turius, quam constituerant, castra ponunt. Suberant
enim montes, atque a milibus passuum v itinera dif-
ficilia atque angusta excipiebant. Hos montes
intrasse cupiebant, ut equitatum effugerent Caesaris
praesidiisque in angustiis collocatis exercitum itinere prohiberent, ipsi sine periculo ac timore Hiberum copias traducerent. Quod fuit illis conandum
atque omni ratione efficiendum; sed totius diei pugna
atque itineris labore defessi rem in posterum diem dis-
tulerunt. Caesar quoque in proximo colle castra ponit.

66 Media circiter nocte eis, qui aquandi causa
longius a castris processerant, ab equitibus cor-
reptis fit ab his certior Caesar duces adversariorum
silentio copias castris educere. Quo cognito signum
dari iubet et vasa militari more conclamari. Illi
exaudito clamore veriti, ne noctu impediti sub onere
confligere cogerentur aut ne ab equitatu Caesaris in
angustiis tenerentur, iter supprimunt copiasque in
castris continent. Postero die Petreius cum paucis
equitibus occulte ad exploranda loca proficiscitur.

they overtook before the ninth hour of the day those who had gone out at the third watch.

And when Afranius with Petreius beheld these 65 troops, whom he caught sight of from a distance, he was dismayed by an event so startling, and halting on higher ground drew up his line. Caesar re-forms his army on the plains that he may not expose it to battle exhausted with fatigue. When they again attempt to advance he follows and checks them. The foe of necessity pitch their camp earlier than they had intended, for the hills were close by and difficult and narrow routes awaited them only five miles off. These hills they were eager to penetrate in order to escape Caesar's cavalry and, by placing outposts in the defiles, to stop the march of his army, and themselves to conduct their forces across the Ebro without danger and alarm. This they should have attempted and carried out by every possible means, but worn out by a whole day's fighting and the toil of their march, they postponed the business till the next day. Caesar also pitches camp on the nearest hill.

About midnight, when some men who had gone 66 some distance from their camp to fetch water were seized by his horsemen, Caesar is informed by them that the officers of the enemy are silently leading their forces out of camp. Having learnt this, he bids the signal be given and the usual military order for striking camp to be proclaimed. The foe, having caught the sound of the proclamation, fearing lest, impeded and over-burdened, they should be compelled to engage by night, or lest they should be held up by Caesar's cavalry in the defiles, stop their march and keep their forces in camp. Next day Petreius sets forth secretly with a few horsemen to explore the district. The same thing

Hoc idem fit ex castris Caesaris. Mittitur L. Decidius Saxa cum paucis, qui loci naturam perspiciat. Uterque idem suis renuntiat: v milia passuum proxima intercedere itineris campestris, inde excipere loca aspera et montuosa; qui prior has angustias occupaverit, ab hoc hostem prohiberi nihil esse negotii.

67 Disputatur in consilio a Petreio atque Afranio et tempus profectionis quaeritur. Plerique censebant, ut noctu iter facerent: posse prius ad angustias veniri, quam sentiretur. Alii, quod pridie noctu conclamatum esset in Caesaris castris, argumenti sumebant loco non posse clam exiri. Circumfundi noctu equitatum Caesaris atque omnia loca atque itinera obsidere; nocturnaque proelia esse vitanda, quod perterritus miles in civili dissensione timori magis quam religioni consulere consuerit. At lucem multum per se pudorem omnium oculis, multum etiam tribunorum militum et centurionum praesentiam afferre[1]; quibus rebus coërceri milites et in officio contineri soleant. Quare omni ratione esse interdiu perrumpendum: etsi aliquo accepto detrimento, tamen summa exercitus salva locum, quem petant, capi posse. Haec vincit in consilio sententia, et prima luce postridie constituunt proficisci.

68 Caesar exploratis regionibus albente caelo omnes copias castris educit magnoque circuitu nullo certo itinere exercitum ducit. Nam quae itinera ad Hiberum atque Octogesam pertinebant castris hostium oppositis tenebantur. Ipsi erant transcendendae

[1] *There is certainly some corruption in the text of this sentence.*

is done from Caesar's camp. L. Decidius Saxa is sent with a few men to reconnoitre the character of the place. Each brings back the same message to his people: that nearest them there lie five miles of level route, then follows rugged and hilly ground, that there is no difficulty in the enemy being stopped by whosoever first occupies these defiles.

Petreius and Afranius hold a discussion in council, 67 the question before them being the time of starting. Many thought that they should march by night, urging that they could reach the defiles before it was noticed. Others took the fact that the cry had been raised the previous night in Caesar's camp as a proof that secret departure was impossible. They pointed out that Caesar's horsemen poured around at night and beset every place and every path; that night battles should be avoided because the soldiers in the terror of civil strife are wont to consider their fears rather than their obligations. But daylight, they urged, in itself brings a sense of shame when all are looking on, and the presence of military tribunes and centurions also contributes much, and that it was by such considerations that troops are wont to be restrained and kept in allegiance. On every ground, therefore, they must break through by day: though some loss should be sustained, yet the place they are after can be captured without impairing the army as a whole. This opinion prevails in the council and they determine to set out next day at early dawn.

Caesar after reconnoitring the district leads all his 68 forces out of camp when the sky grows light and, making a wide circuit, conducts his army by no clearly marked route. For the roads that led to the Ebro and to Octogesa were blocked by the interposition of the enemy's camp. He himself had to cross

valles maximae ac difficillimae; saxa multis locis praerupta iter impediebant, ut arma per manus necessario traderentur, militesque inermes sublevatique alii ab aliis magnam partem itineris conficerent. Sed hunc laborem recusabat nemo, quod eum omnium laborum finem fore existimabant, si hostem Hibero intercludere et frumento prohibere potuissent.

69   Ac primo Afraniani milites visendi causa laeti ex castris procurrebant contumeliosisque vocibus prosequebantur nostros: necessarii victus inopia coactos fugere atque ad Ilerdam reverti. Erat enim iter a proposito diversum, contrariamque in partem iri videbatur. Duces vero eorum consilium suum laudibus efferebant, quod se castris tenuissent; multumque eorum opinionem adiuvabat, quod sine iumentis impedimentisque ad iter profectos videbant, ut non posse inopiam diutius sustinere confiderent. Sed, ubi paulatim retorqueri agmen ad dextram conspexerunt iamque primos superare regionem castrorum animum adverterunt, nemo erat adeo tardus aut fugiens laboris, quin statim castris exeundum atque occurrendum putaret. Conclamatur ad arma, atque omnes copiae paucis praesidio relictis cohortibus exeunt rectoque ad Hiberum itinere contendunt.

70   Erat in celeritate omne positum certamen, utri prius angustias montesque occuparent; sed exercitum Caesaris viarum difficultates tardabant, Afranii copias equitatus Caesaris insequens morabatur. Res

very large and difficult valleys, steep rocks in many
places impeded their march, so that arms were of
necessity passed from hand to hand, and the men
accomplished a great part of their way unarmed and
helped up one by another. But no one shirked this
toil, because they thought it would prove the end of
all their labours, if only they should be able to cut
off the foe from the Ebro and prevent him from
foraging.

And first of all the Afranian soldiers joyfully ran   69
out of their camp to see the spectacle and pursued our
men with insulting cries, saying that they were fleeing
under the stress of lack of necessary food, and were
on their way back to Ilerda. For the direction of
their march was different from that proposed, and
they seemed to be going in the contrary direction.
The Afranian officers extolled their own policy in
having kept themselves in camp, and their opinion was
greatly strengthened by the fact that they saw the
foe started on their way without any baggage train,
so that they were confident that they could not hold
out much longer against privation. But when they
saw the column gradually wheeling to the right and
observed the vanguard already outflanking the line
of their own camp, no one was so slow, so impatient
of labour, as not to feel that they must at once leave
the camp and go to meet the foe. The cry "To
arms!" is raised, and the whole force, a few cohorts
only being left on guard, goes forth and hurries on
a straight course to the Ebro.

The whole contest turned on speed—which of the   70
two would first seize the defiles and the hills—but
the difficulties of the roads delayed Caesar's army,
while Caesar's pursuing cavalry hindered the forces
of Afranius. Matters, however, had of necessity come

tamen ab Afranianis huc erat necessario deducta,
ut, si priores montes, quos petebant, attigissent, ipsi
periculum vitarent, impedimenta totius exercitus
cohortesque in castris relictas servare non possent;
quibus interclusis exercitu Caesaris auxilium ferri
nulla ratione poterat. Confecit prior iter Caesar
atque ex magnis rupibus nactus planitiem in hac
contra hostem aciem instruit. Afranius, cum ab
equitatu novissimum agmen premeretur, ante se
hostem videret, collem quendam nactus ibi constitit.
Ex eo loco iiii cetratorum cohortes in montem, qui
erat in conspectu omnium excelsissimus, mittit.
Hunc magno cursu concitatos iubet occupare, eo
consilio, uti ipse eodem omnibus copiis contenderet
et mutato itinere iugis Octogesam perveniret. Hunc
cum obliquo itinere cetrati peterent, conspicatus
equitatus Caesaris in cohortes impetum fecit; nec
minimam partem temporis equitum vim cetrati sustinere potuerunt omnesque ab eis circumventi in conspectu utriusque exercitus interficiuntur.

71   Erat occasio bene gerendae rei. Neque vero id
Caesarem fugiebat, tanto sub oculis accepto detrimento perterritum exercitum sustinere non posse,
praesertim circumdatum undique equitatu, cum in loco
aequo atque aperto confligeretur; idque ex omnibus
partibus ab eo flagitabatur. Concurrebant legati,
centuriones tribunique militum: ne dubitaret proelium committere; omnium esse militum paratissimos

to such a pass with the Afranians that, if they should first reach the hills that they aimed at, they would themselves escape peril, while they would be unable to save the baggage of the whole army and the cohorts left in the camp; for when these were cut off by Caesar's army it was by no means possible for assistance to be conveyed to them. Caesar completed the distance first, and finding a plain after crossing the great rocks, he draws up his line therein opposite the enemy. Afranius, seeing the foe in front of him, while his rear was being harassed by the cavalry, finding a hill near, halted on it. From this spot he dispatches four light-armed cohorts to a mountain which was the loftiest of all in sight. He orders them to hurry at full speed and occupy it, with the intention of himself hastening thither with all his forces, and by a change of route arriving at Octogesa by the ridge. When the light-armed men were making for this by an oblique route, Caesar's horsemen, perceiving it, charged the cohorts; nor could they, with their small shields, hold out for ever so short a time against the cavalry attack, but are all surrounded by them and slain in the sight of both armies.

There was now opportunity for a successful 71 action. Nor, indeed, did it escape Caesar that an army demoralized by such a loss received under their eyes could not hold out, especially as they were surrounded on every side by cavalry, since the engagement was taking place in level and open country; and such action was demanded of him from every quarter. Legates, centurions, and tribunes hurried to him begging him not to hesitate to join battle; they pointed out that the spirits of the whole force were as keen as possible; on the

97

animos. Afranianos contra multis rebus sui timoris signa misisse: quod suis non subvenissent, quod de colle non decederent, quod vix equitum incursus sustinerent collatisque in unum locum signis conferti neque ordines neque signa servarent. Quod si iniquitatem loci timeret, datum iri tamen aliquo loco pugnandi facultatem, quod certe inde decedendum esset Afranio nec sine aqua permanere posset.

72 Caesar in eam spem venerat, se sine pugna et sine vulnere suorum rem conficere posse, quod re frumentaria adversarios interclusisset. Cur etiam secundo proelio aliquos ex suis amitteret? cur vulnerari pateretur optime de se meritos milites? cur denique fortunam periclitaretur? praesertim cum non minus esset imperatoris consilio superare quam gladio. Movebatur etiam misericordia civium, quos interficiendos videbat; quibus salvis atque incolumibus rem obtinere malebat. Hoc consilium Caesaris plerisque non probabatur: milites vero palam inter se loquebantur, quoniam talis occasio victoriae dimitteretur, etiam cum vellet Caesar, sese non esse pugnaturos. Ille in sua sententia perseverat et paulum ex eo loco digreditur, ut timorem adversariis minuat. Petreius atque Afranius oblata facultate in castra sese referunt. Caesar praesidiis montibus

other hand, the Afranians had in many ways shown signs of fear, by the fact that they had not succoured their own men, that they were not going down from the hill, that they were scarcely holding their ground against the cavalry charges, and that, crowded together, with their colours congregated in one spot, they were keeping neither to their ranks nor to their standards. If it was the inequality of site that he feared, yet an opportunity of fighting in some place or other would be afforded him, because Afranius was certainly bound to come down from his position, and could not continue to hold it without water.

Caesar had entertained the hope that, having cut 72 off his adversaries from their food supply, he would be able to finish the business without exposing his men to fighting or bloodshed. Why should he lose any of his men even in a successful battle? Why should he suffer soldiers who had served him so well to be wounded? Why, in a word, should he make trial of fortune? Especially as it was as much the duty of a commander to win by policy as by the sword. He was moved, moreover, by compassion for his fellow-citizens whose slaughter he saw to be inevitable. He preferred to gain his object without loss or harm to them. This policy of his did not commend itself to the majority; in fact, the soldiers said openly among themselves that, since such an opportunity of victory was being let slip, they would not fight even when Caesar wished them to. He adheres to his intention, and moves a little way from his position so as to diminish the alarm of the foe. Petreius and Afranius return to their camp when the chance is offered them. Caesar, after distributing outposts on the hills, shutting off every route to the

dispositis omni ad Hiberum intercluso itinere quam
proxime potest hostium castris castra communit.

73 Postero die duces adversariorum perturbati, quod
omnem rei frumentariae fluminisque Hiberi spem
dimiserant, de reliquis rebus consultabant. Erat
unum iter, Ilerdam si reverti vellent; alterum, si
Tarraconem peterent. Haec consiliantibus eis nun-
tiantur aquatores ab equitatu premi nostro. Qua
re cognita crebras stationes disponunt equitum et
cohortium alariarum legionariasque intericiunt cohortes vallumque ex castris ad aquam ducere incipiunt, ut intra munitionem et sine timore et sine
stationibus aquari possent. Id opus inter se Petreius
atque Afranius partiuntur ipsique perficiundi operis
causa longius progrediuntur.

74 Quorum discessu liberam nacti milites colloquiorum
facultatem vulgo procedunt, et quem quisque in
castris notum aut municipem habebat conquirit atque
evocat. Primum agunt gratias omnibus, quod sibi
perterritis pridie pepercissent: eorum se beneficio
vivere. Deinde de imperatoris fide[1] quaerunt, rectene
se illi sint commissuri, et quod non ab initio fecerint
armaque cum hominibus necessariis et consanguineis
contulerint, queruntur. His provocati sermonibus
fidem ad imperatore de Petreii atque Afranii vita
petunt, ne quod in se scelus concepisse neu suos

---

[1] MSS. deinde imperatoris fidem: *corrected by Madvig.*

Ebro, entrenches himself as near as possible to the enemy's camp.

On the next day the enemy's officers, dismayed at 73 having lost all prospect of supplies and of reaching the Ebro, took counsel on their other measures. There was one route in case they wished to return to Ilerda, another if they made for Tarraco. While deliberating thereon, word is brought them that their water-carriers are being harassed by our cavalry. Having ascertained this, they distribute numerous outposts of horsemen and auxiliary cohorts, and between them place cohorts of the legions, and set about making a line of rampart from the camp to the water, so that they might be able to get water within their defences, both without alarm and without outposts. Petreius and Afranius share this task between them, and themselves proceed to some distance for the purpose of carrying out the work.

At their departure the soldiers, getting a free 74 opportunity for conversation, come out everywhere, and each one inquires after any acquaintance or fellow-townsman that he had in Caesar's camp and summons him forth. First they all express gratitude to the others collectively for having spared them the day before, when they were in a state of panic: "To your kindness," they said, "we owe our life." Then they inquire about the good faith of the general, whether they would be justified in committing themselves to him, and express regret that they did not do so at first, and that they engaged in a conflict with friends and kinsmen. Stirred by such speeches, the men demand a solemn promise from the general for the life of Petreius and Afranius, fearing lest they should seem to have conceived some crime in their hearts or to have betrayed their party.

prodidisse videantur. Quibus confirmatis rebus se
statim signa translaturos confirmant legatosque de
pace primorum ordinum centuriones ad Caesarem
mittunt. Interim alii suos in castra invitandi causa
adducunt, alii ab suis abducuntur, adeo ut una castra
iam facta ex binis viderentur; compluresque tribuni
militum et centuriones ad Caesarem veniunt seque ei
commendant. Idem hoc fit a principibus Hispaniae,
quos evocaverant et secum in castris habebant obsidum
loco. Hi suos notos hospitesque quaerebant, per
quem quisque eorum aditum commendationis haberet
ad Caesarem. Afranii etiam filius adulescens de sua
ac parentis sui salute cum Caesare per Sulpicium
legatum agebat. Erant plena laetitia et gratulatione
omnia, eorum, qui tanta pericula vitasse, et eorum,
qui sine vulnere tantas res confecisse videbantur,
magnumque fructum suae pristinae lenitatis omnium
iudicio Caesar ferebat, consiliumque eius a cunctis
probabatur.

75   Quibus rebus nuntiatis Afranius ab instituto opere
discedit seque in castra recipit, sic paratus, ut
videbatur, ut, quicumque accidisset casus, hunc
quieto et aequo animo ferret. Petreius vero non de-
serit sese. Armat familiam; cum hac et praetoria
cohorte cetratorum barbarisque equitibus paucis,
beneficiariis suis, quos suae custodiae causa habere
consuerat, improviso ad vallum advolat, colloquia
militum interrumpit, nostros repellit a castris, quos
deprendit interficit. Reliqui coëunt inter se et

If these conditions are assured they guarantee to transfer their colours at once and send centurions of the first rank to Caesar as deputies to treat of peace. Meanwhile some bring their friends into the camp to entertain them, others are led off by their acquaintances, so that the two camps seemed already fused into one, and many military tribunes and centurions come to Caesar and commend themselves to him. The same thing is done by the Spanish chieftains whom the enemy had called out and were keeping with them in camp as hostages. These sought for their own acquaintances and guest-friends by whom they might severally have an opportunity of being commended to the notice of Caesar. The youthful son of Afranius also pleaded with Caesar through the envoy Sulpicius for his own and his father's safety. The whole place was full of rejoicing and congratulation, on the one side of those who were deemed to have avoided such perils, on the other of those who were seen to have wrought such achievements without bloodshed; and Caesar in the general estimation reaped a great advantage from his traditional leniency, and his policy met with the approval of all.

When these events were announced Afranius aban- 75 dons the work that he had begun and returns to camp, apparently resolved to bear with a quiet and equal mind whatever chance should befall. But Petreius does not fail himself. He arms his retinue; with this and his official staff of light-armed men and with a few barbarian horsemen, his own retainers, whom he had been wont to maintain to guard his person, he makes a sudden onset on the rampart, interrupts the soldiers' colloquies, drives our men from the camp, and slays all he catches. The rest gather together and, terri-

repentino periculo exterriti sinistras sagis involvunt gladiosque destringunt atque ita se a cetratis equitibusque defendunt castrorum propinquitate confisi seque in castra recipiunt et ab eis cohortibus, quae erant in statione ad portas, defenduntur.

76 Quibus rebus confectis flens Petreius manipulos circumit militesque appellat, neu se neu Pompeium, imperatorem suum, adversariis ad supplicium tradant, obsecrat. Fit celeriter concursus in praetorium. Postulat, ut iurent omnes se exercitum ducesque non deserturos neque prodituros neque sibi separatim a reliquis consilium capturos. Princeps in haec verba iurat ipse; idem iusiurandum adigit Afranium; subsequuntur tribuni militum centurionesque; centuriatim producti milites idem iurant. Edicunt, penes quem quisque sit Caesaris miles, ut producatur: productos palam in praetorio interficiunt. Sed plerosque ei, qui receperant, celant noctuque per vallum emittunt. Sic terror oblatus a ducibus, crudelitas in supplicio, nova religio iurisiurandi spem praesentis deditionis sustulit mentesque militum convertit et rem ad pristinam belli rationem redegit.

77 Caesar, qui milites adversariorum in castra per tempus colloquii venerant, summa diligentia conquiri et remitti iubet. Sed ex numero tribunorum militum centurionumque nonnulli sua voluntate apud eum remanserunt. Quos ille postea magno

fied by the sudden peril, wrap their left hands in their cloaks, draw their swords, and thus defend themselves from the light infantry and horsemen, trusting in the proximity of their camp, and retire to it, defended by the cohorts which are on guard at the gates.

When this action was over Petreius goes the round 76 of the maniples and calls on his men, beseeching them with tears not to hand over himself or their commander Pompeius to the foe for punishment. A crowd quickly gathers at the general's headquarters. He demands that all should swear not to desert or betray the army and its officers, nor to take measures for their own safety apart from the rest. He first takes this oath himself, and also compels Afranius to take the same. Next come the military tribunes and centurions; the rank and file come forward and take the oath century by century. They issue orders that any soldier of Caesar who is in the company of one of their men should be brought forward by him. When produced they kill him publicly at the headquarters. But many of them are concealed by those who had entertained them, and are let go at night through the ramparts. Thus the intimidation employed by the generals, cruelty in punishment, and the obligation of their fresh oath removed all prospect of present surrender, changed the inclination of the soldiery, and brought matters back to the old condition of hostility.

Caesar gives orders that the men of the other side 77 who had come into his camp at the time of the colloquy should be sought for with the utmost diligence and sent back. But out of their number several military tribunes and centurions remained with him of their own accord. These he afterwards

in honore habuit; centuriones in priores ordines, equites Romanos in tribunicium restituit honorem.

78 Premebantur[1] Afraniani pabulatione, aquabantur aegre. Frumenti copiam legionarii nonnullam habebant, quod dierum XXII[2] ab Ilerda frumentum iussi erant efferre, cetrati auxiliaresque nullam, quorum erant et facultates ad parandum exiguae et corpora insueta ad onera portanda. Itaque magnus eorum cotidie numerus ad Caesarem perfugiebat. In his erat angustiis res. Sed ex propositis consiliis duobus explicitius videbatur Ilerdam reverti, quod ibi paulum frumenti reliquerant. Ibi se reliquum consilium explicaturos confidebant. Tarraco aberat longius; quo spatio plures rem posse casus recipere intellegebant. Hoc probato consilio ex castris proficiscuntur. Caesar equitatu praemisso, qui novissimum agmen carperet atque impediret, ipse cum legionibus subsequitur. Nullum intercedebat tempus, quin extremi cum equitibus proeliarentur.

79 Genus erat hoc pugnae. Expeditae cohortes novissimum agmen claudebant pluresque in locis campestribus subsistebant.[3] Si mons erat ascendendus, facile ipsa loci natura periculum repellebat, quod ex locis superioribus, qui antecesserant, suos ascendentes protegebant; cum vallis aut locus declivis suberat, neque ei, qui antecesserant, moran-

[1] premebantur *MSS.*: prohibebantur *Paul.*
[2] XXII *MSS. The number cannot be right; perhaps* VII *or* VIII *or* XII *should be read.*
[3] *The text of this passage is open to doubt.*

106

held in high honour; centurions he restored to their former ranks, Roman knights to the post of tribune. [1]

The Afranians were in straits with their foraging 78 and were getting water with difficulty. The legionaries had some store of corn because they had been ordered to bring a twenty-two days' supply from Ilerda; the light-armed and auxiliaries had none, since their opportunities for providing it were scanty and their bodies were not trained to carry burdens. And so a great number of them fled to Caesar every day. Such were the straits of the enemy's situation. But of the two plans set before them the simpler seemed to be to return to Ilerda, because they had left a little corn there. They were confident that they would there evolve their plans for the future. Tarraco was a long way off, and they understood that in so long a journey their fortune might meet with various mischances. This plan having approved itself, they depart from the camp. Caesar, after sending forward his cavalry to annoy and hinder their rear, himself follows with the legions. No moment passed without their rearguard having to fight with the horsemen.

Their method of fighting was as follows: lightly 79 equipped cohorts closed in their rearguard and several of these kept halting in the level districts; if a hill had to be climbed, the nature of the ground in itself averted peril, since from the higher ground those who had gone in front protected their comrades who were ascending; whenever a valley or a slope lay before them and those who had gone on in front could not bring aid to those who were delayed, while

---

[1] The *tribuni militum* were *equites Romani*. Caesar means that he restored the military tribunes to the rank that they had previously held in Pompeius' army.

tibus opem ferre poterant, equites vero ex loco
superiore in aversos tela coniciebant, tum magno
erat in periculo res. Relinquebatur, ut, cum eius-
modi locis esset appropinquatum, legionum signa
consistere iuberent magnoque impetu equitatum re-
pellerent, eo submoto repente incitati cursu sese
in valles universi demitterent atque ita transgressi
rursus in locis superioribus consisterent. Nam tantum
ab equitum suorum auxiliis aberant, quorum numerum habebant magnum, ut eos superioribus perterritos proeliis in medium reciperent agmen ultroque
eos tuerentur; quorum nulli ex itinere excedere licebat, quin ab equitatu Caesaris exciperetur.

80   Tali dum pugnatur modo, lente atque paulatim
proceditur, crebroque, ut sint auxilio suis, subsistunt;
ut tum accidit. Milia enim progressi IIII vehementiusque peragitati ab equitatu montem excelsum
capiunt ibique una fronte contra hostem castra muniunt neque iumentis onera doponunt. Ubi Caesaris
castra posita tabernaculaque constituta et dimissos
equites pabulandi causa animum adverterunt, sese
subito proripiunt hora circiter sexta eiusdem diei et
spem nacti morae discessu nostrorum equitum iter
facere incipiunt. Qua re animum adversa Caesar
refectis[1] legionibus subsequitur, praesidio impedimentis paucas cohortes relinquit; hora X subsequi
pabulatores equitesque revocari iubet. Celeriter equitatus ad cotidianum itineris officium revertitur. Pugnatur acriter ad novissimum agmen, adeo ut paene
terga convertant, compluresque milites, etiam non-

_____
[1] refectis *Hoffmann:* relictis *MSS.*

the horsemen from higher ground kept hurling missiles against them from behind, then indeed the position was most critical. The only course left for them was, whenever they approached such places, to order a halt of the legions and to repel the cavalry by a vigorous charge, and when they had dislodged it, starting forward immediately at a run, to descend in a body into the valleys, and so, after crossing them, again to halt on the higher ground. For they were so far from being aided by their cavalry, of whom they had a considerable number, that they actually received them for protection, demoralized as they were by the previous battles, into the centre of their column, and none of them could stray from the route without being caught by Caesar's horse.

Fighting in this way, men advance slowly and 80 tentatively, frequently halting to support their comrades, and so it happened on this occasion. For after proceeding four miles and being seriously harassed by the cavalry, they occupy a lofty hill and there entrench a camp with one front only facing the foe, and do not unload their baggage animals. When they observed Caesar's camp pitched, his tents set up, and the horsemen dispersed on foraging duty, they suddenly sally forth about the sixth hour of the same day and, hoping that the pursuit would be delayed by the departure of our cavalry, begin their march. On observing this, Caesar, having rested his legions, follows them up and leaves a few cohorts to guard the baggage. He orders the foragers to follow on at the tenth hour and the horsemen to be recalled. The cavalry quickly returns to its daily employment during the march. Keen fighting goes on in the rear of the foe so that they are almost put to flight, and many men from the ranks, also several centurions,

nulli centuriones, interficiuntur. Instabat agmen Caesaris atque universum imminebat.

81 Tum vero neque ad explorandum idoneum locum castris neque ad progrediendum data facultate consistunt necessario et procul ab aqua et natura iniquo loco castra ponunt. Sed isdem de causis Caesar, quae supra sunt demonstratae, proelio non lacessit et eo die tabernacula statui passus non est, quo paratiores essent ad insequendum omnes, sive noctu sive interdiu erumperent. Illi animadverso vitio castrorum tota nocte munitiones proferunt castraque castris convertunt. Hoc idem postero die a prima luce faciunt totumque in ea re diem consumunt. Sed quantum opere processerant et castra protulerant, tanto aberant ab aqua longius, et praesenti malo aliis malis remedia dabantur. Prima nocte aquandi causa nemo egreditur ex castris; proximo die praesidio in castris relicto universas ad aquam copias educunt, pabulatum emittitur nemo. His eos suppliciis male haberi Caesar et necessariam subire deditionem quam proelio decertare malebat. Conatur tamen eos vallo fossaque circummunire, ut quam maxime repentinas eorum eruptiones demoretur; quo necessario descensuros existimabat. Illi et inopia pabuli adducti et, quo essent expeditiores,[1] omnia sarcinaria iumenta interfici iubent.

82 In his operibus consiliisque biduum consumitur; tertio die magna iam pars operis Caesaris processerat.

[1] ad id expeditiores *MSS.*: ad iter *Manutius, perhaps rightly.*

are slain. Meanwhile Caesar's main force was pressing on and threatening them in mass.

Then, indeed, having no opportunities of searching 81 for a suitable place for their camp nor of advancing, they are obliged to halt and pitch their camp far from water and in a place unfavourable by nature. But, for the same reasons that are set forth above, Caesar no longer harasses them with hostilities, and on that day he did not allow tents to be set up, in order that his men might all be more ready to pursue, in case they should break out either by night or by day. Observing the faulty position of their camp, the enemy push forward outworks throughout the night and exchange one camp for another. They engage in the same task next day from early dawn, and spend the whole day over it. But the more they advanced with their work and pushed forward their camp, the further they were from water, and remedies were provided for their present ill only by incurring fresh ills. On the approach of night no one goes out of camp for watering; on the following day, leaving a guard in the camp, they lead out all their forces for water, but no one is sent out for fodder. Caesar preferred that they should be harassed by such sufferings and submit to a compulsory surrender rather than fight a pitched battle. Nevertheless he attempts to fence them in with a rampart and ditch, so as to hinder as far as possible sudden sallies on their part, to which he thought they would necessarily have recourse. And so forced by want of fodder, and to lighten their equipment for marching, they order all their baggage animals to be killed.

In these operations and plans two days are con- 82 sumed; on the third day a great part of Caesar's work had already reached completion. The enemy,

Illi impediendae reliquae munitionis causa hora circiter VIIII signo dato legiones educunt aciemque sub castris instruunt. Caesar ab opere legiones revocat, equitatum omnem convenire iubet, aciem instruit; contra opinionem enim militum famamque omnium videri proelium defugisse magnum detrimentum afferebat. Sed eisdem de causis, quae sunt cognitae, quo minus dimicare vellet, movebatur, atque hoc etiam magis, quod spatii brevitate etiam in fugam coniectis adversariis non multum ad summam victoria iuvare poterat. Non enim amplius pedum milibus duobus ab castris castra distabant; hinc duas partes acies occupabant duae; tertia vacabat ad incursum atque impetum militum relicta. Si proelium committeretur, propinquitas castrorum celerem superatis ex fuga receptum dabat. Hac de causa constituerat signa inferentibus resistere, prior proelio non lacessere.

83 Acies erat Afraniana duplex legionum V; tertium in subsidiis locum alariae cohortes obtinebant; Caesaris triplex; sed primam aciem quaternae cohortes ex V legionibus tenebant, has subsidiariae ternae et rursus aliae totidem suae cuiusque legionis subsequebantur; sagittarii funditoresque media continebantur acie, equitatus latera cingebat. Tali instructa acie tenere uterque propositum videbatur: Caesar, ne nisi coactus proelium committeret; ille, ut opera Caesaris impediret. Producitur tamen res,

112

in order to hinder the rest of the defences, giving
the signal about the ninth hour, lead out the legions
and draw up their line close to the camp. Caesar
recalls his legions from their work, orders all the
cavalry to assemble, and draws up his line; for to
appear to have shunned a battle against the general
sentiment of the troops, and his credit in the eyes of
the world, involved serious detriment to his cause.
But, for the same reasons that have been already
made known, he was led to object to a pitched battle,
and all the more because by reason of the narrow
intervening space, even if the enemy were driven to
flight, a victory could not greatly promote his final
success. For the two camps were distant from one
another not more than two thousand paces. The two
lines occupied two-thirds of this space; the remaining
third was empty, left free for the onset and charge of
the troops. If battle were joined, the propinquity of
the camps afforded the conquered a speedy retreat
in their flight. For this reason he had made up his
mind to resist them if they advanced their colours,
but not to be the first to attack.

The Afranian line was a double one of five legions. 83
The third line of reserves was occupied by the auxiliary
cohorts. Caesar's line was threefold, but the first
line was held by four cohorts from each of the five
legions, next to these came three reserve cohorts,
and again three more, each from its respective legion;
the bowmen and slingers were enclosed in the
centre of the force, while cavalry protected the
flanks. The battle array being thus drawn out, each
commander seemed to have gained his purpose,
Caesar not to engage in battle unless compelled,
Afranius to hinder Caesar's works. However, the
situation is prolonged and the battle array is main-

113

aciesque ad solis occasum continentur; inde utrique
in castra discedunt. Postero die munitiones institutas
Caesar parat perficere; illi vadum fluminis Sicoris
temptare, si transire possent. Qua re animadversa
Caesar Germanos levis armaturae equitumque partem
flumen traicit crebrasque in ripis custodias disponit.

84   Tandem omnibus rebus obsessi, quartum iam diem
sine pabulo retentis iumentis, aquae, lignorum,
frumenti inopia colloquium petunt et id, si fieri
possit, semoto a militibus loco. Ubi id a Caesare
negatum et, palam si colloqui vellent, concessum
est, datur obsidis loco Caesari filius Afranii. Veni-
tur in eum locum, quem Caesar delegit. Audiente
utroque exercitu loquitur Afranius: non esse aut
ipsis aut militibus succensendum, quod fidem erga
imperatorem suum Cn. Pompeium conservare volue-
rint. Sed satis iam fecisse officio satisque supplicii
tulisse perpessos omnium rerum inopiam; nunc vero
paene ut feras circummunitos prohiberi aqua, prohiberi ingressu, neque corpore dolorem neque animo
ignominiam ferre posse. Itaque se victos confiteri;
orare atque obsecrare, si qui locus misericordiae re-
linquatur, ne ad ultimum supplicium progredi necesse
habeat. Haec quam potest demississime et subiec-
tissime exponit.

85   Ad ea Caesar respondit: nulli omnium has partes
vel querimoniae vel miserationis minus convenisse.
Reliquos enim omnes officium suum praestitisse: se,

tained till sunset; then each side withdraws to camp. On the next day Caesar prepares to complete the defence works he had started; the enemy make trial of the ford of the River Sicoris to see if they could cross. Observing this, Caesar throws his light-armed Germans and part of his cavalry across the river and places frequent outposts along the banks.

At last blockaded in every way, their baggage 84 animals now kept without fodder for four days, through their want of water, firewood, and forage, they beg for a conference, and that too, if possible, in a place out of reach of the soldiers. When this stipulation was refused by Caesar, but permission was granted provided they chose to confer in public, the son of Afranius is offered to Caesar as a hostage. They come to a place which Caesar chose. In the hearing of each army Afranius speaks. "You must not be angry with us or our men because we have chosen to keep faith with our commander Gn. Pompeius. But we have already done enough for duty and we have suffered punishment enough by enduring the want of every necessary; now indeed, hemmed in almost like wild beasts, we are kept from water, kept from moving, and cannot bear the pain in our bodies or the shame in our minds. And so we confess ourselves beaten: we pray and beseech, if any room for compassion is left, that you should not think it necessary to proceed to the extreme of punishment." Such are the sentiments he expresses in the most humble and submissive language.

To this Caesar replied: "No one in the whole 85 army could have played this part, whether of querulous lament or of self-commiseration, less suitably than you. All the rest have done their duty: I,

qui etiam bona condicione, et loco et tempore aequo, confligere noluerit, ut quam integerrima essent ad pacem omnia; exercitum suum, qui iniuria etiam accepta suisque interfectis, quos in sua potestate habuerit, conservarit et texerit; illius denique exercitus milites, qui per se de concilianda pace egerint; qua in re omnium suorum vitae consulendum putarint. Sic omnium ordinum partes in misericordia constitisse: ipsos duces a pace abhorruisse; eos neque colloquii neque indutiarum iura servasse et homines imperitos et per colloquium deceptos crudelissime interfecisse. Accidisse igitur his, quod plerumque hominum nimia pertinacia atque arrogantia accidere soleat, uti eo recurrant et id cupidissime petant, quod paulo ante contempserint. Neque nunc se illorum humilitate neque aliqua temporis opportunitate postulare, quibus rebus opes augeantur suae; sed eos exercitus, quos contra se multos iam annos aluerint, velle dimitti. Neque enim sex legiones alia de causa missas in Hispaniam septimamque ibi conscriptam neque tot tantasque classes paratas neque submissos duces rei militaris peritos. Nihil horum ad pacandas Hispanias, nihil ad usum provinciae provisum, quae propter diuturnitatem pacis nullum auxilium desiderarit. Omnia haec iam pridem contra se parari; in se novi generis imperia constitui, ut idem ad portas

who was unwilling to fight even when conditions were favourable, time and place suitable, that there might be absolutely nothing to prejudice the chances of peace; my army, which preserved and protected those whom it held in its power, even when it had been injured and its soldiers slain; lastly, the men of your army who voluntarily pleaded for reconciliation, a matter wherein they thought it right to have regard to the life of all their comrades. Thus the part played by all ranks has been based on compassion, but the leaders themselves have shrunk from peace; they have observed the rights neither of conference nor of truce, and with utmost cruelty have slain men who through want of experience were deceived by a pretended colloquy. So that has happened to them which is usually wont to happen to men of overmuch obstinacy and arrogance—namely, to recur to that which they have a little while before despised and to make that the chief object of their desire. Nor do I now make demands whereby my resources may be increased by reason of your humiliation or some fortunate conjuncture of events, but I wish the armies which you have now maintained against me for so many years to be disbanded. For no other reason but this were six legions sent into Spain and a seventh levied there, or so many large fleets equipped or leaders of military experience sent to the front. None of these provisions were made for the pacifying of the Spanish provinces, none for the advantage of the province, which from the long continuance of peace required no assistance. All these measures have been for long in course of preparation against me; against me imperial powers of a novel kind are set up, such as that one and the same person should preside

urbanis praesideat rebus et duas bellicosissimas provincias absens tot annis obtineat; in se iura magistratuum commutari, ne ex praetura et consulatu, ut
semper, sed per paucos probati et electi in provincias
mittantur; in se etiam aetatis excusationem nihil
valere, cum superioribus bellis probati ad obtinendos
exercitus evocentur; in se uno non servari, quod sit
omnibus datum semper imperatoribus, ut rebus feli-
citer gestis aut cum honore aliquo aut certe sine
ignominia domum revertantur exercitumque dimittant. Quae tamen omnia et se tulisse patienter et
esse laturum; neque nunc id agere, ut ab illis abductum exercitum teneat ipse, quod tamen sibi difficile non sit, sed ne illi habeant, quo contra se uti
possint. Proinde, ut esset dictum, provinciis excederent exercitumque dimitterent; si id sit factum, se
nociturum nemini. Hanc unam atque extremam esse
pacis condicionem.

86   Id vero militibus fuit pergratum et iucundum, ut
ex ipsa significatione cognosci potuit, ut, qui aliquid
iusti incommodi exspectavissent, ultro praemium
missionis ferrent. Nam cum de loco et tempore eius
rei controversia inferretur, et voce et manibus
universi ex vallo, ubi constiterant, significare coepe-

over city affairs outside the gates[1] and should hold in absence two of the most warlike provinces for so many years; against me are the rights of magistrates subverted, so that they are not sent into the provinces as always hitherto after the praetorship and consulship, but as approved and elected by a small clique; against me even the plea of age is of no avail to prevent men approved[2] in former wars being called out to control armies; in my case alone the rule is not observed which has always been allowed to all commanders, that when they have conducted affairs successfully they should return home, either with some distinction or at any rate without ignominy, and disband their army. Yet I have borne all these wrongs patiently and will bear them, nor is it my present object to retain for myself an army taken from you, which, however, it would not be difficult for me to do, but to prevent you from having one that you can use against me. So then, as has been said, let us quit our provinces and disband our army; if that is so arranged I will injure no one. This is my one and final condition of peace."

Now it was very acceptable and pleasant to the troops, as could be known merely by the indications they gave, that men who had expected some merited penalty should win the boon of discharge without asking for it. For when a discussion was introduced about the place and time of the arrangement, the whole body of men began to signify by voice and hand from the rampart where they stood that they

[1] Early in 49 Pompeius was outside Rome, endeavouring to control affairs within the city, which, as proconsul and armed with the imperium, he was not allowed to enter.
[2] Veteran officers might reasonably claim exemption from further service. The text of this sentence is, however, uncertain.

runt, ut statim dimitterentur, neque omni interposita
fide firmum esse posse, si in aliud tempus differretur.
Paucis cum esset in utramque partem verbis disputa-
tum, res huc deducitur, ut ei, qui habeant domicilium
aut possessionem in Hispania, statim, reliqui ad
Varum flumen dimittantur; ne quid eis noceatur,
neu quis invitus sacramentum dicere cogatur, a
Caesare cavetur.

87   Caesar ex eo tempore, dum ad flumen Varum
veniatur, se frumentum daturum pollicetur. Addit
etiam, ut, quod quisque eorum in bello amiserit, quae
sint penes milites suos, eis, qui amiserint, restituatur;
militibus aequa facta aestimatione pecuniam pro his
rebus dissolvit. Quascumque postea controversias
inter se milites habuerunt, sua sponte ad Caesarem
in ius adierunt. Petreius atque Afranius cum stipendium ab legionibus paene seditione facta flagitarentur,
cuius illi diem nondum venisse dicerent, Caesar ut
cognosceret, postulatum est, eoque utrique, quod
statuit, contenti fuerunt. Parte circiter tertia exercitus eo biduo dimissa duas legiones suas antecedere,
reliquas subsequi iussit, ut non longo inter se spatio
castra facerent, eique negotio Q. Fufium Calenum
legatum praeficit. Hoc eius praescripto ex Hispania
ad Varum flumen est iter factum, atque ibi reliqua
pars exercitus dimissa est.

should be discharged at once, and that the under-taking could not be assured if it were put off to another time, whatever pledges might be given in the interval. When the point had been briefly dis-cussed in either sense, the final result was that those who had a domicile or holding in Spain should be discharged at once, the rest at the River Varus. Pledges are given by Caesar that no wrong should be done to them, and that no one should be compelled to take the oath of allegiance against his will.

Caesar promises to provide them with corn from 87 that time while on their way to the River Varus. He also adds that whatever any one of them has lost in war, when such property is in the hands of his own soldiers, should be restored to the losers; after making a fair valuation, he pays the men a sum of money for these effects. Hereafter whatever dis-putes the soldiers had amongst themselves, of their own accord they came to Caesar for final decision. When the legions on the verge of mutiny were de-manding their pay from Petreius and Afranius, who said that the time for it had not yet come, a request was made that Caesar should investigate the point, and each was satisfied with his decision. About a third of the army having been discharged within two days, Caesar ordered his own two legions to march first, the rest to follow close, so as to encamp at no great distance apart, and set the legate, Q. Fufius Calenus, in charge of this duty. In accordance with this instruction they marched from Spain to the River Varus, and there the rest of the army was disbanded.

BOOK II

LIBER II

1 DUM haec in Hispania geruntur, C. Trebonius
legatus, qui ad oppugnationem Massiliae relictus
erat, duabus ex partibus aggerem, vineas turresque
ad oppidum agere instituit. Una erat proxima portui
navalibusque, altera ad portam, qua est aditus ex
Gallia atque Hispania, ad id mare, quod adiacet ad
ostium Rhodani. Massilia enim fere tribus ex oppidi
partibus mari alluitur; reliqua quarta est, quae aditum habeat ab terra. Huius quoque spatii pars ea,
quae ad arcem pertinet, loci natura et valle altissima
munita longam et difficilem habet oppugnationem.
Ad ea perficienda opera C. Trebonius magnam iumentorum atque hominum multitudinem ex omni
provincia vocat; vimina materiamque comportari
iubet. Quibus comparatis rebus aggerem in altitudinem pedum LXXX exstruit.

2 Sed tanti erant antiquitus in oppido omnium rerum
ad bellum apparatus tantaque multitudo tormentorum, ut eorum vim nullae contextae viminibus
vineae sustinere possent. Asseres enim pedum XII
cuspidibus praefixi atque hi maximis ballistis missi
per IIII ordines cratium in terra defigebantur. Itaque

BOOK II

WHILE this is going on in Spain, the legate, G.   1
Trebonius, who had been left behind for the siege of
Massilia,[1] began to push up to the town on two sides
an earthwork, penthouses, and towers. One side was
quite close to the harbour and docks, the other to
the gate by which lies the approach from Gaul and
Spain, towards that part of the sea which is adjacent
to the mouth of the Rhone. For Massilia is washed
by the sea on three sides of the town, more or less.
There remains the fourth side, admitting of approach
by land. Of this space, too, the part extending to the
citadel, strengthened by the natural character of the
site and a very deep valley, involves a long and difficult
blockade. To carry out these works, G. Trebonius
requisitions a great multitude of baggage animals and
men from the whole province, and orders rushes and
timber to be got together. When these supplies are
collected he builds an earthwork eighty feet in height.

But there had been in the town from early days   2
such huge military stores of every kind, and such a
multitude of engines, that no penthouses woven with
osiers could withstand their assault. For beams
twelve feet long with spiked ends, discharged by
enormous catapults, often fixed themselves in the earth
after passing through four layers of hurdles. So the
roofs of the penthouses were protected by timbers a

[1] See plan of Massilia.

pedalibus lignis coniunctis inter se porticus intege-
bantur, atque hac agger inter manus proferebatur.
Antecedebat testudo pedum LX aequandi loci causa
facta item ex fortissimis lignis, convoluta omnibus
rebus, quibus ignis iactus et lapides defendi possent.
Sed magnitudo operum, altitudo muri atque turrium,
multitudo tormentorum omnem administrationem tardabat. Crebrae etiam per Albicos eruptiones fiebant
ex oppido ignesque aggeri et turribus inferebantur;
quae facile nostri milites repellebant magnisque ultro
illatis detrimentis eos, qui eruptionem fecerant, in
oppidum reiciebant.

3 Interim L. Nasidius, a Cn. Pompeio cum classe
navium XVI, in quibus paucae erant aeratae, L.
Domitio Massiliensibusque subsidio missus, freto
Siciliae imprudente atque inopinante Curione per-
vehitur appulsisque Messanam navibus atque inde
propter repentinum terrorem principum ac senatus
fuga facta navem ex navalibus eorum deducit. Hac
adiuncta ad reliquas naves cursum Massiliam versus
perficit praemissaque clam navicula Domitium Mas-
siliensesque de suo adventu certiores facit eosque
magnopere hortatur, ut rurus cum Bruti classe additis suis auxiliis confligant.

4 Massilienses post superius incommodum veteres
ad eundem numerum ex navalibus productas naves
refecerant summaque industria armaverant (remigum, gubernatorum magna copia suppetebat) pis-
catoriasque adiecerant atque contexerant, ut essent
126

foot square clamped together, and beneath this shelter material for the earthwork was carried forward from hand to hand. In front went a tortoise sixty feet in height, for the levelling of the ground, also made of very stout timbers, and wrapped over with everything that could serve to keep off showers of firebrands and stones. But the greatness of the works, the height of the wall and the towers, the multitude of engines, hindered the whole of our operations. Moreover, frequent sorties from the town were made by the Albici, and firebrands were flung upon the earthwork and the towers—all of which assaults our troops repelled with ease, and kept driving back into the town those who had made a sortie, even inflicting great losses on them.

Meanwhile L. Nasidius, who had been sent by 3 Gn. Pompeius with a fleet of sixteen ships, a few of which had brazen beaks, to the support of L. Domitius and the Massilians, voyages along the Sicilian strait, without Curio knowing or suspecting it, and bringing his ships to anchor at Messana, when the sudden panic had caused the flight of the chiefs and the senate, removes a ship from their docks. Adding this to the rest, he finishes his course towards Massilia, and, secretly sending a small vessel in advance, informs Domitius and the Massilians of his approach and strongly urges them, now that they have received his reinforcements, again to join battle with the fleet of Brutus.

After their previous disaster the Massilians had 4 brought out of the docks and repaired an equivalent number of old ships and equipped them with the utmost industry—there was an abundant supply of rowers and helmsmen—and had added to them some fishing-vessels which they had furnished with decks,

ab ictu telorum remiges tuti; has sagittariis tormentisque compleverunt. Tali modo instructa classe omnium seniorum, matrum familiae, virginum precibus et fletu excitati, extremo tempore civitati subvenirent, non minore animo ac fiducia, quam ante dimicaverant, naves conscendunt. Communi enim fit vitio naturae, ut inusitatis atque incognitis rebus magis confidamus vehementiusque exterreamur; ut tum accidit. Adventus enim L. Nasidii summa spe et voluntate civitatem compleverat. Nacti idoneum ventum ex portu exeunt et Tauroënta, quod est castellum Massiliensium, ad Nasidium perveniunt ibique naves expediunt rursusque se ad confligendum animo confirmant et consilia communicant. Dextra pars attribuitur Massiliensibus, sinistra Nasidio.

5   Eodem Brutus contendit aucto navium numero. Nam ad eas, quae factae erant Arelate per Caesarem, captivae Massiliensium accesserant sex. Has superioribus diebus refecerat atque omnibus rebus instruxerat. Itaque suos cohortatus, quos integros superavissent ut victos contemnerent, plenus spei bonae atque animi adversus eos proficiscitur. Facile erat ex castris C. Trebonii atque omnibus superioribus locis prospicere in urbem, ut omnis iuventus, quae in oppido remanserat, omnesque superioris aetatis cum liberis atque uxoribus ex publicis locis custodiisque[1] aut e muro ad caelum manus tenderent, aut templa deorum immortalium adirent et ante simu-

---

[1] publicis custodiisque *MSS. I adopt a probable restoration.*

to protect the rowers from the blows of missiles, while they also manned them with archers and catapults. When the fleet was thus equipped, stimulated by the prayers and tears of all the older men, matrons and virgins, beseeching them to succour the state in its extremity, they embark with no less courage and confidence than they had shown in the previous battle. For, by a defect which is common to human nature, we are apt in unusual and unfamiliar circumstances to be too confident or too violently alarmed; and so it happened then. For the arrival of L. Nasidius had filled the community with the utmost hope and goodwill. Finding the wind favourable, they quit the port and reach Nasidius at Taurois, a Massilian fortress, and there get their ships into trim and again make up their minds to the struggle and join in arranging their plans. Operations on the right are assigned to the Massilians, on the left to Nasidius.

Brutus hurries to the same place with the number 5 of his fleet enlarged. For six captured Massilian ships had been added to those which had been constructed by Caesar at Arelate. These he had repaired and fully equipped during the preceding days. And so, exhorting his men to despise as now conquered those whom they had worsted when unscathed, he sets out against them full of good hope and courage. It was easy to get a view into the city from the camp of G. Trebonius and from all the higher parts, and to see how all the youth that had remained in the town and all the men of more advanced age with their children and wives in the public places and guard-houses or on the wall were stretching their hands to heaven or visiting the temples of the immortal gods and, prostrate before their shrines, were

lacra proiecti victoriam ab diis exposcerent. Neque
erat quisquam omnium, quin in eius diei casu suarum
omnium fortunarum eventum consistere existimaret.
Nam et honesti ex iuventute et cuiusque aetatis
amplissimi nominatim evocati atque obsecrati naves
conscenderant, ut, si quid adversi accidisset, ne ad
conandum quidem sibi quicquam reliqui fore viderent; si superavissent, vel domesticis opibus vel
externis auxiliis de salute urbis confiderent.

6   Commisso proelio Massiliensibus res nulla ad virtutem defuit; sed memores eorum praeceptorum, quae
paulo ante ab suis acceperant, hoc animo decertabant,
ut nullum aliud tempus ad conandum habituri viderentur, et quibus in pugna vitae periculum accideret,
non ita multo se reliquorum civium fatum antecedere
existimarent, quibus urbe capta eadem esset belli
fortuna patienda. Diductisque nostris paulatim navibus et artificio gubernatorum et mobilitati navium
locus dabatur, et si quando nostri facultatem nacti
ferreis manibus iniectis navem religaverant, undique
suis laborantibus succurrebant. Neque vero coniuncti
Albici[1] comminus pugnando deficiebant neque multum cedebant virtute nostris. Simul ex minoribus
navibus magna vis eminus missa telorum multa nostris de improviso imprudentibus atque impeditis vulnera inferebant. Conspicataeque naves triremes duae
navem D. Bruti, quae ex insigni facile agnosci poterat,
duabus ex partibus sese in eam incitaverant. Sed

---

[1] Albici *Heller:* Albicis *MSS.*

beseeching the gods for victory. Nor was there a single one of them all who did not think that the issue of his whole fortunes rested on the chances of that day. For the youths of good birth and the most important men of every age had gone on board, individually called out and entreated to serve, so that if anything untoward should happen they might see that nothing would be left them to venture withal, but might be confident of securing the safety of the city, whether by domestic resources or by foreign aid, if they should win the victory.

When the battle had begun the Massilians showed 6 no lack of valour, but, mindful of the precepts they had just received from their friends, they fought with such spirit as to resemble men who were likely to have no other opportunity for effort, and who thought that they who risked their life in battle did not anticipate by so very much the fate of the rest of the citizens, who, if the city were captured, would have to suffer the same fortune of war. And when our ships had been gradually drawn apart, scope was allowed for the skill of the pilots and the handiness of the ships, and whenever, meeting with an opportunity, our men had secured a ship by casting the grappling-irons on it, the foe went from every side to the succour of their distressed comrades. Nor indeed did the Albici, who took part in the engagement, fail in hand-to-hand fighting or fall short of our men in valour. At the same time a great shower of missiles hurled from the smaller vessels at a distance inflicted many wounds on our men, who were unexpectedly taken off their guard and embarrassed. And two triremes, having sighted the ship of D. Brutus, which could be easily recognized from its standard, threw themselves upon it from two sides. But Brutus, seeing

tantum re provisa Brutus celeritate navis enisus est, ut parvo momento antecederet. Illae adeo graviter inter se incitatae conflixerunt, ut vehementissime utraque ex concursu laborarent, altera vero praefracto rostro tota collabefieret. Qua re animadversa, quae proximae ei loco ex Bruti classe naves erant, in eas impeditas impetum faciunt celeriterque ambas deprimunt.

7   Sed Nasidianae naves nullo usui fuerunt celeriterque pugna excesserunt; non enim has aut conspectus patriae aut propinquorum praecepta ad extremum vitae periculum adire cogebant. Itaque ex eo numero navium nulla desiderata est: ex Massiliensium classe v sunt depressae, iv captae, una cum Nasidianis profugit; quae omnes citeriorem Hispaniam petiverunt. At ex reliquis una praemissa Massiliam huius nuntii perferendi gratia cum iam appropinquaret urbi, omnis sese multitudo ad cognoscendum effudit, et re cognita tantus luctus excepit, ut urbs ab hostibus capta eodem vestigio videretur. Massilienses tamen nihilo secius ad defensionem urbis reliqua apparare coeperunt.

8   Est animadversum ab legionibus, qui dextram partem operis administrabant, ex crebris hostium eruptionibus magno sibi esse praesidio posse, si ibi pro castello ac receptaculo turrim ex latere sub muro fecissent. Quam primo ad repentinos incursus humilem parvamque fecerunt. Huc se referebant; hinc, si qua maior oppresserat vis, propugnabant;

what was coming, made so vigorous an effort, thanks to the speed of his ship, that a brief thrust carried him ahead of them. They, borne down on one another, collided so heavily that each was seriously damaged by the crash, and one of them, having its beak broken off, collapsed altogether. When this was observed, the ships of Brutus' fleet which were nearest to the spot set upon them while thus disabled and quickly sank them both.

But the ships of Nasidius were of no use and quickly retired from the battle; for neither the sight of their fatherland nor the promptings of kinsmen urged them to incur the supreme peril of life. Consequently from that detachment of ships none was missed; out of the fleet of the Massilians five were sunk, four captured, and one fled with the Nasidian ships, and they all made for hither Spain. And when one of the rest, sent forward to Massilia to convey this news, was now approaching the city, the whole multitude poured forth to learn the event, and when they had learnt it such a lamentation followed that it seemed as if the city had been forthwith captured by the enemy. However, the Massilians none the less began to make the other necessary preparations for the defence of the town.

In consequence of the frequent sorties of the enemy, it was noticed by the legionaries who were conducting operations on the right that it could be a great protection to them if they made there a tower of brick under the wall to serve as a stronghold and place of retreat. This they constructed at first of low elevation and small size to meet sudden sallies. To this they used to retire; from this shelter they fought if a stronger assault pressed them; from

hinc ad repellendum et prosequendum hostem procurrebant. Patebat haec quoquo versus pedes XXX, sed parietum crassitudo pedes V. Postea vero, ut est rerum omnium magister usus, hominum adhibita sollertia inventum est magno esse usui posse, si haec esset in altitudinem turris elata. Id hac ratione perfectum est.

9 Ubi turris altitudo perducta est ad contabulationem, eam in parietes instruxerunt, ita ut capita tignorum extrema parietum structura tegerentur, ne quid emineret, ubi ignis hostium adhaeresceret. Hanc super contignationem, quantum tectum plutei ac vinearum passum est, laterculo adstruxerunt supraque eum locum duo tigna transversa iniecerunt non longe ab extremis parietibus, quibus suspenderent eam contignationem, quae turri tegimento esset futura, supraque ea tigna directo transversas trabes iniecerunt easque axibus religaverunt (has trabes paulo longiores atque eminentiores, quam extremi parietes erant, effecerant, ut esset, ubi tegimenta praependere possent ad defendendos ictus ac repellendos, cum infra eam contignationem parietes exstruerentur) eamque contabulationem summam lateribus lutoque constraverunt, ne quid ignis hostium nocere posset, centonesque insuper iniecerunt, ne aut tela tormentis immissa tabulationem perfringerent, aut saxa ex catapultis latericium

134

this they issued forth to repel and pursue the foe.
Its dimensions were thirty feet each way, but the
thickness of the walls was five feet. But afterwards, as experience is the guide of all conduct,
by applying their wits they discovered that it could
be of great service to them if this tower were raised
to a height. This was accomplished in the following
manner.

When the height of the tower reached the level   9
of a story they built the floor into the walls in such
a way that the heads of the beams were hidden in
the outside structure of the walls, to prevent any
projection on which the firebrands of the enemy
could lodge. Above this timber-work they built up
with brick, only so far as the shelter afforded by the
shed and the penthouses allowed, and above this
part they laid across two beams not far from the
outer walls, whereon to raise aloft the wooden frame
which was to serve as the roof of the tower,[1] and
over these beams they laid joists across at right
angles and fixed them in place by tie-beams.
The joists they made rather longer and projecting
beyond the outside of the walls, so that there might
be a place to hang out screens to ward off and repel
blows while the walls were being built up below
this timber frame; and on the top of this flooring they
made a layer of bricks and clay so that the firebrands
of the enemy might do no harm. And they further
laid thereon mattresses, that missiles hurled by
engines might not crash through the flooring or

[1] When the level of the second floor was reached a timber
framework was placed on the top of the walls, but not built into
them or fastened to them. This framework, serving, with its
hanging fenders, to protect the workmen, was raised by leverage
as occasion required, till at last it reached the top and formed
the roof of the six-storied tower.

discuterent. Storias autem ex funibus ancorariis tres
in longitudinem parietum turris latas IIII pedes
fecerunt easque ex tribus partibus, quae ad hostes
vergebant, eminentibus trabibus circum turrim prae-
pendentes religaverunt; quod unum genus tegimenti
aliis locis erant experti nullo telo neque tormento
traici posse. Ubi vero ea pars turris, quae erat perfecta, tecta atque munita est ab omni ictu hostium,
pluteos ad alia opera abduxerunt; turris tectum per
se ipsum pressionibus ex contignatione prima supen-
dere ac tollere coeperunt. Ubi, quantum storiarum
demissio patiebatur, tantum elevarant, intra haec
tegimenta abditi atque muniti parietes lateribus ex-
struebant rursusque alia pressione ad aedificandum sibi
locum expediebant. Ubi tempus alterius contabula-
tionis videbatur, tigna item ut primo tecta extremis
lateribus instruebant exque ea contignatione rursus
summam contabulationem storiasque elevabant. Ita
tuto ac sine ullo vulnere ac periculo sex tabulata ex-
struxerunt fenestrasque, quibus in locis visum est, ad
tormenta mittenda in struendo reliquerunt.

10   Ubi ex ea turri, quae circum essent opera, tueri se
posse confisi sunt, musculum pedes LX longum ex
materia bipedali, quem a turri latericia ad hostium
turrim murumque perducerent, facere instituerunt;
cuius musculi haec erat forma. Duae primum trabes
in solo aeque longae distantes inter se pedes IIII col-
locantur, inque eis columellae pedum in altitudinem

stones from catapults dislodge the brickwork. They made moreover three fenders four feet broad out of anchor-ropes to cover the length of the walls of the tower and fastened these on the three sides towards the enemy from the beams projecting round the tower. This was the only kind of protection that they had found by experience in other places to be impervious to any missile or catapult. But when that part of the tower which was finished was protected and defended from every weapon cast by the enemy they removed their sheds to other works, and began to poise and lift the roof of the tower independently by leverage from the first-floor stage. When they had raised it to the height allowed by the hanging fenders, being thus concealed and protected within these defences they proceeded to build up the walls with brick, and again by further leverage made themselves space for fresh building. When the opportunity came for a second story they built in beams, just as at first, concealed in the outside of the walls, and from this flooring again they proceeded to raise the topmost story and the protecting fenders. So safely and without any wounds or peril they built up six stories, and in the course of erection they left openings, where it seemed suitable, for the discharge of darts from catapults.

When they were sure that from the tower they 10 could protect all the surrounding works, they set about making out of timber two feet square a covered gallery sixty feet long, to be carried from the brick tower to the enemy's tower and wall. And the form of the gallery was as follows. First of all two beams of equal length are laid on the ground with a distance of four feet between them, and in these posts are fixed five feet in height. These posts they con-

v defiguntur. Has inter se capreolis molli fastigio
coniungunt, ubi tigna, quae musculi tegendi causa
ponant, collocentur. Eo super tigna bipedalia
iniciunt eaque laminis clavisque religant. Ad extremum musculi tectum trabesque extremas quad-
ratas regulas IIII patentes digitos difigunt, quae
lateres, qui super musculo struantur, contineant. Ita
fastigato atque ordinatim structo, ut trabes erant in
capreolis collocatae,[1] lateribus lutoque musculus, ut
ab igni, qui ex muro iaceretur, tutus esset, conte-
gitur. Super lateres coria inducuntur, ne canalibus
aqua immissa lateres diluere posset. Coria autem,
ne rursus igni ac lapidibus corrumpantur, centonibus conteguntur. Hoc opus omne tectum vineis ad
ipsam turrim perficiunt subitoque inopinantibus hostibus machinatione navali, phalangis subiectis, ad
turrim hostium admovent, ut aedificio iungatur.

11 Quo malo perterriti subito oppidani saxa quam
maxima possunt vectibus promovent praecipitataque
muro in musculum devolvunt. Ictum firmitas
materiae sustinet, et quicquid incidit fastigio musculi elabitur. Id ubi vident, mutant consilium: cupas
taeda ac pice refertas incendunt easque de muro in
musculum devolvunt. Involutae labuntur, delapsae
ab lateribus longuriis furcisque ab opere removentur.

[1] *The text of this sentence is corrupt, and the meaning uncertain:* tecto *should probably be inserted after* structo.

nect by rafters of low elevation whereon to place the boarding to be laid for the roofing of the gallery. Over these rafters they lay two-foot beams and fasten them with plates and bolts. On the outside of the roof of the gallery and on the edges of these beams they fasten three-inch-square shingles[1] to keep in place the bricks to be laid on the roof. Thus when it had all been sloped and duly constructed, after the beams had been laid on the rafters, the gallery is roofed with tiles and clay, so as to be safe from fire that might be thrown from the wall. Hides are drawn over the bricks lest water discharged at them through pipes should wash them out. The hides, too, are covered over with patchwork lest they in their turn should be spoilt by fire and stones. The whole of this work, protected by mantlets, they complete up to the tower itself, and suddenly, when the enemy were off their guard, they put rollers under it—a nautical appliance—and push it forward to the tower of the enemy, so as to join on to the structure.

Dismayed at this sudden calamity, the townsmen 11 bring forward with cranes the largest possible stones, and roll them headlong from the wall on to the gallery. The strength of the timber bears the blow, and everything that falls on it slips off owing to the sloping roof of the gallery. Observing this, they change their plan and set on fire barrels filled with pine-wood and pitch, and roll them down from the wall on to the gallery. When, however, they had rolled on to it they slip off and, having fallen from the tiles, are removed from the work by poles and forks. Meanwhile some soldiers under the

---

[1] Shingles (or "shindles") are thin rectangular slabs of wood. A fringe of these was placed round the edge of the roof of the shed.

Interim sub musculo milites vectibus infima saxa turris hostium, quibus fundamenta continebantur, convellunt. Musculus ex turri latericia a nostris telis tormentisque defenditur; hostes ex muro ac turribus submoventur: non datur libera muri defendendi facultas. Compluribus iam lapidibus ex ea, quae suberat, turri subductis repentina ruina pars eius turris concidit, pars reliqua consequens procumbebat: cum hostes urbis direptione perterriti inermes cum infulis se porta foras universi proripiunt, ad legatos atque exercitum supplices manus tendunt.

12 Qua nova re oblata omnis administratio belli consistit, militesque aversi a proelio ad studium audiendi et cognoscendi feruntur. Ubi hostes ad legatos exercitumque pervenerunt, universi se ad pedes proiciunt; orant, ut adventus Caesaris exspectetur: captam suam urbem videre: opera perfecta, turrim subrutam; itaque ab defensione desistere. Nullam exoriri moram posse, quo minus, cum venisset, si imperata non facerent ad nutum, e vestigio diriperentur. Docent, si omnino turris concidisset, non posse milites contineri, quin spe praedae in urbem irrumperent urbemque delerent. Haec atque eiusdem generis complura ut ab hominibus doctis magna cum misericordia fletuque pronuntiantur.

13 Quibus rebus commoti legati milites ex opere deducunt, oppugnatione desistunt; operibus cus-

gallery prise out with crowbars the lowest stones of the enemy's tower which served to hold the foundations together. The gallery is defended by our men from the brick tower with missiles and catapults, the enemy are dislodged from their wall and towers, no free opportunity of defending their wall is allowed them. When now a number of stones had been withdrawn from the tower next the gallery, a part of it suddenly collapsed and fell. The rest was beginning to follow it and fall forward, when the enemy, terrified at the sacking of their city, without their arms and wearing fillets, fling themselves in a mass outside the gate and stretch out their hands as suppliants to the legates and the army.

In the face of this new occurrence all military 12 operations cease, and the men turning from the fight are drawn to satisfy their longing to hear and learn the news. When the enemy reached the legates and the army they fling themselves in a body at their feet, and beseech them to wait for Caesar's arrival: they say that they behold their city captured, the works of investment completed, their tower undermined, and so they desist from their defence. Nothing can now arise to prevent their being plundered forthwith on his arrival if they do not carry out orders at his beck. They point out that if the tower should collapse altogether the soldiers could not be withheld from bursting into the town in hope of plunder and utterly destroying it. These and many such like words, as might be expected from men of intelligence, are uttered with much pathetic appeal and weeping.

Stirred by these events, the legates withdraw their 13 men from the work and abandon the siege, leaving

141

todias relinquunt. Indutiarum quodam genere
misericordia facto adventus Caesaris exspectatur.
Nullum ex muro, nullum a nostris mittitur telum;
ut re confecta omnes curam et diligentiam remittunt.
Caesar enim per litteras Trebonio magnopere mandaverat, ne per vim oppidum expugnari pateretur,
ne gravius permoti milites et defectionis odio et con-
temptione sui et diutino labore omnes puberes interficerent; quod se facturos minabantur, aegreque
tunc sunt retenti, quin oppidum irrumperent, gravi-
terque eam rem tulerunt, quod stetisse per Trebonium, quo minus oppido potirentur, videbatur.

14   At hostes sine fide tempus atque occasionem
fraudis ac doli quaerunt interiectisque aliquot diebus
nostris languentibus atque animo remissis subito
meridiano tempore, cum alius discessisset, alius ex
diutino labore in ipsis operibus quieti se dedisset,
arma vero omnia reposita contectaque essent, portis
se foras erumpunt, secundo magnoque vento ignem
operibus inferunt. Hunc sic distulit ventus, uti uno
tempore agger, plutei, testudo, turris, tormenta
flammam conciperent et prius haec omnia con-
sumerentur, quam, quemadmodum accidisset, animad-
verti posset. Nostri repentina fortuna permoti arma,
quae possunt, arripiunt; alii ex castris sese incitant.
Fit in hostes impetus; sed de muro sagittis tormentisque fugientes persequi prohibentur. Illi sub
murum se recipiunt ibique musculum turrimque
latericiam libere incendunt. Ita multorum mensium

sentries to guard the works. Some kind of truce having been arranged out of compassion, they wait for Caesar's arrival. No missile is cast from the wall, none by our men; as though the business were finished, all relax their care and diligence. For Caesar in his dispatch had strongly urged Trebonius not to suffer the town to be taken by storm, lest the troops, deeply moved by hatred of the revolt, by the contempt shown for themselves, and by their continuous labour, should slay all the youths; which in fact they were constantly threatening to do, and were now with difficulty restrained from breaking into the town, and resented the fact because it appeared to be the fault of Trebonius that they did not get possession of the town.

But the enemy, with no sense of honour, sought for 14 time and opportunity for fraud and treachery, and after an interval of several days, when our men were weary and slack in spirit, suddenly at noon, after some had gone away and others after their long toil had surrendered themselves to sleep among the siege works, and all their arms had been put away out of sight, broke forth from the gates and set fire to the works, the wind being strong and favourable. The wind spread the fire to such an extent that the mound, the sheds, the tortoise, the machines all caught fire at once, and they were all consumed before it could be ascertained how it had happened. Our men, alarmed by the sudden mischance, snatch up such arms as they can, others fling themselves from the camp. They charge the enemy, but are prevented from following the fugitives by arrows and catapults from the wall. The foe retire beneath their wall, and there without hindrance set fire to the gallery and the brick tower. So the labour of many

labor hostium perfidia et vi tempestatis puncto temporis interiit. Temptaverunt hoc idem Massilienses postero die. Eandem nacti tempestatem maiore cum fiducia ad alteram turrim aggeremque eruptione pugnaverunt multumque ignem intulerunt. Sed ut superioris temporis contentionem nostri omnem remiserant, ita proximi diei casu admoniti omnia ad defensionem paraverant. Itaque multis interfectis reliquos infecta re in oppidum reppulerunt.

15 Trebonius ea, quae sunt amissa, multo maiore militum studio administrare et reficere instituit. Nam ubi tantos suos labores et apparatus male cecidisse viderunt indutiisque per scelus violatis suam virtutem irrisui fore perdoluerunt, quod, unde agger omnino comportari posset, nihil erat reliquum, omnibus arboribus longe lateque in finibus Massiliensium excisis et convectis aggerem novi generis atque inauditum ex latericiis duobus muris senum pedum crassitudine atque eorum murorum contignatione facere instituerunt aequa fere altitudine, atque ille congesticius ex materia fuerat agger. Ubi aut spatium inter muros aut imbecillitas materiae postulare videretur, pilae interponuntur, traversaria tigna iniciuntur, quae firmamento esse possint, et quicquid est contignatum cratibus consternitur, crates luto integuntur. Sub tecto miles dextra ac sinistra muro tectus, adversus plutei obiectu, operi quaecumque sunt usui sine periculo supportat.

months perished in a moment through the perfidy of the enemy and the violence of the storm. The Massilians made a like attempt the next day. In similar weather they sallied forth and fought with greater confidence at the second tower and earthwork and cast much fire on them. But though our men had relaxed all the keen vigilance of an earlier period, yet, warned by the previous day's disaster, they had made every preparation for defence. So after slaying many they drove back the rest into the town and prevented them from accomplishing their purpose.

Trebonius began to apply himself to the task of repairing his losses, with a great increase of zeal on the part of his troops. For they saw that all their labours and appliances had turned out ill, and were highly indignant that owing to the wicked violation of the truce their valour would be a mark for derision; and so, since there was no place left from which material for a rampart could possibly be collected, because all the trees far and wide in the Massilian district had been cut down and brought in, they set about making an earthwork of a novel kind that no one had heard of before out of two brick walls each six feet thick, and roofing these walls over, so that the width was about the same as that of the former earthwork piled up with timber. Wherever either the space between the walls or the weakness of the timber seemed to require it, piles are placed between them, cross-beams are put in to serve as a strengthening, and all the part roofed is spread over with hurdles, and the hurdles are covered with clay. Under this cover the soldiers, sheltered to right and left by the wall, in front by the defence of a screen, bring up without danger whatever is of use for the

15

145

Celeriter res administratur; diuturni laboris detrimentum sollertia et virtute militum brevi reconciliatur.   Portae, quibus locis videtur, eruptionis causa in muro relinquuntur.

16   Quod ubi hostes viderunt, ea, quae vix longinquo spatio[1] refici non posse sperassent, paucorum dierum opera et labore ita refecta, ut nullus perfidiae neque eruptioni locus esset nec quicquam omnino relinqueretur, qua aut telis militibus aut igni operibus noceri posset, eodemque exemplo sentiunt totam urbem, qua sit aditus ab terra, muro turribusque circumiri posse, sic ut ipsis consistendi in suis munitionibus locus non esset, cum paene inaedificata muris ab exercitu nostro moenia viderentur ac telum manu coniceretur, suorumque tormentorum usum, quibus ipsi magna speravissent, spatio propinquitatis interire parique condicione ex muro ac turribus bellandi data se virtute nostris adaequare non posse intellegunt, ad easdem deditionis condiciones recurrunt.

17   M. Varro in ulteriore Hispania initio cognitis eis rebus, quae sunt in Italia gestae, diffidens Pompeianis rebus amicissime de Caesare loquebatur: praeoccupatum sese legatione ab Cn. Pompeio teneri obstrictum fide; necessitudinem quidem sibi nihilo minorem cum Caesare intercedere, neque se igno-

[1] diu longoque spatio *MSS.—an impossible phrase, yet Paul is the only editor who alters it.*

work. The business is conducted with speed; the wastage of their long-continued labour is soon made up by the skill and energy of the soldiers. Gates are left in the wall wherever seems suitable to allow of a sortie.

And when the enemy saw that the losses which 16 they had hoped could hardly be repaired within a long period of time had been so thoroughly repaired by the work and toil of a few days, that there was now no opportunity for treachery or sortie, and that no possible chance was left for any injury to be done either to the men by weapons or to the works by fire; and when they become aware that in a like manner the whole city, where there is an approach to it by land, can be so thoroughly invested by wall and towers that there was no chance for themselves of standing their ground on their own defences, since the investing walls seemed to have been built by our army almost on to their own town walls, and missiles were being hurled by hand; and that the use of their own engines, on which they had laid great hopes, was coming to nothing owing to the narrow space that separated them; and when they understand that if equal conditions of fighting from wall and towers are afforded they cannot equal our men in valour: then they recur to the same terms of surrender.

M. Varro, at first in further Spain, when he learnt 17 of the events that had happened in Italy, mistrusting the fortunes of Pompeius, began to speak in the most friendly terms of Caesar. He pointed out that, having been previously secured by Gn. Pompeius as his legate, he was held bound by a pledge of loyalty, yet that no less strong a tie of intimacy existed between himself and Caesar, and that he was not unaware what

147

rare, quod esset officium legati, qui fiduciariam operam obtineret, quae vires suae, quae voluntas erga Caesarem totius provinciae. Haec omnibus ferebat sermonibus neque se in ullam partem movebat. Postea vero, cum Caesarem ad Massiliam detineri cognovit, copias Petreii cum exercitu Afranii esse coniunctas, magna auxilia convenisse, magna esse in spe atque exspectari et consentire omnem citeriorem provinciam, quaeque postea acciderant, de angustiis ad Ilerdam rei frumentariae, accepit, atque haec ad eum latius atque inflatius Afranius perscribebat, se quoque ad motus fortunae movere coepit.

18   Delectum habuit tota provincia, legionibus completis duabus cohortes circiter XXX alarias addidit. Frumenti magnum numerum coëgit, quod Massiliensibus, item quod Afranio Petreioque mitteret. Naves longas X Gaditanis ut facerent imperavit, complures praeterea Hispali faciendas curavit. Pecuniam omnem omniaque ornamenta ex fano Herculis in oppidum Gades contulit; eo sex cohortes praesidii causa ex provincia misit Gaiumque Gallonium, equitem Romanum, familiarem Domitii, qui eo procurandae hereditatis causa venerat missus a Domitio, oppido Gadibus praefecit; arma omnia privata ac publica in domum Gallonii contulit. Ipse habuit graves in Caesarem contiones. Saepe ex tribunali praedicavit adversa Caesarem proelia fecisse, magnum numerum ab eo militum ad Afranium perfu-

was the duty of a legate who held a post of trust, what his own strength was, and what was the feeling of the whole province towards Caesar. These opinions he used to express in all his talk, but meanwhile made no movement towards either side. But afterwards, when he learnt that Caesar was being detained at Massilia, that the forces of Petreius had been united with the army of Afranius, that large auxiliary forces had assembled, that other large reinforcements were in prospect and constantly expected, and that the whole hither province was unanimous; and when he heard of what had afterwards happened about the dearth of provisions at Ilerda, and when Afranius kept writing to him about this in a large and exaggerated style, he began himself to move in response to the movements of fortune.

He held a levy throughout his province, and when 18 he had made up two legions he added about thirty auxiliary cohorts. He collected a great store of corn to be sent to the Massilians, some also to Afranius and Petreius. He ordered the Gaditanians to make ten ships of war and contracted for the building of many others at Hispalis. He bestowed in the town of Gades all the money and all the treasures from the temple of Hercules; he sent thither from his province six cohorts on garrison duty, and put in charge of the town of Gades Gaius Gallonius, a Roman knight, a friend of Domitius, who had gone thither commissioned by Domitius to take possession of an inheritance; all weapons, private and public, he bestowed in the house of Gallonius. He delivered incriminating speeches against Caesar. He often asserted from his tribunal that Caesar had fought unsuccessful battles, that a great number of soldiers had deserted him for Afranius; that he had ascer-

gisse: haec se certis nuntiis, certis auctoribus
comperisse. Quibus rebus perterritos cives Romanos
eius provinciae sibi ad rem publicam administrandam
HS ⌐CLXXX⌐ et argenti pondo XX milia, tritici mo-
dium CXX milia polliceri coëgit. Quas Caesari esse
amicas civitates arbitrabatur, his graviora onera
iniungebat praesidiaque eo deducebat et iudicia in
privatos reddebat qui verba atque orationem adversus rem publicam habuissent: eorum bona in
publicum addicebat. Provinciam omnem in sua et
Pompei verba iusiurandum adigebat. Cognitis eis
rebus, quae sunt gestae in citeriore Hispania, bellum
parabat. Ratio autem haec erat belli, ut se cum II
legionibus Gades conferret, naves frumentumque
omne ibi contineret; provinciam enim omnem Caesaris rebus favere cognoverat. In insula frumento
navibusque comparatis bellum duci non difficile existimabat. Caesar, etsi multis necessariisque rebus in
Italiam revocabatur, tamen constituerat nullam partem belli in Hispaniis relinquere, quod magna esse
Pompei beneficia et magnas clientelas in citeriore
provincia sciebat.

19   Itaque duabus legionibus missis in ulteriorem Hispaniam cum Q. Cassio, tribuno plebis, ipse DC cum
equitibus magnis itineribus progreditur edictumque
praemittit, ad quam diem magistratus principesque
omnium civitatum sibi esse praesto Cordubae vellet.
Quo edicto tota provincia pervulgato nulla fuit civitas, quin ad id tempus partem senatus Cordubam

tained this by trustworthy messengers, on trustworthy authority. He compelled the Roman citizens
of the province, terrified by such proceedings, to
promise him for the administration of public affairs
18,000,000 sesterces and 20,000 pounds of silver and
120,000 measures of wheat. On all the communities
that he thought friendly to Caesar he proceeded to
impose very heavy burdens, to move garrisons into
them, and to deliver judgments against private
persons who had uttered words or made speeches
against the commonwealth; their property he confiscated for public purposes. He went on to compel
his whole province to swear allegiance to himself
and Pompeius. When he had ascertained what had
happened in hither Spain he began to prepare war.
His plan of campaign was to go to Gades with two
legions, and to retain there the ships and all the
corn, for he had found out that the whole of his
province favoured the side of Caesar. If the corn
and ships were collected in the island he thought it
would not be difficult for the war to be prolonged.
Caesar, though many urgent affairs were summoning
him back to Italy, had nevertheless determined to
abandon no section of the war in the two Spains,
because he knew how great were the benefactions of
Pompeius and what large bodies of retainers he had
in the hither province.

So, having sent two legions into further Spain with 19
Q. Cassius, tribune of the people, he himself proceeds
ahead with six hundred horsemen by forced marches,
and sends on an order stating on what date he wished
the magistrates and chief men of all the communities to meet him at Corduba. When this edict was
promulgated throughout the province there was no
community that did not send a portion of its council

mitteret, non civis Romanus paulo notior, quin ad
diem conveniret. Simul ipse Cordubae conventus
per se portas Varroni clausit, custodias vigiliasque
in turribus muroque disposuit, cohortes duas, quae
colonicae appellabantur, cum eo casu venissent, tuendi
oppidi causa apud se retinuit. Eisdem diebus Carmonenses, quae est longe firmissima totius provinciae
civitas, deductis tribus in arcem oppidi cohortibus a
Varrone praesidio, per se cohortes eiecit portasque
praeclusit.

20   Hoc vero magis properare Varro, ut cum legionibus quam primum Gades contenderet, ne itinere aut
traiectu intercluderetur: tanta ac tam secunda in
Caesarem voluntas provinciae reperiebatur. Pro-
gresso ei paulo longius litterae Gadibus redduntur:
simulatque sit cognitum de edicto Caesaris, consen-
sisse Gaditanos principes cum tribunis cohortium,
quae essent ibi in praesidio, ut Gallonium ex oppido
expellerent, urbem insulamque Caesari servarent.
Hoc inito consilio denuntiavisse Gallonio, ut sua
sponte, dum sine periculo liceret, excederet Gadibus; si id non fecisset, sibi consilium capturos. Hoc
timore adductum Gallonium Gadibus excessisse. His
cognitis rebus altera ex duabus legionibus, quae ver-
nacula appellabatur, ex castris Varronis adstante
et inspectante ipso signa sustulit seseque Hispalim
recepit atque in foro et porticibus sine maleficio

to Corduba, no Roman citizen of any repute who did not come on the appointed day. At the same time the Roman burgess-body at Corduba of its own accord shut the gates against Varro, set outposts and sentries on the towers and walls, and detained for the defence of the town two cohorts called "Colonial"[1] which had come there by chance. About the same time the people of Carmona, which is by far the strongest community in the whole province, of its own accord thrust out three cohorts which had been introduced into the citadel by Varro as a garrison, and closed its gates against them.

And this made Varro hurry all the more to reach 20 Gades with his legions as soon as possible, that he might not be cut off from his route or from the crossing, so great and enthusiastic did he find the feeling of the province in favour of Caesar. When he had advanced a little further a dispatch from Gades is handed him stating that, as soon as it was known about Caesar's edict, the chief men of Gades had conspired with the tribunes of the cohorts which were there on garrison duty to expel Gallonius from the town and to secure the city and island for Caesar: that on forming this design they had told Gallonius to quit Gades voluntarily while he could do so without danger; if he did not do so they would take measures for themselves: that Gallonius under the influence of this fear had quitted Gades. When these events became known one of the two legions, which was called the Native[2] Legion, removed its colours from Varro's camp while he was standing by and looking on, and, withdrawing to Hispalis, bivouacked in the forum and porticoes

---

[1] So called because raised in a Roman colony.
[2] Consisting of native provincials.

consedit. Quod factum adeo eius conventus cives
Romani comprobaverunt, ut domum ad se quisque
hospitio cupidissime reciperet. Quibus rebus perterritus Varro, cum itinere converso sese Italicam
venturum praemisisset, certior ab suis factus est
praeclusas esse portas. Tum vero omni interclusus
itinere ad Caesarem mittit, paratum se esse legionem,
cui iusserit, tradere. Ille ad eum Sextum Caesarem
mittit atque huic tradi iubet. Tradita legione Varro
Cordubam ad Caesarem venit; relatis ad eum publicis cum fide rationibus quod penes eum est pecuniae tradit et, quid ubique habeat frumenti et navium,
ostendit.

21   Caesar contione habita Cordubae omnibus generatim gratias agit: civibus Romanis, quod oppidum
in sua potestate studuissent habere; Hispanis, quod
praesidia expulissent; Gaditanis, quod conatus adversariorum infregissent seseque in libertatem vin-
dicassent; tribunis militum centurionibusque, qui eo
praesidii causa venerant, quod eorum consilia sua
virtute confirmassent. Pecunias, quas erant in publicum Varroni cives Romani polliciti, remittit; bona
restituit eis, quos liberius locutos hanc poenam tulisse
cognoverat. Tributis quibusdam populis[1] publicis
privatisque praemiis reliquos in posterum bona spe
complet biduumque Cordubae commoratus Gades
proficiscitur; pecunias monumentaque, quae ex fano

---

[1] *The MSS. vary between* populis *and* publicis. *I follow Meusel in adopting both words.*

without harming anyone. The Roman citizens of
the district approved this action so highly that
every one of them most eagerly welcomed the men
with hospitable entertainment in his own house.
Varro, alarmed by these events, after sending on
word that he had changed his route and was coming
to Italica, was informed by his friends that the gates
were shut against him. Thereupon, being shut off from
every route, he sends word to Caesar that he is ready
to hand over his legion to whomsoever he shall ap-
point. Caesar sends Sex. Caesar to him, bidding him
hand it over to him. When the legion was given up
Varro comes to Caesar at Corduba; after faithfully
rendering him a statement of the public accounts, he
hands over the money in his possession and explains
what he has in the way of corn and ships, wherever
it may be.

Caesar held a public meeting at Corduba and   21
thanked all classes separately—the Roman citizens
for their zeal in keeping the town under his control,
the Spaniards for having cast out the garrisons, the
Gaditanians for having crushed the attempts of his
adversaries and having vindicated their own liberty,
the military tribunes and centurions who had come
there on garrison duty for having confirmed the
resolutions of the others by their own valour. He
remits the sums of money which the Roman citizens
had promised to Varro for public purposes; he
restores their property to those whom he understood
to have been thus penalized for their freedom of
speech. Having bestowed on certain communities
public and private rewards, he fills the rest with
good hope for the future, and after a stay of two
days at Corduba sets out for Gades, where he orders
the moneys and memorial offerings that had been

Herculis collata erant in privatam domum, referri in
templum iubet.   Provinciae Q. Cassium praeficit;
huic IIII legiones attribuit.   Ipse eis navibus, quas
M. Varro quasque Gaditani iussu Varronis fecerant,
Tarraconem paucis diebus pervenit.   Ibi totius fere
citerioris provinciae legationes Caesaris adventum
exspectabant.   Eadem ratione privatim ac publice
quibusdam civitatibus habitis honoribus Tarracone
discedit pedibusque Narbonem atque inde Massiliam
pervenit.   Ibi legem de dictatore latam seseque
dictatorem dictum a M. Lepido praetore cognoscit.

22   Massilienses omnibus defessi malis, rei frumentariae ad summam inopiam adducti, bis navali proelio
superati, crebris eruptionibus fusi, gravi etiam pestilentia conflictati ex diutina conclusione et mutatione
victus (panico enim vetere atque hordeo corrupto
omnes alebantur, quod ad huiusmodi casus antiquitus
paratum in publicum contulerant) deiecta turri,
labefacta magna parte muri, auxiliis provinciarum et
exercituum desperatis, quos in Caesaris potestatem
venisse cognoverant, sese dedere sine fraude constituunt.   Sed paucis ante diebus L. Domitius
cognita Massiliensium voluntate navibus III comparatis, ex quibus duas familiaribus suis attribuerat,
unam ipse conscenderat nactus turbidam tempestatem profectus est.   Hunc conspicatae naves, quae
iussu Bruti consuetudine cotidiana ad portum excu-
babant, sublatis ancoris sequi coeperunt.   Ex his

brought from the shrine of Hercules to a private house to be restored to the temple, and sets Q. Cassius over the province, assigning him four legions. In a few days he arrives at Tarraco with the ships which M. Varro had built and those which the Gaditanians had built on Varro's order. There embassies from nearly the whole of the hither province were awaiting Caesar's arrival. Having in the same way conferred honours privately and publicly on certain communities, he leaves Tarraco and makes his way by land to Narbo and thence to Massilia. There he learns that a law had been passed about a dictator, and that he himself had been nominated dictator by the praetor M. Lepidus.

The Massilians, worn out by every form of ill, 22 reduced to the extremest scarcity of provisions, twice beaten in a naval battle, routed in their frequent sorties, harassed moreover by a serious pestilence resulting from their long confinement and change of food—for they were all supporting themselves on an old stock of millet and stale barley which they had long ago collected for such emergencies and put in a public store—their tower overthrown, a great part of their wall in ruins, with no hope of reinforcements from the provinces and the armies, which they had been informed had fallen under Caesar's control, determined to make a loyal surrender. But a few days before L. Domitius, learning of the intention of the Massilians, having got together three ships, two of which he had assigned to his friends, himself embarking on the other, departed in stormy weather. The ships which by order of Brutus were keeping watch off the port according to their daily custom, catching sight of him, weighed anchor and began the pursuit.

unum ipsius navigium contendit et fugere perseveravit auxilioque tempestatis ex conspectu abiit, duo perterrita concursu nostrarum navium sese in portum receperunt. Massilienses arma tormentaque ex oppido, ut est imperatum, proferunt, naves ex portu navalibusque educunt, pecuniam ex publico tradunt. Quibus rebus confectis Caesar magis eos pro nomine et vetustate, quam pro meritis in se civitatis conservans duas ibi legiones praesidio relinquit, ceteras in Italiam mittit; ipse ad urbem proficiscitur.

23   Eisdem temporibus C. Curio in Africam profectus ex Sicilia et iam ab initio copias P. Attii Vari despiciens duas legiones ex IIII, quas a Caesare acceperat, D equites transportabat biduoque et noctibus tribus navigatione consumptis appellit ad eum locum, qui appellatur Anquillaria. Hic locus abest a Clupeis passuum XXII milia habetque non incommodam aestate stationem et duobus eminentibus promuntoriis continetur. Huius adventum L. Caesar filius cum X longis navibus ad Clupea praestolans, quas naves Uticae ex praedonum bello subductas P. Attius reficiendas huius belli causa curaverat, veritus navium multitudinem ex alto refugerat appulsaque ad proximum litus trireme constrata et in litore relicta pedibus Adrumetum perfugerat. Id oppidum C. Considius Longus unius legionis praesidio tuebatur. Reliquae Caesaris naves eius fuga se Adrumetum receperunt. Hunc secutus Marcius Rufus quaestor navibus XII, quas praesidio onerariis

The ship which belonged to Domitius himself held steadily on its course in flight and, aided by the storm, passed out of sight; two, terrified by the united onset of our ships, took shelter in the harbour. The Massilians produce from the town their arms and engines according to orders, bring out their ships from the port and docks, and hand over their money from the treasury. When all this was done, Caesar, sparing them more on account of the name and antiquity of their state than for anything they had deserved of him, leaves two legions there as a garrison, sends the rest to Italy, and himself sets out for Rome.

At the same period G. Curio, who had set out from Sicily for Africa,[1] despising at the very outset the forces of P. Attius Varus, was transporting two of the four legions which he had received from Caesar and five hundred horsemen, and after spending two days and three nights on the voyage touches at the place called Anquillaria. This place is distant twenty-two miles from Clupea, and has an anchorage not unsuitable in summer, and is enclosed by two projecting promontories. The young L. Caesar, awaiting his arrival at Clupea with ten ships of war (which, having been laid up at Utica after the pirate war, P. Attius had caused to be repaired for the purpose of this war) being alarmed at the number of the ships, had fled from the high sea, and beaching his decked trireme on the nearest shore and leaving it there, had fled by land to Hadrumetum, a town which G. Considius Longus was protecting with a garrison of one legion; and on his flight the rest of Caesar's ships betook themselves to Hadrumetum. The quaestor Marcius Rufus, following him with twelve ships which Curio had brought from Sicily to protect the

23

[1] See map of Curio's campaign in Africa.

navibus Curio ex Sicilia eduxerat, postquam in litore relictam navem conspexit, hanc remulco abstraxit; ipse ad C. Curionem cum classe redit.

24 Curio Marcium Uticam navibus praemittit; ipse eodem cum exercitu proficiscitur biduique iter progressus ad flumen Bagradam pervenit. Ibi C. Caninium Rebilum legatum cum legionibus reliquit; ipse cum equitatu antecedit ad castra exploranda Cornelia, quod is locus peridoneus castris habebatur. Id autem est iugum directum eminens in mare, utraque ex parte praeruptum atque asperum, sed tamen paulo leniore fastigio ab ea parte, quae ad Uticam vergit. Abest directo itinere ab Utica paulo amplius passuum milibus III. Sed hoc itinere est fons, quo mare succedit longius, lateque is locus restagnat; quem si qui vitare voluerit, sex milium circuitu in oppidum pervenit.

25 Hoc explorato loco Curio castra Vari conspicit muro oppidoque coniuncta ad portam, quae appellatur Belica,[1] admodum munita natura loci, una ex parte ipso oppido Utica, altero a theatro, quod est ante oppidum, substructionibus eius operis maximis, aditu ad castra difficili et angusto. Simul animadvertit multa undique portari atque agi plenissimis viis, quae repentini tumultus timore ex agris in urbem conferantur. Huc equitatum mittit, ut diriperet atque haberet loco praedae; eodemque tempore his rebus subsidio DC equites Numidae ex oppido peditesque CCCC mittuntur a Varo, quos auxilii causa rex

---

[1] *MSS.* bellica, *corrected by H. Hartz.*

merchant-vessels, on seeing the ship left on the shore, dragged it off with a tow-rope and himself returned to G. Curio with his fleet.

Curio sends Marcius on to Utica with his fleet; 24 he himself sets out thither with his army, and having completed a two days' march, arrived at the River Bagrada. There he left the legate G. Caninius Rebilus with the legions, and himself goes on in front with his cavalry to explore the Cornelian Camp, because that spot seemed particularly suitable for a camp. Now this was a straight ridge projecting into the sea, abrupt and rugged on either side, but with a somewhat gentler slope on the side facing Utica. The distance from Utica in a straight line is a little more than three miles, but in this direction a stream rises, by the bed of which the sea runs up for some distance, and the place becomes a wide marsh, and anyone wishing to avoid this only reaches the town by a circuit of six miles.

Reconnoitring this place, Curio sees the camp of 25 Varus joined on to the wall and town near the so-called gate of Baal, strongly protected by the nature of the ground—on one side by the town of Utica itself, on the other by the amphitheatre in front of the town, the substructions of this work being very large, rendering approach to the camp difficult and narrow. At the same time he notices that all along the densely crowded roads there is much carrying and hurrying of property that is being conveyed from the country into the town in fear of a sudden tumult. Hither he sends the cavalry to seize and retain it as booty, and at the same time to protect this property six hundred Numidian horsemen and four hundred foot-soldiers, whom King Juba had sent to Utica by way of aid a few days before, are dispatched

Iuba paucis diebus ante Uticam miserat. Huic et paternum hospitium cum Pompeio et simultas cum Curione intercedebat, quod tribunus plebis legem promulgaverat, qua lege regnum Iubae publicaverat. Concurrunt equites inter se; neque vero primum impetum nostrorum Numidae ferre potuerunt, sed interfectis circiter CXX reliqui se in castra ad oppidum receperunt. Interim adventu longarum navium Curio pronuntiare onerariis navibus iubet, quae stabant ad Uticam numero circiter CC, se in hostium habiturum loco, qui non e vestigio ad castra Cornelia naves traduxisset. Qua pronuntiatione facta temporis puncto sublatis ancoris omnes Uticam relinquunt et quo imperatum est transeunt. Quae res omnium rerum copia complevit exercitum.

26   His rebus gestis Curio se in castra ad Bagradam recipit atque universi exercitus conclamatione imperator appellatur posteroque die exercitum Uticam ducit et prope oppidum castra ponit. Nondum opere castrorum perfecto equites ex statione nuntiant magna auxilia equitum peditumque ab rege missa Uticam venire; eodemque tempore vis magna pulveris cernebatur, et vestigio temporis primum agmen erat in conspectu. Novitate rei Curio permotus praemittit equites, qui primum impetum sustineant ac morentur; ipse celeriter ab opere deductis legionibus aciem instruit. Equitesque committunt proelium et, priusquam plane legiones explicari et consistere

from the town by Varus. Juba had hereditary ties of hospitality with Pompeius, and between him and Curio there was a quarrel because, as tribune of the people, Curio had promulgated a law by which he had confiscated Juba's realm. The cavalry meet in conflict, nor could the Numidians withstand the first onset of our men, but when about a hundred and twenty of them had been killed the rest retreated towards the town to their camp. Meanwhile on the approach of the warships Curio bids proclamation be made to the merchant-vessels that were stationed at Utica to the number of about two hundred that he would treat anyone as an enemy who did not forthwith transfer his ships to the Cornelian Camp. On the issue of this proclamation they all immediately weigh anchor, leave Utica, and cross over whither they are bidden. This supplied the army with an abundance of all necessaries.

After these achievements Curio withdraws to the   26 camp by the Bagrada and is saluted as "Imperator"[1] by the acclamations of the whole army, and on the next day leads his army to Utica and pitches his camp near the town. Before the work of entrenching was completed horsemen on picket duty bring word that large reinforcements of cavalry and infantry sent by the king are on their way to Utica, and at the same time a great mass of dust was seen and forthwith the van appeared in sight. Curio, disturbed by the unexpected event, sends forward horsemen to meet and check the first onset, and himself, hastily withdrawing his legions from their work, draws up his line of battle. The cavalry engage, and before the legions could be fully deployed and take up their

---

[1] It was customary for troops after a victory to salute their commander as Imperator.

possent, tota auxilia regis impedita ac perturbata, quod nullo ordine et sine timore iter fecerant, in fugam coniciunt equitatuque omni fere incolumi, quod se per litora celeriter in oppidum recepit, magnum peditum numerum interficiunt.

27 Proxima nocte centuriones Marsi duo ex castris Curionis cum manipularibus suis XXII ad Attium Varum perfugiunt. Hi, sive vere quam habuerant opinionem ad eum perferunt, sive etiam auribus Vari serviunt (nam, quae volumus, et credimus libenter et, quae sentimus ipsi, reliquos sentire speramus), confirmant quidem certe totius exercitus animos alienos esse a Curione maximeque opus esse in conspectum exercitus venire et colloquendi dare facultatem. Qua opinione adductus Varus postero die mane legiones ex castris educit. Facit idem Curio, atque una valle non magna interiecta suas uterque copias instruit.

28 Erat in exercitu Vari Sextus Quintilius Varus, quem fuisse Corfinii supra demonstratum est. Hic dimissus a Caesare in Africam venerat, legionesque eas traduxerat Curio, quas superioribus temporibus Corfinio receperat Caesar, adeo ut paucis mutatis centurionibus eidem ordines manipulique constarent. Hanc nactus appellationis causam Quintilius circuire aciem Curionis atque obsecrare milites coepit, ne primam sacramenti, quod apud Domitium atque apud se quaestorem dixissent, memoriam deponerent, neu contra eos arma ferrent, qui eadem essent usi fortuna eademque in obsidione perpessi, neu pro

positions, they threw all the king's reinforcements into confusion and panic, since they had been marching in no order and without fear, and routed them; and though the cavalry sustained scarcely any loss, owing to their retiring quickly along the coast to the town, they slew a great number of the infantry.

On the following night two Marsic centurions 27 from Curio's camp, with twenty-two of their men, desert to Attius Varus. Whether they convey to him the opinion that they really held, or whether they only flatter his ears—for what we desire we gladly believe, and what we ourselves feel we hope that others feel too—at any rate they assure him that the hearts of the whole army are estranged from Curio, and that it is highly necessary that he should come within sight of the army and afford an opportunity of conference. Varus, influenced by this judgment, leads his legions out of camp early the next day. Curio does the same, and each draws up his forces with only one small valley between them.

In the army of Varus was Sex. Quintilius Varus, 28 who, as explained above, had been at Corfinium. Dismissed by Caesar, he had come to Africa, and Curio had brought across the legions which Caesar had at an earlier period recovered from Corfinium, without altering the establishment of officers and men, though a few centurions were changed. Having this excuse for appealing to them, Quintilius began to go the round of Curio's force and beseech the soldiers not to lay aside their early memory of the oath that they had sworn before Domitius and before himself as quaestor, nor bear arms against those who had experienced the same fortune and suffered the same hardships in the siege,

his pugnarent, a quibus cum contumelia perfugae appellarentur. Huc pauca ad spem largitionis addidit, quae ab sua liberalitate, si se atque Attium secuti essent, exspectare deberent. Hac habita oratione nullam in partem ab exercitu Curionis fit significatio, atque ita suas uterque copias reducit.

29 At in castris Curionis magnus omnium incessit timor animis. Is variis hominum sermonibus celeriter augetur. Unusquisque enim opiniones fingebat et ad id, quod ab alio audierat, sui aliquid timoris addebat. Hoc ubi uno auctore ad plures permanaverat, atque alius alii tradiderat, plures auctores eius rei videbantur. Civile bellum; genus hominum, cui liceret libere facere et sequi, quod vellet; legiones eae, quae paulo ante apud adversarios fuerant, nam etiam Caesaris beneficium mutaverat consuetudo, qua offerrentur; municipia etiam diversis partibus coniuncta, namque ex Marsis Pelignisque veniebant ei qui superiore nocte: haec in contuberniis commilites que nonnulli graviora; sermones militum dubii durius accipiebantur, nonnulli etiam ab eis, qui diligentiores videri volebant, fingebantur. [1]

30 Quibus de causis consilio convocato de summa rerum deliberare incipit. Erant sententiae, quae

[1] *The text of the whole passage from* Civile bellum *to* fingebantur *is too imperfect to admit of restoration. The translation must, therefore, be regarded as only an approximate rendering of the fragmentary text.*

nor fight for those by whom they were insultingly styled deserters. To this he adds a few words to arouse hope of bounty—such rewards as they were bound to expect from his liberality if they should follow himself and Attius. On the delivery of this speech no sign is made either way by Curio's army, and so each commander leads back his forces.

But in Curio's camp great alarm took possession of the minds of all, and this alarm is quickly increased by various popular rumours. For each person invented imaginary views and added something of his own fear to whatever he had heard from another. When the story had spread from the first who vouched for it to a number of others, each handing it on to his fellow, there appeared at last to be several who could vouch for its truth. It was a civil war, they said; the men were of a class which was permitted to do freely what it liked and to follow its bent; the legions were those which a little while before had been in the hands of their foes, for the custom of constantly offering gifts had depreciated even the bounty of Caesar; the municipal communities, too, were attached to different sides, for men came equally from the Marsi and the Peligni, as, for instance, those who had deserted the night before. In the tents some of the soldiers proposed strong measures. Doubtful speeches on the part of the men were harshly interpreted; some reports were even invented by those who wished to seem more zealous than their fellows.

For these reasons a council is summoned, and Curio opens a discussion on the general position. Opinions were delivered expressing the view that a

conandum omnibus modis castraque Vari oppugnanda censerent, quod in huiusmodi militum consiliis otium maxime contrarium esse arbitrarentur;
postremo praestare dicebant per virtutem in pugna
belli fortunam experiri, quam desertos et circumven-
tos ab suis gravissimum supplicium perpeti. Erant,
qui censerent de tertia vigilia in castra Cornelia
recedendum, ut maiore spatio temporis interiecto
militum mentes sanarentur, simul, si quid gravius
accidisset, magna multitudine navium et tutius et
facilius in Siciliam receptus daretur.

31   Curio utrumque improbans consilium, quantum
alteri sententiae deesset animi, tantum alteri super-
esse dicebat: hos turpissimae fugae rationem habere,
illos etiam iniquo loco dimicandum putare. "Qua
enim," inquit, "fiducia et opere et natura loci munitissima castra expugnari posse confidimus? Aut
vero quid proficimus, si accepto magno detrimento
ab oppugnatione castrorum discedimus? Quasi non
et felicitas rerum gestarum exercitus benevolentiam
imperatoribus et res adversae odia colligant! Castrorum autem mutatio quid habet nisi turpem fugam
et desperationem omnium et alienationem exercitus?
Nam neque pudentes suspicari oportet sibi parum
credi, neque improbes scire sese timeri, quod his
licentiam timor augeat noster, illis studia deminuat."
"Quod si iam," inquit, "haec explorata habeamus,
quae de exercitus alienatione dicuntur, quae quidem

bold attempt should by all means be made and the camp of Varus attacked, because in the present temper of the soldiery they thought inaction particularly inopportune; lastly, they said that it was better to tempt the fortune of war by valour in battle than, deserted and cheated by their comrades, to undergo the severest penalties. Some there were who proposed a retirement at the third watch to the Cornelian Camp, so that by the interposition of a longer interval of time the minds of the troops might be restored to sanity, and that, at the same time, if anything serious should occur, a withdrawal to Sicily might be more safely and easily secured owing to the great number of ships.

Curio, disapproving of each plan, remarked that in 31 proportion as the one lacked spirit the other had too much of it; the one party had in view an utterly disgraceful flight, the other were thinking that they should fight even in an unfavourable position. "Pray on what grounds of assurance are we confident," said he, "that a camp so strongly fortified both by works and by the nature of the position can be taken by storm? Or indeed what do we gain if after sustaining serious losses we abandon the siege of the camp? As if it were not success in action that brought a commander the goodwill, and reverses that brought him the hatred, of his army! What does a change of camp imply but a discreditable flight and general despair and the estrangement of the army? For the honourable ought not to suspect that they are insufficiently trusted, nor the dishonest know that they are feared, because fear on our part increases the licence of the latter and diminishes the zeal of the former. Now if," he continues, "we have full assurance of the statements that are made

ego aut omnino falsa aut certe minora opinione esse
confido, quanto haec dissimulari et occultari, quam
per nos confirmari praestet? An non, uti corporis
vulnera, ita exercitus incommoda sunt tegenda, ne
spem adversariis augeamus? At etiam, ut media
nocte proficiscamur, addunt, quo maiorem, credo,
licentiam habeant, qui peccare conentur. Namque
huiusmodi res aut pudore aut metu tenentur; quibus
rebus nox maxime adversaria est. Quare neque tanti
sum animi, ut sine spe castra oppugnanda censeam,
neque tanti timoris, uti spe deficiam, atque omnia
prius experienda arbitror magnaque ex parte iam me
una vobiscum de re iudicium facturum confido."

32   Dimisso consilio contionem advocat militum.
Commemorat, quo sit eorum usus studio ad Corfinium Caesar, ut magnam partem Italiae beneficio
atque auctoritate eorum suam fecerit. "Vos enim
vestrumque factum omnia," inquit, "deinceps municipia sunt secuta, neque sine causa et Caesar amicissime de vobis et illi gravissime iudicaverunt. Pompeius
enim nullo proelio pulsus vestri facti praeiudicio de-
motus Italia excessit; Caesar me, quem sibi carissi-
mum habuit, provinciam Siciliam atque Africam,
sine quibus urbem atque Italiam tueri non potest,
vestrae fidei commisit. At sunt, qui vos hortentur,

170

about the estrangement of the army, which for my part I am confident are either altogether false or at any rate are less true than is supposed, how much better would it be for these rumours to be ignored and kept hidden than to be confirmed through our action? Is it not true that reverses of an army, like wounds of the body, should be concealed, that we may not increase the hopes of our adversaries? Why, they even add that we should set out at midnight, to give greater licence, I suppose, to those who are striving to do wrong! For misdeeds of this kind are kept in check either by shame or by fear, and to such checks night is in the highest degree unfavourable. Wherefore I am neither a man of such courage as to think that the camp should be attacked without hope of success, nor of such timidity as to be without hope, and so I think that every expedient should be tried before this, and I am confident that in the main you and I together will form a decision on the point at issue."

On the dismissal of the council he calls a meeting 32 of the soldiers. He reminds them how zealous Caesar had found them at Corfinium, how it was, thanks to them and their powerful aid, he made a great part of Italy his own. "All the municipal towns in turn," he said, "followed you and your action, and it was not without reason that Caesar formed the friendliest opinion of you, and the enemy the harshest. For Pompeius, though not beaten in any battle, was thrust away by the predetermining effect of your action and quitted Italy; while Caesar entrusted to your loyalty me, whom he held most dear, and the province of Sicily and Africa, without which he cannot protect the capital and Italy. Yet there are people who urge you to fall apart from us. Why,

ut a nobis desciscatis. Quid enim est illis optatius,
quam uno tempore et nos circumvenire et vos nefario
scelere obstringere? aut quid irati gravius de vobis
sentire possunt, quam ut eos prodatis, qui se vobis
omnia debere iudicant, in eorum potestatem veniatis,
qui se per vos perisse existimant? An vero in Hispania res gestas Caesaris non audistis? duos pulsos
exercitus, duos superatos duces, duas receptas provincias? haec acta diebus XL, quibus in conspectum adversariorum venerit Caesar? An, qui
incolumes resistere non potuerunt, perditi resistant?
vos autem incerta victoria Caesarem secuti diiudicata
iam belli fortuna victum sequamini, cum vestri officii
praemia percipere debeatis? Desertos enim se ac
proditos a vobis dicunt et prioris sacramenti mentionem faciunt. Vosne vero L. Domitium, an vos
Domitius deseruit? Nonne extremam pati fortunam
paratos proiecit ille? nonne sibi clam salutem
fuga petivit? nonne proditi per illum Caesaris beneficio estis conservati? Sacramento quidem vos tenere
qui potuit, cum proiectis fascibus et deposito imperio
privatus et captus ipse in alienam venisset potestatem? Relinquitur nova religio, ut eo neglecto
sacramento, quo tenemini, respiciatis illud, quod
deditione ducis et capitis deminutione sublatum est.
At, credo, si Caesarem probatis, in me offenditis.
Qui de meis in vos meritis praedicaturus non sum,

what do our opponents pray for more than at one and the same time to take us in their toils and to entrammel you by a nefarious crime? Or what harsher idea of you can they form in their anger than that you should betray those who judge that they owe everything to you, and pass under the control of those who think that they were ruined by you? Have you really not heard of Caesar's exploits in Spain—two armies routed, two generals overcome, two provinces recovered—these successes gained within forty days after Caesar came within sight of the enemy? Should those who could not resist when they were unharmed resist now that they are ruined? Again, should you, who followed Caesar when victory was uncertain, now, when the fortune of war is once for all decided, follow the conquered when you ought to be reaping the rewards of your dutiful allegiance? They say in reply that they were deserted and betrayed by you, and they make mention of your former oath. I ask, did you desert L. Domitius, or did Domitius desert you? Did he not cast you off when you were ready to endure the extremity of fortune? Did he not without your knowledge seek safety for himself in flight? When betrayed by him, was it not by Caesar's kindness that you have been preserved? As for the oath, how could he hold you bound by it when, flinging aside his fasces and laying down his military command, he had himself passed, a private person and a captive, into the control of another? A novel obligation is left you, to disregard the oath by which you are bound and look back to that which has been cancelled by the surrender of the general and his civil degradation. But, I suppose, even if you approve of Caesar, you stumble at me. I am not going to talk of my services

quae sunt adhuc et mea voluntate et vestra exspectatione leviora; sed tamen sui laboris milites semper
eventu belli praemia petiverunt, qui qualis sit futurus, ne vos quidem dubitatis: diligentiam quidem
nostram aut, quem ad finem adhuc res processit,
fortunam cur praeteream? An poenitet vos, quod
salvum atque incolumem exercitum nulla omnino
nave desiderata traduxerim? quod classem hostium
primo impetu adveniens profligaverim? quod bis per
biduum equestri proelio superaverim? quod ex portu
sinuque adversariorum CC naves oneratas abduxerim
eoque illos compulerim, ut neque pedestri itinere
neque navibus commeatu iuvari possint? Hac vos
fortuna atque his ducibus repudiatis Corfiniensem
ignominiam, Italiae fugam, Hispaniarum deditionem,
Africi belli praeiudicia, sequimini! Equidem me Caesaris militem dici volui, vos me imperatoris nomine
appellavistis. Cuius si vos poenitet, vestrum vobis
beneficium remitto, mihi meum nomen restituite, ne
ad contumeliam honorem dedisse videamini."

33   Qua oratione permoti milites crebro etiam dicentem interpellabant, ut magno cum dolore infidelitatis
suspicionem sustinere viderentur, discedentem vero
ex contione universi cohortantur, magno sit animo,
necubi dubitet proelium committere et suam fidem
virtutemque experiri. Quo facto commutata omnium
et voluntate et opinione consensu summo constituit
Curio, cum primum sit data potestas, proelio rem
committere posteroque die productos eodem loco,

towards you; at present they are slighter than I could wish or you expect; but still, soldiers have always sought the rewards of their labour by the issue of the war, and what that will be, you, too, have no doubt. As for my diligence—or, so far as things have gone at present, our fortune—why should I pass them over? Are you dissatisfied with my having transported the army safe and sound without the loss of a single ship? With my having scattered the fleet of the enemy on my arrival at the first onset? At my having twice in two days won in a cavalry engagement? At my having taken off two hundred loaded vessels from the recesses of the enemy's harbour, and having driven the foe to such straits that they cannot be replenished with provisions either by a land route or by sea? Repudiating such fortune, such leaders, you follow the disgrace of Corfinium, the flight from Italy, the surrender of the Spains, events which forecast the issue of the African war! I, for my part, wished to be called a soldier of Caesar: you have addressed me by the title of Imperator. If you regret this, I give you back your bounty; restore me my proper name, lest you should seem to have given me an honour only as an insult."

Moved by this speech, the men interrupted him 33 even while speaking, making it evident that they endured with great indignation the suspicion of disloyalty; but on his leaving the assembly they exhort him in a body to be of good courage and on no occasion to hesitate to join battle and test their loyalty and valour. When by this action the feelings and thoughts of the men had been completely changed, Curio determines with their unanimous consent to commit the issue to battle as soon as opportunity is offered, and on the next day he leads them out and arranges them in order of battle in the same

quo superioribus diebus constiterat, in acie collocat.
Ne Varus quidem dubitat copias producere, sive
sollicitandi milites sive aequo loco dimicandi detur
occasio, ne facultatem praetermittat.

34   Erat vallis inter duas acies, ut supra demonstratum
est, non ita magna, at difficili et arduo ascensu. Hanc
uterque, si adversariorum copiae transire conarentur,
exspectabat, quo aequiore loco proelium committeret.
Simul ab sinistro cornu P. Attii equitatus omnis et
una levis armaturae interiecti complures, cum se in
vallem demitterent, cernebantur. Ad eos Curio
equitatum et duas Marrucinorum cohortes mittit;
quorum primum impetum equites hostium non tulerunt, sed admissis equis ad suos refugerunt; relicti
ab his, qui una procurrerant levis armaturae, circum-
veniebantur atque interficiebantur ab nostris. Huc
tota Vari conversa acies suos fugere et concidi videbat. Tunc Rebilus, legatus Caesaris, quem Curio
secum ex Sicilia duxerat, quod magnum habere usum
in re militari sciebat, "perterritum," inquit "hostem
vides, Curio: quid dubitas uti temporis opportunitate?" Ille unum elocutus, ut memoria tenerent
milites ea, quae pridie sibi confirmassent, sequi sese
iubet et praecurrit ante omnes. Adeo erat impedita
vallis, ut in ascensu nisi sublevati a suis primi non
facile eniterentur. Sed praeoccupatus animus At-
tianorum militum timore et fuga et caede suorum
nihil de resistendo cogitabat, omnesque se iam ab

place in which he had taken up his position on the previous days. Nor does Varus hesitate to lead out his forces, that he may not let slip an opportunity, if chance is given him, either of tampering with Curio's men or of fighting in a favourable position.

Between the two lines there was, as explained 34 above, a valley, not very large, but with a difficult and steep ascent. Each commander was waiting to see whether the enemy's forces would attempt to cross this, in order that he might join battle on more level ground. At the same time on the left wing the whole cavalry force of P. Attius and a number of light-armed troops placed among them were seen as they were descending into the valley. Against them Curio sends his cavalry and two cohorts of the Marrucini. Their first charge the enemy's horse failed to withstand, but fled back at a gallop to their comrades. The light-armed men who had advanced with them, being abandoned by them, were surrounded and slain by our men. The whole of Varus' array turned and saw their men being cut down in flight. Then Rebilus, Caesar's legate, whom Curio had brought with him from Sicily, knowing him to be possessed of great experience in warfare, said: "You see the enemy panic-stricken, Curio: why do you hesitate to use the opportunity of the moment?" Curio, merely exclaiming that the troops should bear in mind the assurances that they had given him the day before, bids them follow him and hurries ahead of them all. Now the valley was so difficult that the front men could not easily win their way up unless assisted by their comrades. But the minds of the Attian soldiers, preoccupied by their fear and the flight and slaughter of their comrades, never gave a thought to resistance, and they all imagined

equitatu circumveniri arbitrabantur. Itaque priusquam telum abici posset, aut nostri propius acce-
derent, omnis Vari acies terga vertit seque in castra
recepit.

35   Qua in fuga Fabius Pelignus quidam ex infimis
ordinibus de exercitu Curionis primus agmen fugientium consecutus magna voce Varum nomine appellans requirebat, uti unus esse ex eius militibus et
monere aliquid velle ac dicere videretur. Ubi ille
saepius appellatus aspexit ac restitit et, quis esset
aut quid vellet, quaesivit, umerum apertum gladio
appetit paulumque afuit, quin Varum interficeret;
quod ille periculum sublato ad eius conatum scuto
vitavit. Fabius a proximis militibus circumventus
interficitur. Hac fugientium multitudine ac turba
portae castrorum occupantur atque iter impeditur,
pluresque in eo loco sine vulnere quam in proelio
aut fuga intereunt, neque multum afuit, quin etiam
castris expellerentur, ac nonnulli protinus eodem
cursu in oppidum contenderunt. Sed cum loci
natura et munitio castrorum aditum prohibebant,
tum quod ad proelium egressi Curionis milites eis
rebus indigebant, quae ad oppugnationem castrorum
erant usui. Itaque Curio exercitum in castra reducit
suis omnibus praeter Fabium incolumibus, ex numero
adversariorum circiter DC interfectis ac mille vulneratis; qui omnes discessu Curionis multique
praeterea per simulationem vulnerum ex castris in
oppidum propter timorem sese recipiunt. Qua re
animadversa Varus et terrore exercitus cognito buci-
natore in castris et paucis ad speciem tabernaculis

178

that they were being already surrounded by cavalry.
And so before a weapon could be cast or our men
could approach nearer, the whole of Varus' line
turned to flight and withdrew to the camp.

In this flight one Fabius, a Pelignian, of the lowest 35
rank of centurions in Curio's army, being the first man
to overtake the fugitive column, kept looking for Varus,
calling him with a loud voice by name, so as to seem
to be one of his men and to be wishing to make some
suggestion and statement. When Varus on being
frequently addressed stopped and looked at him and
asked who he was or what he wanted, he struck at
his exposed shoulder with a sword and came within
a little of killing Varus, who avoided the peril by
raising his shield to meet the attempted stroke.
Fabius is surrounded and killed by the nearest
soldiers. The gates of the camp are beset by this
throng and turmoil of fugitives and the road blocked,
and more perish in this spot without wounds than in
the battle or the flight; they were indeed very near
being driven even out of the camp, and some, without
checking their course, hurried straight into the town.
But not only did the nature of the ground and the
defences of the camp prohibit access, but also the
fact that Curio's men, having marched out for a battle,
lacked the appliances that were required for the
siege of a camp. And so Curio brings back his army
into camp with all his men safe except Fabius, while
of the number of the foe about six hundred were slain
and a thousand wounded. And on Curio's departure
all these, and many others feigning wounds, retreat
from the camp into the town by reason of their
fear. And observing this and aware of the terror
of his army, Varus, leaving a trumpeter in his camp
and a few tents for the sake of appearance, silently

relictis de tertia vigilia silentio exercitum in oppidum reducit.

36   Postero die Curio obsidere Uticam et vallo circummunire instituit. Erat in oppido multitudo insolens belli diuturnitate otii, Uticenses pro quibusdam Caesaris in se beneficiis illi amicissimi, conventus is, qui ex variis generibus constaret, terror ex superioribus proeliis magnus. Itaque de deditione omnes palam loquebantur et cum P. Attio agebant, ne sua pertinacia omnium fortunas perturbari vellet. Haec cum agerentur, nuntii praemissi ab rege Iuba venerunt, qui illum adesse cum magnis copiis dicerent et de custodia ac defensione urbis hortarentur. Quae res eorum perterritos animos confirmavit.

37   Nuntiabantur haec eadem Curioni, sed aliquamdiu fides fieri non poterat: tantam habebat suarum rerum fiduciam. Iamque Caesaris in Hispania res secundae in Africam nuntiis ac litteris perferebantur. Quibus omnibus rebus sublatus nihil contra se regem nisurum existimabat. Sed ubi certis auctoribus comperit minus v et xx milibus longe ab Utica eius copias abesse, relictis munitionibus sese in castra Cornelia recepit. Huc frumentum comportare, castra munire, materiam conferre coepit statimque in Siciliam misit, uti duae legiones reliquusque equitatus ad se mitteretur. Castra erant ad bellum ducendum aptissima natura loci et munitione et

leads his army into the town about the third watch.

On the next day Curio sets himself to blockade 36 Utica and invest it with an earthwork. In the town there was a multitude of people unaccustomed to war owing to the long continuance of peace; there were the inhabitants of Utica who were most friendly to Caesar on account of certain benefits that he had conferred on them; there was the Roman burgess-body, consisting of various classes, and there was also great alarm in consequence of the previous battles. And so all now began to speak openly about surrender and to plead with P. Attius that he should not allow the fortunes of all to be upset by his own obstinacy. While this was going on some messengers sent on by King Juba arrived to say that he was close at hand with large forces and to exhort them to guard and defend the city. This strengthened their panic-stricken spirits.

The same news was conveyed to Curio, but for 37 some time he could not be induced to believe it, such confidence had he in his own fortunes. By now, too, news of Caesar's successes in Spain was being brought by messengers and dispatches to Africa. Elated by all this, he imagined that the king would attempt nothing against him. But when he found out on sure authority that his forces were twenty-four miles from Utica, he left his defences and withdrew to the Cornelian Camp. Here he began to bring together corn, to entrench a camp, to collect timber, and at once sent word to Sicily that two legions and the rest of the cavalry should be sent to him. The camp was most suitable for carrying on a prolonged war both from the nature of the site and from its defensive works, and also on account of the nearness

maris propinquitate et aquae et salis copia, cuius
magna vis iam ex proximis erat salinis eo congesta.
Non materia multitudine arborum, non frumentum,
cuius erant plenissimi agri, deficere poterat. Itaque
omnium suorum consensu Curio reliquas copias exspectare et bellum ducere parabat.

38   His constitutis rebus probatisque consiliis ex
perfugis quibusdam oppidanis audit Iubam revo-
catum finitimo bello et controversiis Leptitanorum
restitisse in regno, Saburram, eius praefectum, cum
mediocribus copiis missum Uticae appropinquare.
His auctoribus temere credens consilium commutat
et proelio rem committere constituit. Multum ad
hanc rem probandam adiuvat adulescentia, magnitudo animi, superioris temporis proventus, fiducia rei
bene gerendae. His rebus impulsus equitatum omnem
prima nocte ad castra hostium mittit ad flumen
Bagradam, quibus praeerat Saburra, de quo ante erat
auditum; sed rex omnibus copiis insequebatur et sex
milium passuum intervallo a Saburra consederat.
Equites missi nocte iter conficiunt, imprudentes
atque inopinantes hostes aggrediuntur. Numidae
enim quadam barbara consuetudine nullis ordinibus
passim consederant. Hos oppressos somno et dispersos adorti magnum eorum numerum interficiunt;
multi perterriti profugiunt. Quo facto ad Curionem
equites revertuntur captivosque ad eum reducunt.

of the sea, and the abundance of water and of salt, a great quantity of which had already been stored there from neighbouring salt-works. Timber could not fail, from the multitude of the trees, nor corn, of which the fields were unusually full. And so, with the approval of all his men, Curio prepared to wait for the rest of his forces and to wage a protracted war.

When these arrangements had been made and his **38** measures approved, he learns from some deserting townsmen that Juba, recalled by a neighbouring war and by quarrels with the people of Leptis, had stayed behind in his kingdom, and that his prefect Saburra, who had been sent on with a moderate force, was approaching Utica. Rashly believing their word, he changes his purpose and determines to commit the issue to battle. In his approval of this measure he is greatly aided by his youth, his high spirits, the results of the earlier period, his confidence of success. Urged on by such considerations, he sends all his cavalry at nightfall to the enemy's camp at the River Bagrada. Saburra, of whom he had previously heard, was in command of this camp, but the king was following on with all his forces and had taken up a position at a distance of six miles from Saburra. The cavalry whom Curio sent complete their journey by night and attack the enemy taken off their guard and unawares. For the Numidians, according to some barbarous custom of their own, had taken up their position here and there and in no set order. Attacking them when overcome by sleep and dispersed, they kill a great number of them; many fly panic-stricken. Having achieved this, the cavalry return to Curio and bring him back their captives.

39   Curio cum omnibus copiis quarta vigilia exierat
cohortibus v castris praesidio relictis. Progressus
milia passuum VI equites convenit, rem gestam cognovit; e captivis quaerit, quis castris ad Bagradam
praesit: respondent Saburram. Reliqua studio itineris
conficiendi quaerere praetermittit proximaque respiciens signa, "videtisne," inquit, "milites, captivorum
orationem cum perfugis convenire? abesse regem,
exiguas esse copias missas, quae paucis equitibus
pares esse non potuerint? Proinde ad praedam, ad
gloriam properate, ut iam de praemiis vestris et de
referenda gratia cogitare incipiamus." Erant per se
magna, quae gesserant equitas, praesertim cum
eorum exiguus numerus cum tanta multitudine
Numidarum confertur. Haec tamen ab ipsis inflatius commemorabantur, ut de suis homines laudibus
libenter praedicant. Multa praeterea spolia praefere-
bantur, capti homines equique producebantur, ut,
quicquid intercederet temporis, hoc omne victoriam
morari videretur. Ita spei Curionis militum studia
non deerant. Equites sequi iubet sese iterque
accelerat, ut quam maxime ex fuga perterritos adoriri
posset. At illi itinere totius noctis confecti subsequi
non poterant, atque alii alio loco resistebant. Ne
haec quidem Curionem ad spem morabantur.

40   Iuba certior factus a Saburra de nocturno
proelio II milia Hispanorum et Gallorum equitum,
quos suae custodiae causa circum se habere consue-

Curio had gone out at the fourth watch with all
his forces, leaving five cohorts to guard the camp.
When he had marched six miles he met the cavalry
and learnt of their success. He inquires of the
captives who is in command of the camp at the
Bagrada. They reply, "Saburra." In his zeal to
complete his march he omits other questions, and
looking to the nearest colours, he says: "Do you see,
my men, that the story of the captives agrees with
that of the deserters—that the king is absent, that
scanty forces have been dispatched, insufficient to
cope with a few horsemen? Hasten on then to
plunder and to glory, that we may at last begin
to take thought of your rewards and of the gratitude
that is your due." The exploits of the horsemen were
in fact considerable, especially when their small
number is compared with the great multitude of the
Numidians. But they were related in a somewhat
inflated style by the men themselves, with the usual
delight that men take in proclaiming their own
merits. Moreover, many spoils were displayed,
captured men and horses were produced, so that all
delay that might occur seemed to be a postponement
of the victory. So far was the zeal of the troops from
falling short of Curio's expectations. He bids the
horsemen follow him and hastens his march that he
might attack the foe just when most disordered by
flight. But his men, worn out by the whole night's
march, could not maintain the pursuit, and kept
stopping, one here and another there. Even this did
not check Curio in his aspirations.

Juba, having been informed by Saburra of the
night battle, sends to his relief two thousand Spanish
and Gallic cavalry which he had been wont to keep
round his person as a bodyguard, and that part of

rat, et peditum eam partem, cui maxime confidebat, Saburrae submisit; ipse cum reliquis copiis elephantisque LX lentius subsequitur. Suspicatus praemissis equitibus ipsum affore Curionem Saburra copias equitum peditumque instruit atque his imperat, ut simulatione timoris paulatim cedant ac pedem referant: sese, cum opus esset, signum proelii daturum et, quod rem postulare cognovisset, imperaturum. Curio ad superiorem spem addita praesentis temporis opinione, hostes fugere arbitratus copias ex locis superioribus in campum deducit.

41 Quibus ex locis cum longius esset progressus, confecto iam labore exercitu XII milium spatio constitit. Dat suis signum Saburra, aciem constituit et circumire ordines atque hortari incipit; sed peditatu dumtaxat procul ad speciem utitur, equites in aciem immittit. Non deest negotio Curio suosque hortatur, ut spem omnem in virtute reponant. Ne militibus quidem ut defessis neque equitibus ut paucis et labore confectis studium ad pugnandum virtusque deerat; sed hi erant numero CC, reliqui in itinere substiterant. Hi, quamcumque in partem impetum fecerant, hostes loco cedere cogebant, sed neque longius fugientes prosequi neque vehementius equos incitare poterant. At equitatus hostium ab utroque cornu circuire aciem nostram et aversos proterere incipit. Cum cohortes ex acie procucurrissent, Numidae integri celeritate impetum nostrorum effugie-

the infantry on which he most relied, and himself
follows more slowly with the rest of his forces and
sixty elephants. Saburra, suspecting that after sending forward the cavalry Curio would himself approach,
draws up his forces, horse and foot, and orders them
to feign fear and to give ground gradually and retire,
saying that he himself would give the signal of battle
when necessary and issue such orders as he might
judge the situation to require. Curio, having the
general opinion of the moment to confirm his former
hopes, and thinking that the enemy was in flight,
leads down his forces from the higher ground towards
the plain.

When he had gone a considerable distance from 41
this place, his army being now worn out by toil, he
halted after covering twelve miles. Saburra gives
his men the signal, draws up his line of battle, and
starts going up and down the ranks and exhorting
the men. But he uses his infantry merely to make
a show a little way off and hurls his horse on the
line. Curio is equal to the emergency and encourages
his men, bidding them place all their hopes on valour.
Nor did zeal for the fight or valour fail either the
infantry, weary as they were, or the cavalry, though
they were few and exhausted by toil. But these
were only two hundred in number; the rest had
stopped on the route. They compelled the enemy
to give way at whatever point they charged, but
they could neither follow them when they fled
to a distance nor urge their horses to more strenu-
ous effort. But the enemy's cavalry begins to
surround our force on either wing and to trample
them down from the rear. Whenever cohorts left
the main body and charged, the Numidians by their
swiftness fled unscathed from the assault of our

bant rursusque ad ordines suos se recipientes circuibant et ab acie excludebant. Sic neque in loco manere ordinesque servare neque procurrere et casum subire tutum videbatur. Hostium copiae submissis ab rege auxiliis crebro augebantur; nostros vires lassitudine deficiebant, simul ei, qui vulnera acceperant, neque acie excedere neque in locum tatum referri poterant, quod tota acies equitatu hostium circumdata tenebatur. Hi de sua salute desperantes, ut extremo vitae tempore homines facere consuerunt, aut suam mortem miserabantur aut parentes suos commendabant, si quos ex eo periculo fortuna servare potuisset. Plena erant omnia timoris et luctus.

42 Curio, ubi perterritis omnibus neque cohortationes suas neque preces audiri intellegit, unam ut in miseris rebus spem reliquam salutis esse arbitratus, proximos colles capere universos atque eo signa inferri iubet. Hos quoque praeoccupat missus a Saburra equitatus. Tum vero ad summam desperationem nostri perveniunt et partim fugientes ab equitatu interficiuntur, partim integri procumbunt. Hortatur Curionem Cn. Domitius, praefectus equitum, cum paucis equitibus circumsistens, ut fuga salutem petat atque in castra contendat, et se ab eo non discessurum pollicetur. At Curio numquam se amisso exercitu, quem a Caesare fidei commissum acceperit, in eius conspectum reversurum confirmat atque ita proelians interficitur. Equites ex proelio perpauci se recipiunt; sed ei, quos ad novissimum agmen equorum reficiendorum causa substitisse demon-

men, and, betaking themselves to their own ranks
again, began to surround them and to cut them off
from the main body. Thus it seemed unsafe either
to keep their ground and maintain their ranks or to
charge and risk the chance of conflict. As the king
sent up reinforcements the forces of the enemy were
constantly increasing, while fatigue kept diminishing
the strength of our men, and those who had received
wounds could neither quit the line nor be carried to
a safe place because the whole force was surrounded
and closed in by the enemy's horse. These men, despairing of their safety, after the manner of men in
the extreme crisis of life, were either bewailing their
own death or commending their parents to such as
fortune might be able to rescue from the peril. The
whole place was full of terror and lamentation.

When all were panic-stricken and Curio under- 42
stood that neither his exhortations nor his entreaties
were listened to, considering that in such pitiable
plight only one hope of safety remained, he ordered
them in a body to occupy the nearest hills and the
colours to be transferred thither. These, too, were outstripped by the cavalry sent by Saburra. Then indeed
our men touch the extremity of despair, and some are
slain as they fly from the cavalry, others fall to the
ground unwounded. Gn. Domitius, prefect of the
horse, surrounding Curio with a few horsemen, begs
him to seek safety in flight and hurry to the camp,
promising not to leave him. But Curio declares
that he will never present himself again before the
eyes of Caesar after losing the army that he has
received from him on trust, and so dies fighting.
Very few horsemen come safe out of the battle, but
those who, as was explained, halted in the extreme
rear for the purpose of refreshing their horses,

stratum est, fuga totius exercitus procul animadversa sese incolumes in castra conferunt. Milites ad
unum omnes interficiuntur.

43   His rebus cognitis Marcius Rufus quaestor in castris relictus a Curione cohortatur suos, ne animo deficiant. Illi orant atque obsecrant, ut in Siciliam
navibus reportentur. Pollicetur magistrisque imperat
navium, ut primo vespere omnes scaphas ad litus
appulsas habeant. Sed tantus fuit omnium terror,
ut alii adesse copias Iubae dicerent, alii cum legionibus instare Varum iamque se pulverem venientium
cernere, quarum rerum nihil omnino acciderat, alii
classem hostium celeriter advolaturam suspicarentur.
Itaque perterritis omnibus sibi quisque consulebat.
Qui in classe erant, proficisci properabant. Horum
fuga navium onerariarum magistros incitabat; pauci
lenunculi ad officium imperiumque conveniebant.
Sed tanta erat completis litoribus contentio, qui po-
tissimum ex magno numero conscenderent, ut multitudine atque onere nonnulli deprimerentur, reliqui
hoc timore propius adire tardarentur.

44   Quibus rebus accidit, ut pauci milites patresque
familiae, qui aut gratia aut misericordia valerent aut
naves adnare possent, recepti in Siciliam incolumes
pervenirent. Reliquae copiae missis ad Varum noctu
legatorum numero centurionibus sese ei dediderunt.
Quarum cohortium milites postero die ante oppidum
Iuba conspicatus suam esse praedicans praedam magnam partem eorum interfici iussit, paucos electos in

observing from a distance the flight of the whole army, retreat to the camp unhurt. The foot-soldiers are slain to a man.

On learning of these events Marcius Rufus, the 43 quaestor, who had been left in the camp by Curio, exhorts his men not to lose heart. They beg and beseech him to transport them back by sea to Sicily. Promising to do so, he bids the captains of the ships have all their boats drawn up on shore by the early evening. But so great was the general terror that some declared that the forces of Juba were close at hand, others that Varus was upon them with his legions and that already they saw the dust of their approach, though in reality nothing of the kind had happened; others suspected that the enemy's fleet would quickly hurry up to the attack. And so, amid the universal panic, each took counsel for himself. Those who were in the fleet hastened to depart. Their flight instigated the captains of the merchant-ships; only a few boats gathered at the call of duty and the word of command. But on the closely packed shores so great was the struggle to be the first out of the multitude to embark that some of the boats were sunk by the weight of the crowd, and the rest in fear of this hesitated to approach nearer.

Thus it fell out that only a few soldiers and 44 fathers of families, who prevailed either by influence or by exciting compassion, or who could swim to the ships, were received on board and reached Sicily in safety. The rest of the forces sent centurions by night to Varus in the capacity of ambassadors and surrendered themselves to him. And Juba, seeing the men of these cohorts next day in front of the town, declaring that they were his booty, ordered a great part of them to be slain and sent back

regnum remisit, cum Varus suam fidem ab eo laedi
quereretur neque resistere auderet. Ipse equo in
oppidum vectus prosequentibus compluribus senatoribus, quo in numero erat Ser. Sulpicius et Licinius
Damasippus paucis, quae fieri vellet, Uticae constituit
atque imperavit diebusque post paucis se in regnum
cum omnibus copiis recepit.

a few picked men to his kingdom, Varus the while complaining that his own honour was being injured by Juba, but not venturing to resist. Juba, himself riding into the town with an escort of several senators, among them Ser. Sulpicius and Licinius Damasippus, briefly arranged and ordered what he wanted to be done at Utica, and a few days afterwards withdrew with all his forces to his own kingdom.

BOOK III

LIBER III

1　Dictatore habente comitia Caesare consules crean-
tur Iulius Caesar et P. Servilius: is enim erat annus,
quo per leges ei consulem fieri liceret.　His rebus
confectis, cum fides tota Italia esset angustior neque
creditae pecuniae solverentur, constituit, ut arbitri
darentur; per eos fierent aestimationes possessionum
et rerum, quanti quaeque earum ante bellum fuisset,
atque hae creditoribus traderentur.　Hoc et ad timorem novarum tabularum tollendum minuendumve,
qui fere bella et civiles dissensiones sequi consuevit,
et ad debitorum tuendam existimationem esse aptis-
simum existimavit.　Itemque praetoribus tribunisque
plebis rogationes ad populum ferentibus nonnullos
ambitus Pompeia lege damnatos illis temporibus,
quibus in urbe praesidia legionum Pompeius habuerat, quae iudicia iliis audientibus iudicibus, aliis sententiam ferentibus singulis diebus erant perfecta, in
integrum restituit, qui se illi initio civilis belli
obtulerant, si sua opera in bello uti vellet, proinde
aestimans, ac si usus esset, quoniam sui fecissent

BOOK III

CAESAR as dictator presided over the elections, and
Julius Caesar and P. Servilius were created consuls,
this being the year in which the laws permitted
Caesar to hold the consulship. On the conclusion of
these proceedings, as credit throughout Italy was
somewhat restricted and loans were not being re-
paid, he decided that arbitrators should be appointed
to estimate the value of real and movable property
as it had been before the war, and that the creditors
should be paid on that basis. He considered that this
was the most suitable method at once of removing or
diminishing the fear of that general repudiation of
debts which is apt to follow war and civil strife, and
of maintaining the good faith of the debtors. Moreover, on motions brought before the people by the
praetors and tribunes, he restored to their former
rights persons who, in those critical times when Pompeius had kept in Rome a detachment of his troops
as a bodyguard, had been convicted of bribery under
the Pompeian law, and whose trials had been carried
through, each in a single day, with one set of judges
hearing the evidence and another voting on the
issue. As these persons had offered themselves to
him at the beginning of the civil war in case he
should wish to use their services in the war, he
accounted them as having been actually in his service, since they had placed themselves at his disposal.

potestatem. Statuerat enim prius hos iudicio populi debere restitui, quam suo beneficio videri receptos, ne aut ingratus in referenda gratia aut arrogans in praeripiendo populi beneficio videretur.

2   His rebus et feriis Latinis comitiisque omnibus perficiendis XI dies tribuit dictaturaque se abdicat et ab urbe proficiscitur Brundisiumque pervenit. Eo legiones XII, equitatum omnem venire iusserat. Sed tantum navium repperit, ut anguste XV milia legionariorum militum, DC equites transportari possent. Hoc unum Caesari ad celeritatem conficiendi belli defuit. Atque hae ipsae copiae hoc infrequentiores imponuntur, quod multi Gallicis tot bellis defecerant, longumque iter ex Hispania magnum numerum deminuerat, et gravis autumnus in Apulia circumque Brundisium ex saluberrimis Galliae et Hispaniae regionibus omnem exercitum valetudine temptaverat.

3   Pompeius annuum spatium ad comparandas copias nactus, quod vacuum a bello atque ab hoste otiosum fuerat, magnam ex Asia Cycladibusque insulis, Corcyra, Athenis, Ponto, Bithynia, Syria, Cilicia, Phoenice, Aegypto classem coëgerat, magnam omnibus locis aedificandam curaverat; magnam imperatam Asiae, Syriae regibusque omnibus et dynastis et tetrarchis et liberis Achaiae populis pecuniam exegerat, magnam societates earum provinciarum, quas ipse obtinebat, sibi numerare coëgerat.

For he had determined that they ought to be restored by a decision of the popular assembly rather than be supposed to be reinstated by his own act of kindness, his object being that he might not appear either ungrateful in the matter of returning a benefit, or too presumptuous in robbing the popular assembly of its right to confer a favour.

He allowed eleven days for carrying out these 2 measures and for holding the Latin festival and all the elections. He then resigned the dictatorship, quitted the city, and went to Brundisium. He had ordered twelve legions and all the cavalry to come there. But he found only enough ships to allow of his transporting in the crowded space fifteen thousand legionary soldiers and five hundred horse. This alone hindered Caesar's speedy conclusion of the war. And even these forces were embarked below their full strength, for many had dropped out in all the Gallic wars, and the long march from Spain had taken off a large number, and the unwholesome autumn in Apulia and round Brundisium, after the extremely healthy districts of Gaul and Spain, had affected the whole army with weakness.

Pompeius, availing himself for the purpose of col- 3 lecting forces of a whole year which had been free from war and without disturbance from an enemy, had gathered a large fleet from Asia and the Cyclades islands, from Corcyra, Athens, Pontus, Bithynia, Syria, Cilicia, Phoenice, Egypt; had contracted for the building of a large fleet wherever possible; had requisitioned a large sum of money from Asia, Syria, and all the kings, potentates, and tetrarchs, and from the free communities of Achaia; and had compelled the tax-farming associations of the provinces of which he was himself in control to pay over the large sums.

4   Legiones effecerat civium Romanorum VIIII:
v ex Italia, quas traduxerat; unam ex Cilicia vete-
ranam, quam factam ex duabus gemellam appellabat;
unam ex Creta et Macedonia ex veteranis militibus,
qui dimissi a superioribus imperatoribus in his provinciis consederant; duas ex Asia, quas Lentulus
consul conscribendas curaverat. Praeterea magnum
numerum ex Thessalia, Boeotia, Achaia Epiroque
supplementi nomine in legiones distribuerat: his
Antonianos milites admiscuerat. Praeter has exspectabat cum Scipione ex Syria legiones II. Sagittarios Creta, Lacedaemone, ex Ponto atque Syria
reliquisque civitatibus III milia numero habebat,
funditorum cohortes sescenarias II, equitum VII
milia. Ex quibus DC Gallos Deiotarus adduxerat,
D Ariobarzanes ex Cappadocia; ad eundem numerum
Cotys ex Thracia dederat et Sadalam filium miserat;
ex Macedonia CC erant, quibus Rhascypolis praeerat,
excellenti virtute; D ex Gabinianis Alexandria, Gallos
Germanosque, quos ibi A. Gabinius praesidii causa
apud regem Ptolomaeum reliquerat, Pompeius filius
cum classe adduxerat; DCCC ex servis suis pasto-
rumque suorum numero coëgerat; CCC Tarcondarius
Castor et Domnilaus ex Gallograecia dederant (horum
alter una venerat, alter filium miserat); CC ex Syria
a Commageno Antiocho, cui magna Pompeius praemia
tribuit, missi erant, in his plerique hippotoxotae.
200

He had made up nine legions of Roman citizens: 4
five from Italy, which he had conveyed across the sea;
one of veterans from Cilicia, which, being formed out
of two legions, he styled the Twin Legion; one from
Crete and Macedonia out of veteran troops which,
when disbanded by their former commanders, had
settled in those provinces; two from Asia, for the
levying of which the consul Lentulus had arranged.
Besides, he had distributed among the legions by way
of supplement a large number of men from Thessaly,
Boeotia, Achaia, and Epirus. With these he had
mixed men who had served under Antonius. Besides
these he was expecting two legions with Scipio from
Syria. He had archers from Crete and Lacedaemon,
from Pontus and Syria and the older states, to the
number of three thousand; also two cohorts, six
hundred strong, of slingers, and seven thousand
horsemen. Of these Deiotarus had brought six
hundred Gauls, and Ariobarzanes five hundred from
Cappadocia; Cotys had provided the same number
from Thrace and had sent his son Sadala; from
Macedonia there were two hundred under the
command of Rhascypolis, a man of marked valour.
The young Pompeius had brought with his fleet five
hundred of the Gabinian troops from Alexandria,
Gauls and Germans, whom A. Gabinius had left
there with King Ptolomaeus on garrison duty. He
had collected eight hundred from his own slaves and
from his list of herdsmen. Tarcondarius Castor and
Domnilaus had provided three hundred from Gallograecia; of these the one had come with his men,
the other had sent his son. From Syria two hundred
had been sent by Antiochus of Commagene, on whom
Pompeius bestowed large rewards, and among them
many mounted archers. To these Pompeius had added

CAESAR

Huc Dardanos, Bessos partim mercenarios, partim imperio aut gratia comparatos, item Macedones, Thessalos ac reliquarum gentium et civitatum adiecerat atque eum, quem supra demonstravimus, numerum expleverat.

5 Frumenti vim maximam ex Thessalia, Asia, Aegypto, Creta, Cyrenis reliquisque regionibus comparaverat. Hiemare Dyrrachii, Apolloniae omnibusque oppidis maritimis constituerat, ut mare transire Caesarem prohiberet, eiusque rei causa omni ora maritima classem disposuerat. Praeerat Aegyptiis navibus Pompeius filius, Asiaticis D. Laelius et C. Triarius, Syriacis C. Cassius, Rhodiis C. Marcellus cum C. Coponio, Liburnicae atque Achaicae classi Scribonius Libo et M. Octavius. Toti tamen officio maritimo M. Bibulus praepositus cuncta administrabat; ad hunc summa imperii respiciebat.

6 Caesar, ut Brundisium venit, contionatus apud milites, quoniam prope ad finem laborum ac periculorum esset perventum, aequo animo mancipia atque impedimenta in Italia relinquerent, ipsi expediti naves conscenderent, quo maior numerus militum posset imponi, omniaque ex victoria et ex sua liberalitate sperarent, conclamantibus omnibus, imperaret, quod vellet, quodcumque imperavisset, se aequo animo esse facturos, II. Non. Ian. naves solvit. Impositae, ut supra demonstratum est, legiones VII. Postridie terram attigit. Inter Cerauniorum[1] saxa et alia loca periculosa quietam nactus stationem et portus omnes timens, quos teneri ab adversariis arbitrabatur, ad eum locum, qui appella-

[1] *MSS.* Germiniorum, *and below* quod . . . arbitrabantur. *The text is extremely doubtful.*

Dardani and Bessi, partly mercenaries, partly secured by his authority or influence, also Macedonians, Thessalians, and men of other nations and states, and had thus filled up the number stated above.

He had collected a very large quantity of corn 5 from Thessaly, Asia, Egypt, Crete, Cyrene, and other districts. He had made up his mind to winter at Dyrrachium, Apollonia, and all the coast towns, so as to prevent Caesar from crossing the sea, and for that reason had distributed his fleet all along the sea-coast. The young Pompeius was in command of the Egyptian ships, D. Laelius and G. Triarius of the Asiatic, C. Cassius of the Syrian, G. Marcellus, with G. Coponius, of the Rhodian, Scribonius Libo and M. Octavius of the Liburnian and Achaean fleet. M. Bibulus, however, was put in charge of the whole maritime operations and controlled everything; in him was centered the supreme command.

Caesar, as soon as he came to Brundisium, after 6 haranguing the troops and bidding them, as they had almost reached the end of their toils and dangers, to leave with a quiet mind their slaves and baggage in Italy, and themselves embark, lightly equipped so that a larger number of men could be put on board, and to hope for everything from victory and his generosity, on their raising a unanimous shout that he should give such commands as he wished, and that whatever he commanded they would do with a quiet mind, on January 4 weighed anchor. Seven legions, as explained above, were on board. On the next day he touched land. Having found a quiet harbourage among the Ceraunian rocks and other dangerous places, and fearing all the ports, which he believed to be in the occupation of the enemy, he

batur Palaeste, omnibus navibus ad unam incolumibus milites exposuit.

7 Erat Orici Lucretius Vespillo et Minucius Rufus cum Asiaticis navibus XVIII, quibus iussu D. Laelii praeerant, M. Bibulus cum navibus CX Corcyrae. Sed neque illi sibi confisi ex portu prodire sunt ausi, cum Caesar omnino XII naves longas praesidio duxisset, in quibus erant constratae IIII, neque Bibulus impeditis navibus dispersisque remigibus satis mature occurrit, quod prius ad continentem visus est Caesar, quam de eius adventu fama omnino in eas regiones perferretur.

8 Expositis militibus naves eadem nocte Brundisium a Caesare remittuntur, ut reliquae legiones equitatusque transportari possent. Huic officio praepositus erat Fufius Calenus legatus, qui celeritatem in transportandis legionibus adhiberet. Sed serius a terra provectae naves neque usae nocturna aura in redeundo offenderunt. Bibulus enim Corcyrae certior factus de adventu Caesaris, sperans alicui se parti onustarum navium occurrere posse, inanibus occurrit et nactus circiter XXX in eas indiligentiae suae ac doloris iracundiam erupit omnesque incendit eodemque igne nautas dominosque navium interfecit, magnitudine poenae reliquos terreri sperans. Hoc confecto negotio a Sasonis ad Curici portum stationes litoraque omnia longe lateque classibus occupavit custodiisque diligentius dispositis ipse gravissima hieme in navibus excubans neque ullum laborem

disembarked his troops at a place called Palaeste without damage to a single one of his ships.

Lucretius Vespillo and Minucius Rufus were at 7 Oricum with eighteen Asiatic ships, of which they had been put in command by D. Laelius; and M. Bibulus was at Corcyra with a hundred and ten ships. But the former had not sufficient confidence in themselves to venture out of port, since Caesar had conveyed thither twelve warships in all to protect the coast, among them four decked ships; and Bibulus, having his ships disorganized and his rowers dispersed, did not come up in time, because Caesar was seen off the mainland before the report of his approach could in any way reach those districts.

The soldiers having been disembarked, the ships are 8 sent back by Caesar to Brundisium the same night, so that the rest of the legions and the cavalry could be transported. Fufius Calenus, the legate, was set over this task, with orders to employ all speed in transporting the legions. But the ships, having started too late from the land and missed the night breeze, met with difficulties on their return. For Bibulus, having been informed at Corcyra of Caesar's approach, hoping to be able to fall in with some portion of the loaded ships, fell in with them empty; and coming across about thirty of them, he vented on them the rage caused by vexation at his own slackness, and burnt them all, slaying in the same fire crews and captains, hoping for the rest to be deterred by the greatness of the punishment. This business accomplished, he occupied with his fleets all the roadsteads and shores far and wide from the port of Saso to that of Curicum, and carefully disposing his outposts, himself lying on board, though the weather was very severe, not shirking any difficulty or duty,

aut munus despiciens, neque subsidium exspectans si in Caesaris complexum venire posset[1] . . .

9 Discessu Liburnarum ex Illyrico M. Octavius cum eis, quas habebat, navibus Salonas pervenit. Ibi concitatis Dalmatis reliquisque barbaris Issam a Caesaris amicitia avertit; conventum Salonis cum neque pollicitationibus neque denuntiatione periculi permovere posset, oppidum oppugnare instituit. Est autem oppidum et loci natura et colle munitum. Sed celeriter cives Romani ligneis effectis turribus his sese munierunt et, cum essent infirmi ad resistendum propter paucitatem hominum crebris confecti vulneribus, ad extremum auxilium descenderunt servosque omnes puberes liberaverunt et praesectis omnium mulierum crinibus tormenta effecerunt. Quorum cognita sententia Octavius quinis castris oppidum circumdedit atque uno tempore obsidione et oppugnationibus eos premere coepit. Illi omnia perpeti parati maxime a re frumentaria laborabant. Cui rei missis ad Caesarem legatis auxilium ab eo petebant; reliqua, ut poterant, incommoda per se sustinebant. Et longo interposito spatio cum diuturnitas oppugnationis neglegentiores Octavianos effecisset, nacti occasionem meridiani temporis discessu eorum pueris mulieribusque in muro dispositis, ne quid cotidianae consuetudinis desideraretur, ipsi manu facta cum eis, quos nuper[2] liberaverant, in proxima Octavii castra irruperunt. His expugnatis

---

[1] *The text is too imperfect to admit of certain restoration.*
[2] *MSS.* nuper maximi (*or* maxime).

nor waiting for reinforcement if only he could come
to the grapple with Caesar . . .

On the departure of the Liburnian galleys from 9
Illyricum, M. Octavius comes to Salonae with the
ships under his command. There he diverts Issa from
its friendship with Caesar, stirring up the Dalmatians
and the rest of the Barbarians. Failing to influence
the Roman citizen body at Salonae, either by promises
or by threatenings of peril, he set himself to besiege
the town. Now, the town was strongly protected by
the nature of its site and by a hill. But the Roman
citizens, rapidly constructing wooden towers, protected themselves with them, and, being weak in
resistance owing to their small numbers, worn out by
constant wounds, betook themselves to the last re-
source of despair and armed all their grown-up slaves,
and cut off the hair of all their women to make
catapult ropes. Octavius, having ascertained their
sentiments, surrounded the town with five camps and
began to press the inhabitants at once by blockade
and by siege operations. Prepared to endure everything, they suffered most in the matter of the corn
supply. To remedy this they sent envoys to Caesar
and begged his aid. The rest of their troubles they
endured by themselves as well as they could. And
after a long interval, when the protracted siege had
made the Octavians rather careless, taking advantage of the opportunity afforded by the hour
of noon when the enemy had withdrawn, they
placed their boys and women on the walls that no
particular of their daily routine might be missed
by the besiegers, and forming themselves into a
band, together with those whom they had just
recently liberated, they burst into the nearest camp
of Octavius. This being taken by storm, with a

eodem impetu altera sunt adorti, inde tertia et
quarta et deinceps reliqua omnibusque eos castris
expulerunt et magno numero interfecto reliquos atque
ipsum Octavium in naves confugere coëgerunt. Hic
fuit oppugnationis exitus. Iamque hiems appropinquabat, et tantis detrimentis acceptis Octavius de-
sperata oppugnatione oppidi Dyrrachium sese ad
Pompeium recepit.

10   Demonstravimus L. Vibullium Rufum, Pompei praefectum, bis in potestatem pervenisse Caesaris atque
ab eo esse dimissum, semel ad Corfinium, iterum in
Hispania. Hunc pro suis beneficiis Caesar idoneum
iudicaverat, quem cum mandatis ad Cn. Pompeium
mitteret, eundemque apud Cn. Pompeium auctoritatem habere intellegebat. Erat autem haec summa
mandatorum: debere utrumque pertinaciae finem
facere et ab armis discedere neque amplius fortunam
periclitari. Satis esse magna utrimque incommoda
accepta, quae pro disciplina et praeceptis habere
possent, ut reliquos casus timerent: illum Italia ex-
pulsum amissa Sicilia et Sardinia duabusque Hispaniis et cohortibus in Italia atque Hispania civium
Romanorum centum atque XXX; se morte Curionis
et detrimento Africani exercitus tanto militumque
deditione ad Curictam. Proinde sibi ac rei publicae
parcerent, cum, quantum in bello fortuna posset, iam
ipsi incommodis suis satis essent documento. Hoc
unum esse tempus de pace agendi, dum sibi uterque
confideret et pares ambo viderentur; si vero alteri
paulum modo tribuisset fortuna, non esse usurum con-

similar onset they attacked the second, then the third and fourth, and the remaining one in its turn, and drove the men out of all the camps, and having slain a great number, forced the rest and Octavius himself to fly to the ships. Such was the end of the siege. And now winter was approaching, and Octavius, despairing of the siege of the town after receiving such heavy losses, retired to Dyrrachium to Pompeius.

We have shown that L. Vibullius Rufus, Pompeius' 10 chief engineer, twice fell into the hands of Caesar and was released by him, once at Corfinium and a second time in Spain. In consideration of the benefits that he had conferred on him Caesar had decided that Vibullius was a suitable person to send with instructions to Gn. Pompeius, and he also understood that he had influence with Gn. Pompeius. Now this was the main purport of his instructions—that each of them ought to put an end to his obstinacy, lay down his arms, and no longer tempt fortune. Sufficiently serious losses had been incurred on both sides, which might serve them as a lesson and warn them to fear further mischances: Pompeius had been driven from Italy after the loss of Sicily and Sardinia and the two Spains, and one hundred and thirty cohorts of Roman citizens in Italy and Spain; he himself had suffered by the death of Curio and the disaster to the African army, and the surrender of Antonius and his troops at Curicta. So let them spare themselves and the republic, since by their own losses they were already a sufficient example to themselves of what fortune could do in war. This was the one time for treating of peace, when each had confidence in himself and both seemed on an equality. But if fortune should show but a little partiality to one of the two,

dicionibus pacis eum, qui superior videretur, neque
fore aequa parte contentum, qui se omnia habiturum
confideret. Condiciones pacis, quoniam antea convenire non potuissent, Romae ab senatu et a populo
peti debere. Interea et rei publicae et ipsis placere
oportere, si uterque in contione statim iuravisset se
triduo proximo exercitum dimissurum. Depositis armis
auxiliisque, quibus nunc confiderent, necessario
populi senatusque iudicio fore utrumque contentum.
Haec quo facilius Pompeio probari possent, omnes
suas terrestres ubique copias dimissurum[1] . . .

11   Vibullius expositus Corcyrae[2] non minus necessarium
esse existimavit de repentino adventu Caesaris Pompeium fieri certiorem, uti ad id consilium capere posset, antequam de mandatis agi inciperetur, atque ideo
continuato nocte ac die itinere atque omnibus oppidis[3]
mutatis ad celeritatem iumentis ad Pompeium contendit, ut adesse Caesarem nuntiaret. Pompeius erat
eo tempore in Candavia iterque ex Macedonia in
hiberna Apolloniam Dyrrachiumque habebat. Sed
re nova perturbatus maioribus itineribus Apolloniam
petere coepit, ne Caesar orae maritimae civitates
occuparet. At ille expositis militibus eodem die
Oricum proficiscitur. Quo cum venisset, L. Torquatus, qui iussu Pompei oppido praeerat praesidiumque
ibi Parthinorum habebat, conatus portis clausis oppidum defendere, cum Graecos murum ascendere atque
arma capere iuberet, illi autem se contra imperium

---

[1] *The text of this last sentence is imperfect.*
[2] expositus Corcyrae *Madvig:* his expositis Corcyrae
MSS.: his expositis (*these instructions having been given him*)
Nipperdey, which may be right.
[3] oppidis *Lipsius:* copiis *MSS.:* locis *Menge.*

the one who should seem superior would not adopt terms of peace, nor would he who was sure that he would have everything be contented with an equal division. Conditions of peace should now be sought at Rome from the senate and the people, since it had not been possible to agree on them before. Meanwhile it ought to satisfy the republic and themselves if each should at once swear in a public assembly that he would disband his army within the next three days. If they laid aside their arms and gave up the reinforcements on which they now relied, each would necessarily be contented with the judgment of the people and the senate. That these proposals might be more easily approved by Pompeius, he said that he would disband all his land forces.

Vibullius, having disembarked at Corcyra, thought 11 it no less necessary that Pompeius should be informed of the sudden approach of Caesar, that he might be able to take counsel thereon before they should begin to discuss the instructions, and so, continuing his journey night and day and changing horses at every town to gain speed, he hurried to Pompeius to announce Caesar's approach. Pompeius was at that time in Candavia, and was on his way from Macedonia to Apollonia and Dyrrachium to winter quarters. But, disturbed by the fresh crisis, he began to make for Apollonia by longer marches, lest Caesar should occupy the towns on the sea-coast. But Caesar, after landing his troops, set out for Oricum on the same day. When he had come there, L. Torquatus, who was in control of the town by Pompeius' order and had in it a garrison of Parthini, endeavoured to defend the town by closing the gates; but on his bidding the Greeks to mount the wall and take up arms, and on their refusing to fight against the

populi Romani pugnaturos esse negarent, oppidani
autem etiam sua sponte Caesarem recipere conaren
tur, desperatis omnibus auxiliis portas aperuit et s
atque oppidum Caesari dedit incolumisque ab e
conservatus est.

12   Recepto Caesar Orico nulla interposita mor
Apolloniam proficiscitur.   Cuius adventu audit
L. Staberius, qui ibi praeerat, aquam comportare i
arcem atque eam munire obsidesque ab Apollonia
tibus exigere coepit.   Illi vero daturos se negare
neque portas consuli praeclusuros, neque sibi iudiciur
sumpturos contra atque omnis Italia populusqu
Romanus iudicavisset.   Quorum cognita voluntat
clam profugit Apollonia Staberius.   Illi ad Caesarer
legatos mittunt oppidoque recipiunt.   Hos sequuntu
Bullidenses, Amantini et reliquae finitimae civitate
totaque Epiros et legatis ad Caesarem missis, qua
imperaret, facturos pollicentur.

13   At Pompeius cognitis his rebus, quae erant Oric
atque Apolloniae gestae, Dyrrachio timens diurni
eo nocturnisque itineribus contendit.   Simul Caesa
appropinquare dicebatur, tantusque terror incid
eius exercitui, quod properans noctem diei coniunxe
rat neque iter intermiserat, ut paene omnes ex Epir
finitimisque regionibus signa relinquerent, complure
arma proicerent ac fugae simile iter videretur.   Se
cum prope Dyrrachium Pompeius constitisset cas
traque metari iussisset, perterrito etiam tum exercit
princeps Labienus procedit iuratque se eum no

212

imperial power of the Roman people, while the townsmen also of their own accord attempted to admit Caesar, despairing of all aid he opened the gates and surrendered himself and the town to Caesar and was kept by him safe and unharmed.

On the recovery of Oricum Caesar with no interval 12 of delay set out for Apollonia. Hearing of his approach, L. Staberius, who was in command there, began to collect a supply of water for the citadel, and to fortify it and to exact hostages from the inhabitants. But they refused to give them or to shut their gates against the consul, or to decide anything for themselves that should be contrary to the decision of the whole of Italy and of the Roman people. Having ascertained their sentiments, Staberius secretly fled from Apollonia. The inhabitants sent envoys to Caesar and admitted him into the town. Their lead was followed by the Byllidenses, the Amantini, and the rest of the neighbouring communities and the whole of Epiros, and sending envoys to Caesar they promised to do his bidding.

But Pompeius, when he learnt of what had 13 happened at Oricum and Apollonia, fearing for Dyrrachium, hurried there, marching night and day. At the same time Caesar was said to be approaching, and so great a terror fell on the army of Pompeius, because their leader, joining night to day in his hurry, had never paused in his march, that nearly all the men from Epiros and the neighbouring districts abandoned the colours, many flung away their arms, and the march resembled a flight. But when Pompeius had halted near Dyrrachium and had ordered his camp to be measured out, his army being still in a state of panic, Labienus is the first to come forward and swear that he will not desert him and

deserturum eundemque casum subiturum, quemcumque ei fortuna tribuisset. Hoc idem reliqui iurant legati; tribuni militum centurionesque sequuntur, atque idem omnis exercitus iurat. Caesar praeoccupato itinere ad Dyrrachium finem properandi facit castraque ad flumen Apsum ponit in finibus Apolloniatium, ut bene meritae civitates tutae essent praesidio,[1] ibique reliquarum ex Italia legionum adventum exspectare et sub pellibus hiemare constituit. Hoc idem Pompeius fecit et trans flumen Apsum positis castris eo copias omnes auxiliaque conduxit.

14   Calenus legionibus equitibusque Brundisii in naves impositis, ut erat praeceptum a Caesare, quantum navium facultatem habebat, naves solvit paulumque a portu progressus litteras a Caesare accipit, quibus est certior factus portus litoraque omnia classibus adversariorum teneri. Quo cognito se in portum recipit navesque omnes revocat. Una ex his, quae perseveravit neque imperio Caleni obtemperavit, quod erat sine militibus privatoque consilio administrabatur, delata Oricum atque a Bibulo expugnata est; qui de servis liberisque omnibus ad impuberes supplicium sumit et ad unum interficit. Ita exiguo tempore magnoque casu totius exercitus salus constitit.

15   Bibulus, ut supra demonstratum est, erat cum classe ad Oricum et, sicuti mari portibusque Caesarem prohibebat, ita ipse omni terra earum regionum prohibebatur; praesidiis enim dispositis omnia litora

[1] ut castellis vigiliisque bene meritae civitates tutae essent praesidio *MSS.: either* castellis vigiliisque *or* praesidio *must be omitted.*

that he will undergo any hazard, no matter what, that fortune may bestow on his leader. The rest of the legates swear the same oath; they are followed by the tribunes and centurions, and the whole army takes the same pledge. Caesar, finding himself forestalled in his march to Dyrrachium, stays his rapid advance and pitches his camp by the River Apsus, in the territory of the Apolloniates, that the communities which had deserved well of him might be protected by a garrison, and decides to wait there for the arrival of the rest of his legions from Italy and to winter in tents. Pompeius did the same, and, pitching his camp the other side of the River Apsus, conveyed thither all his forces and auxiliaries.

Calenus, having put on board his legions and 14 cavalry at Brundisium as Caesar had ordered him, as far as his supply of ships allowed, weighed anchor, and when he had gone a little way from the port he received a dispatch from Caesar which informed him that all the harbours and shores were occupied by the fleets of the enemy. Learning this, he returns to the port and recalls all his ships. One of these, which kept on its way and did not attend to the command of Calenus, because it was without soldiers and was under private management, was carried to Oricum and attacked and taken by Bibulus, who inflicted punishment on slaves and freemen, even down to beardless boys, and killed them all without exception. Thus on a brief conjuncture and supreme moment of crisis hung the safety of the whole army.

Bibulus, as shown above, was with his fleet at 15 Oricum, and just as he was excluding Caesar from the sea and the harbour, so he was himself being excluded from all landing in that district, for all

a Caesare tenebantur, neque lignandi atque aquandi neque naves ad terram religandi potestas fiebat. Erat res in magna difficultate, summisque angustiis rerum necessariarum premebantur, adeo ut cogerentur sicuti reliquum commeatum ita ligna atque aquam Corcyra navibus onerariis supportare; atque etiam uno tempore accidit, ut difficilioribus usi tempestatibus ex pellibus, quibus erant tectae naves, nocturnum excipere rorem cogerentur; quas tamen difficultates patienter atque aequo animo ferebant neque sibi nudanda litora et relinquendos portus existimabant. Sed cum essent in quibus demonstravi angustiis, ac se Libo cum Bibulo coniunxisset, loquuntur ambo ex navibus cum M. Acilio et Statio Murco legatis; quorum alter oppidi muris, alter praesidiis terrestribus praeerat: velle se de maximis rebus cum Caesare loqui, si sibi eius rei facultas detur. Huc addunt pauca rei confirmandae causa, ut de compositione acturi viderentur. Interim postulant ut sint indutiae, atque ab eis impetrant. Magnum enim, quod afferebant, videbatur, et Caesarem id summe sciebant cupere, et profectum aliquid Vibullii mandatis existimabatur.

16 Caesar eo tempore cum legione una profectus ad recipiendas ulteriores civitates et rem frumentariam expediendam, qua angusta utebatur, erat ad Buthrotum, oppidum oppositum Corcyrae. Ibi certior ab Acilio

the shores were occupied by Caesar with garrisons placed at intervals, nor was any opportunity given him of procuring wood or water, or of mooring his ships ashore. The position was one of great difficulty, as they were oppressed by extreme scarcity of necessaries, to such an extent that they were obliged to bring up by merchant-ships from Corcyra supplies of wood and water as of other stores, and it even happened at the same time that, experiencing rather rough weather, they were compelled to catch the night's moisture in the skins with which the ships were covered. Yet these difficulties they bore with patience and equanimity and thought it their duty not to expose their shores nor abandon their harbours. But being in such straits as I have explained, and Libo having joined Bibulus, both commanders held a colloquy from their ships with the legates M. Acilius and Statius Murcus, one of whom was in command of the walls of the town, the other of the land garrisons, stating that if opportunity is offered them they are willing to confer with Caesar on matters of the highest importance. To this they add a few words by way of confirming their action, so that it might be evident that they were intending to treat about an arrangement. Meanwhile they demand a truce, and the others grant their request. For what they proposed seemed of importance, and they were aware that Caesar was particularly anxious for this, and something was thought to have been gained by the instructions of Vibullius.

Caesar, who had set out at that time with one 16 legion to recover the more distant communities and to expedite the food supply, which he was finding insufficient, was at Buthrotum, a town over against Corcyra. There informed by letter by Acilius and

et Murco per litteras factus de postulatis Libonis et
Bibuli legionem relinquit; ipse Oricum revertitur.
Eo cum venisset, evocantur illi ad colloquium. Prodit Libo atque excusat Bibulum, quod is iracundia
summa erat inimicitiasque habebat etiam privatas
cum Caesare ex aedilitate et praetura conceptas:
ob eam causam colloquium vitasse, ne res maximae
spei maximaeque utilitatis eius iracundia impedirentur. Suam summam[1] esse ac fuisse semper
voluntatem, ut componeretur atque ab armis discederetur, sed potestatem eius rei nullam habere,
propterea quod de consilii sententia summam belli
rerumque omnium Pompeio permiserint. Sed postulatis Caesaris cognitis missuros ad Pompeium, atque
illum reliqua per se acturum hortantibus ipsis.
Interea manerent indutiae, dum ab illo rediri posset,
neve alter alteri noceret. Huc addit pauca de causa
et de copiis auxiliisque suis.

17 Quibus rebus neque tum respondendum Caesar
existimavit, neque nunc, ut memoriae prodantur,
satis causae putamus. Postulabat Caesar, ut legatos
sibi ad Pompeium sine periculo mittere liceret, idque
ipsi fore reciperent aut acceptos per se ad eum perducerent. Quod ad indutias pertineret, sic belli
rationem esse divisam, ut illi classe naves auxiliaque
sua impedirent, ipse ut aqua terraque eos prohiberet.

---

[1] suam summam *Elberling:* Pompei summam *MSS.*

Murcus about the demands of Libo and Bibulus, he leaves his legion and himself returns to Oricum. On his arrival there they are invited to a conference. Libo comes out and makes excuses for Bibulus because he was of extremely passionate character and had also a private feud with Caesar contracted in his aedileship and praetorship. For this reason he said Bibulus had avoided a colloquy lest issues of the highest prospects and advantage should be hindered by his irascibility. He said that his own desire for a settlement and the laying down of arms was and always had been extreme, but that he had no influence in the matter, because by the advice of their council they had entrusted the entire control of war and everything else to Pompeius. But now that they had ascertained Caesar's demands they would send to Pompeius, and he would carry out the rest of the negotiations by himself with their encouragement. Meanwhile the truce should hold good till the messengers could return from Pompeius, and the one side should do no injury to the other. To this he adds a few words about the cause and about his own forces and auxiliaries.

Caesar did not consider at the time that any reply 17 was needed to these remarks, nor do we now think that there is any sufficient reason for recording them. Caesar's demand was that he should be allowed to send envoys to Pompeius under safe conduct, and that they should undertake that this should be done or should themselves receive the envoys and conduct them to him. As regards a truce, there was this distinction between them in their conduct of the war: they with their fleet were hindering his ships and reinforcements; he was preventing them from watering and from landing. If they desired any concession

Si hoc sibi remitti vellent, remitterent ipsi de
maritimis custodiis; si illud tenerent, se quoque id
retenturum. Nihilo minus tamen agi posse de compositione, ut haec non remitterentur, neque hanc
rem illi esse impedimento. Libo neque legatos
Caesaris recipere neque periculum praestare eorum
sed totam rem ad Pompeium reicere: unum instare
de indutiis vehementissimeque contendere. Quem
ubi Caesar intellexit praesentis periculi atque inopiae
vitandae causa omnem orationem instituisse neque
ullam spem aut condicionem pacis afferre, ad reliquam
cogitationem belli sese recepit.

18   Bibulus multos dies terra prohibitus et graviore
morbo ex frigore et labore implicitus, cum neque
curari posset neque susceptum officium deserere
vellet, vim morbi sustinere non potuit. Eo mortuo
ad neminem unum summa imperii redit, sed separatim
suam quisque classem ad arbitrium suum administrabat. Vibullius sedato tumultu, quem repentinus
adventus Caesaris concitaverat, ubi primum e re visum
est, adhibito Libone et L. Lucceio et Theophane
quibuscum communicare de maximis rebus Pompeius
consueverat, de mandatis Caesaris agere instituit.
Quem ingressum in sermonem Pompeius interpellavit
et loqui plura prohibuit. "Quid mihi," inquit, "aut
vita aut civitate opus est, quam beneficio Caesaris
habere videbor? cuius rei opinio tolli non poterit

in this respect, let them make some concessions themselves about their surveillance by sea; if they retained that, he would retain his position also. Nevertheless it was possible, he said, to treat of an arrangement without making any such concessions, nor did these considerations hinder that treatment. Libo neither receives Caesar's envoys nor agrees to grant them safe convoy, but refers the whole question to Pompeius; one point he urges, about the truce, and contends for it with the utmost eagerness. And when Caesar understood that his whole speech was framed with a view to the present danger and the avoidance of want, and that he offered no prospect or proposal of peace, he returned to the consideration of his further plan of campaign.

Bibulus, being prevented from landing for many 18 days and being attacked by a serious disease caused by cold and hard work, since he could not be successfully treated nor was willing to abandon the duty he had undertaken, failed to hold out against the severity of his illness. On his death the chief command fell to no one person, but each controlled his own fleet separately at his own discretion. After the tumult which had been aroused by the sudden approach of Caesar had quieted down, Vibullius, as soon as it seemed suitable, taking into his confidence Libo and L. Lucceius and Theophanes, whom Pompeius had been in the habit of consulting about his most important affairs, began to treat of Caesar's proposals. As soon as he had begun his discourse Pompeius interrupted him and prevented him from speaking further. "What," said he, "is the use of life or citizenship to me which I shall be supposed to hold by the bounty of Caesar? It will be impossible to remove this opinion when on the con-

cum in Italiam, ex qua profectus sum, reductus existimabor bello perfecto." Ab eis Caesar haec facta cognovit, qui sermoni interfuerunt; conatus tamen nihilo minus est aliis rationibus per colloquia de pace agere.

19 Inter bina castra Pompei atque Caesaris unum flumen tantum intererat Apsus, crebraque inter se colloquia milites habebant, neque ullum interim telum per pactiones loquentium traiciebatur. Mittit P. Vatinium legatum ad ripam ipsam fluminis, qui ea, quae maxime ad pacem pertinere viderentur, ageret et crebro magna voce pronuntiaret, liceretne civibus ad cives de pace legatos mittere, quod etiam fugitivis ab saltu Pyrenaeo praedonibusque licuisset, praesertim cum id agerent, ne cives cum civibus armis decertarent? Multa suppliciter locutus est, ut de sua atque omnium salute debebat, silentioque ab utrisque militibus auditus. Responsum est ab altera parte Aulum Varronem profiteri se altera die ad colloquium venturum atque una visurum, quemadmodum tuto legati venire et quae vellent exponere possent; certumque ei rei tempus constituitur. Quo cum esset postero die ventum, magna utrimque multitudo convenit, magnaque erat exspectatio eius rei, atque omnium animi intenti esse ad pacem videbantur. Qua ex frequentia Titus Labienus prodit, sed missa oratione[1] de pace, loqui atque altercari cum Vatinio incipit. Quorum mediam orationem interrumpunt subito undique tela immissa;

[1] I adopt, with hesitation, Terpstra's alteration of a corrupt passage.

clusion of the war I shall be thought to have been fetched back to Italy, from which I set out." Caesar learned of these doings from those who were present at the conversation. Nevertheless he endeavoured in other ways to treat of peace by means of conferences.

The River Apsus alone separated the two camps of 19 Pompeius and Caesar, and the men engaged in frequent conversations, nor meanwhile did a single missile cross the line, by a compact made between the speakers. Caesar sends his legate P. Vatinius to the bank of the river to urge points that seemed most conducive to peace and to exclaim frequently in a loud voice: "Should not citizens be permitted to send envoys in safety to their fellow-citizens about peace, a privilege granted even to fugitive slaves from the Pyrenean forests and to pirates, especially when their object is to prevent citizens from contending in arms against citizens?" Much he said in the suppliant tones that he was bound to use in the interests of his own and the general safety, and was heard in silence by both forces. A reply came from the other side that Aulus Varro professed his intention of coming to a conference the next day and considering with them how envoys could come safely and explain what they wanted, and a fixed time is arranged for this. And when they came on the next day, a great multitude came together from both sides, and there was great suspense about the result, and the minds of all seemed earnestly turned towards peace. From among this concourse Titus Labienus comes forward, who begins to talk and dispute with Vatinius, but says nothing about peace. A sudden shower of missiles from every quarter breaks off their discourse; protected by the arms of the soldiers, he avoided

quae ille obtectus armis militum vitavit; vulnerantur
tamen complures, in his Cornelius Balbus, M. Plotius, L. Tiburtius, centuriones militesque nonnulli.
Tum Labienus: "desinite ergo de compositione
loqui; nam nobis nisi Caesaris capite relato pax esse
nulla potest."

20   Eisdem temporibus M. Caelius Rufus praetor causa
debitorum suscepta initio magistratus tribunal suum
iuxta C. Treboni, praetoris urbani, sellam collocavit
et, si quis appellavisset de aestimatione et de solu-
tionibus, quae per arbitrum fierent, ut Caesar prae-
sens constituerat, fore auxilio pollicebatur.   Sed
fiebat aequitate decreti et humanitate Treboni, qui
his temporibus clementer et moderate ius dicendum
existimabat, ut reperiri non possent, a quibus
initium appellandi nasceretur.   Nam fortasse inopiam excusare et calamitatem aut propriam suam
aut temporum queri et difficultates auctionandi pro-
ponere etiam mediocris est animi; integras vero
tenere possessiones, qui se debere fateantur, cuius
animi aut cuius impudentiae est?   Itaque, hoc qui
postularet reperiebatur nemo.   Atque ipsis, ad quorum commodum pertinebat, durior inventus est
Caelius.   Et ab hoc profectus initio, ne frustra
ingressus turpem causam videretur, legem promul-
gravit, ut sexenni die sine usuris creditae pecuniae
solvantur.

21   Cum resisteret Servilius consul reliquique magistratus, et minus opinione sua efficeret, ad hominum

them, but many are wounded, among them Cornelius
Balbus, M. Plotius, L. Tiburtius, and some centurions
and soldiers. Then Labienus exclaimed: "Cease
then to talk about a settlement, for there can be
no peace for us till Caesar's head is brought in."

About the same time the praetor M. Caelius Rufus,   20
espousing the cause of the debtors, at the beginning
of his magistracy placed his tribunal close to the
chair of G. Trebonius, the city praetor, and promised
to assist anyone who should appeal about the valuation and the payments to be fixed by an arbitrator,
in accordance with Caesar's arrangements when
present in Rome.   But through the equitable
decrees and humanity of Trebonius, who was of
opinion that in this crisis law should be administered with clemency and moderation, it happened that none could be found to originate an
appeal.   For to make the excuse of poverty and to
complain either of one's own calamities or of the
calamitous times and to set forth the difficulties of
sale is possible for a man of merely ordinary spirit,
but for persons who admit their indebtedness to
cling to the whole of their possessions, what an
audacious, what a shameless spirit does that mark!
And thus no one was found to make this demand.
And so Caelius proved himself harder to deal with
than the very persons whose interests were concerned; and, lest he should seem to have taken up
a disgraceful cause to no purpose, his next step was
to promulgate a law that the money owed shall be
paid without accumulation of interest on that day six
years.

As the consul Servilius with the rest of the   21
magistrates opposed this, and Caelius effected less
than he expected, to kindle general enthusiasm he

excitanda studia sublata priore lege duas promul-
gavit: unam, qua mercedes habitationum annuas
conductoribus donavit, aliam tabularum novarum,
impetuque multitudinis in C. Trebonium facto et
nonnullis vulneratis eum de tribunali deturbavit.
De quibus rebus Servilius consul ad senatum ret-
tulit, senatusque Caelium ab re publica removendum
censuit. Hoc decreto eum consul senatu prohibuit
et contionari conantem de rostris deduxit. Ille
ignominia et dolore permotus palam se proficisci ad
Caesarem simulavit; clam nuntiis ad Milonem missis,
qui Clodio interfecto eo nomine erat damnatus, atque
eo in Italiam evocato, quod magnis muneribus datis
gladiatoriae familiae reliquias habebat,[1] sibi coniunxit atque eum in Thurinum ad sollicitandos pastores praemisit. Ipse cum Casilinum venisset, uno-
que tempore signa eius militaria atque arma Capuae
essent comprensa et familia Neapoli visa, quae pro-
ditionem oppidi appararet,[2] patefactis consiliis ex-
clusus Capua et periculum veritus, quod conventus
arma ceperat atque eum hostis loco habendum
existimabat, consilio destitit atque eo itinere sese
avertit.

22   Interim Milo dimissis circum municipia litteris,
se ea, quae faceret, iussu atque imperio facere
Pompei, quae mandata ad se per Vibullium delata
essent, quos ex aere alieno laborare arbitrabatur,

    [1] *There is considerable uncertainty about the text of this
passage.*
    [2] *The reading is uncertain. Most MSS. have* visaque prodi-
tione oppidi apparere.

cancelled his former law and promulgated two others, one whereby he made a free gift of a year's rent of houses to the hirers, another authorizing a repudiation of debts; and when the mob made a rush at G. Trebonius and some persons were wounded, Caelius drove him from his tribunal. The consul Servilius brought a motion before the senate dealing with these events, and the senate decided that Caelius should be removed from the service of the state. In accordance with this decree the consul excluded him from the senate, and on his attempting to make a speech in public removed him from the platform. Deeply moved by the smart of his disgrace, he made a public pretence of going to Caesar, but secretly sent messages to Milo, who after the murder of Clodius had been condemned on that charge, and summoning him into Italy—because Milo, having given public shows on a large scale, had with him the residue of a school of gladiators—associated him with himself and sent him on in front to the Thurine district to raise the farmers. When he had himself reached Casilinum, and when at one and the same time his military standards and arms were seized at Capua and the gladiators, who were preparing the betrayal of the town, were seen at Naples, finding himself shut out from Capua by the detection of his designs and fearing danger, because the Roman citizen body, considering that he should be regarded as a public enemy, had taken up arms, he abandoned his design and turned aside from his journey.

Meanwhile Milo, after sending dispatches round the 22 municipal towns to the effect that in what he was doing he was acting by the order and authority of Pompeius, on instructions conveyed to him through Vibullius, began to stir up those whom he supposed to be

sollicitabat. Apud quos cum proficere nihil posset, quibusdam solutis ergastulis Cosam in agro Thurino oppugnare coepit. Eo cum a Q. Pedio praetore cum legione . . . lapide ictus ex muro periit.[1] Et Caelius profectus, ut dictitabat, ad Caesarem pervenit Thurios. Ubi cum quosdam eius municipii sollicitaret equitibusque Caesaris Gallis atque Hispanis, qui eo praesidii causa missi erant, pecuniam polliceretur, ab his est interfectus. Ita magnarum initia rerum, quae occupatione magistratuum et temporum[2] sollicitam Italiam habebant, celerem et facilem exitum habuerunt.

23   Libo profectus ab Orico cum classe, cui praeerat, navium L, Brundisium venit insulamque, quae contra portum Brundisinum est, occupavit, quod praestare arbitrabatur unum locum, qua necessarius nostris erat egressus, quam omnia litora ac portus custodia clausos teneri. Hic repentino adventu naves onerarias quasdam nactus incendit et unam frumento onustam abduxit magnumque nostris terrorem iniecit et noctu militibus ac sagittariis in terram expositis praesidium equitum deiecit et adeo loci opportunitate profecit, uti ad Pompeium litteras mitteret, naves reliquas, si vellet, subduci et refici iuberet: sua classe auxilia sese Caesaris prohibiturum.

24   Erat eo tempore Antonius Brundisii; is virtute militum confisus scaphas navium magnarum circiter LX cratibus pluteisque contexit eoque milites delectos imposuit atque eas in litore pluribus locis

---

[1] *The incomplete sentence cannot be restored with certainty.*
[2] et temporum *MSS.:* legitimorum *Kübler:* et imperiorum *Paul. Possibly some word like* difficultate *or* calamitate *has fallen out.*

oppressed by debt. When he could make no progress with them he let loose some slaves from their dungeons and began to besiege Cosa, in the Thurine district. There meeting with the praetor Q. Pedius at the head of a legion, he was struck by a stone from the wall and perished. And Caelius, setting forth, as he gave out, to Caesar, reached Thurii. There, on trying to tamper with certain inhabitants of the municipality and promising money to Caesar's Gallic and Spanish horsemen who had been sent there on garrison duty, he was killed by them. Thus the first outbreak of a serious movement, which kept Italy harassed by the burden of work imposed on the magistrates by the crisis, came promptly and easily to an end.

Libo, setting out from Oricum with the fleet of 23 fifty ships under his command, came to Brundisium and occupied the island over against the port of Brundisium, because he thought it better to guard one place by which our men would necessarily have to go out than to keep all the shores and harbours closely blockaded. Approaching suddenly, he found some merchantmen; these he burned, and one loaded with corn he towed off, filling our men with great terror. Then landing by night some soldiers and archers, he dislodged the cavalry outpost and made such good use of the opportunities of his position that he sent a dispatch to Pompeius saying that, if he liked, he might order the rest of his ships to be beached and repaired, and that with his own fleet he would keep off Caesar's reinforcements.

Antonius was at that time at Brundisium; and having 24 confidence in the valour of his soldiers, he protected with fascines and screens about sixty row-boats belonging to his large ships, and, putting picked men

separatim disposuit navesque triremes duas, quas
Brundisii faciendas curaverat, per causam exercen-
dorum remigum ad fauces portus prodire iussit. Has
cum audacius progressas Libo vidisset, sperans inter-
cipi posse, quadriremes v ad eas misit. Quae cum
navibus nostris appropinquassent, nostri veterani
in portum refugiebant: illi studio incitati incautius
sequebantur. Iam ex omnibus partibus subito Anto-
nianae scaphae signo dato se in hostes incitaverunt
primoque impetu unam ex his quadriremibus cum
remigibus defensoribusque suis ceperunt, reliquas tur-
piter refugere coëgerunt. Ad hoc detrimentum accessit,
ut equitibus per oram maritimam ab Antonio dispositis aquari prohiberentur. Qua necessitate et ignominia permotus Libo discessit a Brundisio obsessio-
nemque nostrorum omisit.

25   Multi iam menses erant et hiems praecipitaverat,
neque Brundisio naves legionesque ad Caesarem
veniebant. Ac nonnullae eius rei praetermissae
occasiones Caesari videbantur, quod certi saepe
flaverant venti, quibus necessario committendum
existimabat. Quantoque eius amplius processerat
temporis, tanto erant alacriores ad custodias, qui
classibus praeerant, maioremque fiduciam prohi-
bendi habebant, et crebris Pompei litteris castiga-
bantur, quoniam primo venientem Caesarem non
prohibuissent, ut reliquos eius exercitus impedirent,
duriusque cotidie tempus ad transportandum lenio-
ribus ventis exspectabant. Quibus rebus permotus

on board, stationed them singly at various places along the coast, and gave orders that two triremes which he had caused to be built at Brundisium should go out to the mouth of the harbour under the pretence of exercising the rowers. When Libo saw them advance so boldly he sent five quadriremes against them, hoping that they could be intercepted. On their approaching our ships, our veteran crews began to retreat to the harbour, while the foe, impelled by their zeal, incautiously followed. Then suddenly, the signal being given, the Antonian rowboats threw themselves on the foe from every side, and at the first onset captured one of these quadriremes with its rowers and fighting men and compelled the rest to a discreditable flight. In addition to this loss they were prevented from watering by horsemen stationed by Antonius along the sea-coast, and Libo, moved by this need and by his disgrace, departed from Brundisium and abandoned the blockade of our men.

Many months had now passed and winter was far 25 advanced, yet his ships and legions did not come to Caesar from Brundisium. And in fact some opportunities for this seemed to Caesar to have been passed over, since steady winds had often blown by which, in his opinion, they should without fail have set their course. And the further this period of time extended the more keen were the officers of the enemy's fleet in their vigilance, and the greater confidence they had of stopping him. They were upbraided, too, by frequent letters from Pompeius urging them to hinder the rest of his forces, since they had not stopped Caesar on his first arrival, and every day they were expecting a more difficult season for transport, as the winds were slackening. Moved

CAESAR

Caesar Brundisium ad suos severius scripsit, nacti
idoneum ventum ne occasionem navigandi dimitterent, sive ad litora Apolloniatium sive ad Labeatium[1] cursum dirigere atque eo naves eicere possent.
Haec a custodiis classium loca maxime vacabant,
quod se longius a portibus committere non audebant.

26   Illi adhibita audacia et virtute administrantibus
M. Antonio et Fufio Caleno, multum ipsis militibus
hortantibus neque ullum periculum pro salute
Caesaris recusantibus nacti austrum naves solvunt
atque altero die Apolloniam praetervehuntur. Qui
cum essent ex continenti visi, Coponius, qui
Dyrrachii classi Rhodiae praeerat, naves ex portu
educit, et cum iam nostris remissiore vento appropinquasset, idem auster increbuit nostrisque praesidio
fuit. Neque vero ille ob eam causam conatu desistebat,
sed labore et perseverantia nautarum etiam vim
tempestatis superari posse sperabat praetervectosque
Dyrrachium magna vi venti nihilo secius sequebatur.
Nostri usi fortunae beneficio tamen impetum classis
timebant, si forte ventus remisisset. Nacti portum,
qui appellatur Nymphaeum, ultra Lissum milia
passuum III, eo naves introduxerunt (qui portus ab
Africo tegebatur, ab austro non erat tutus) leviusque
tempestatis quam classis periculum aestimaverunt.

---

[1] sive ad Labeatium, *not in MSS., is added by F. Hofmann to
complete the sense: E. Hoffmann proposes to insert* sive ad Apsi
ostium *after* dimitterent.

by these considerations, Caesar wrote in severer terms
to his partisans at Brundisium, that when they got a
suitable wind they should not let slip the opportunity
of sailing, whether they were able to direct their
course to the shores of the Apolloniates or to those
of the Labeates, and run their ships ashore there.
These places were mostly out of the range of observation of the enemy's fleet, because they did not
venture to trust themselves too far from the
harbours.

Displaying audacity and valour, with M. Antonius 26
and Fufius Calenus directing operations, and the
soldiers themselves giving much encouragement and
refusing no danger for Caesar's safety, they weigh
anchor with a south wind, and on the second day sail
past Apollonia. When they had been seen from the
mainland, Coponius, who was at Dyrrachium in command of the Rhodian fleet, leads his ships out of
port, and when on the wind falling light he had now
approached near our force, the same south wind rose
again and served to protect our side. Yet he did not
on that account desist from his attempt, but kept
hoping that even the violence of the storm could be
overcome by the toil and perseverance of the sailors,
and though we had been carried past Dyrrachium
by the strong force of the wind, he none the less kept
pursuing us. Our men, though experiencing the
kindness of fortune, nevertheless feared an attack by
the fleet in case the wind should drop. Coming to a
harbour named Nymphaeum, three miles beyond
Lissus, a harbour which was protected from the
south-west wind but was not safe from the south,
they took their ships in there, reckoning the danger
from the storm less than that from the enemy's fleet.
And as soon as they entered there, by an incredible

Quo simulatque introitum est, incredibili felicitate auster, qui per biduum flaverat, in Africum se vertit.

27 Hic subitam commutationem fortunae videre licuit. Qui modo sibi timuerant, hos tutissimus portus recipiebat; qui nostris navibus periculum intulerant, de suo timere cogebantur. Itaque tempore commutato tempestas et nostros texit et naves Rhodias afflixit, ita ut ad unam omnes, constratae numero XVI, eliderentur et naufragio interirent, et ex magno remigum propugnatorumque numero pars ad scopulos allisa interficeretur, pars ab nostris detraheretur; quos omnes conservatos Caesar domum dimisit.

28 Nostrae naves duae tardius cursu confecto in noctem coniectae, cum ignorarent, quem locum reliquae cepissent, contra Lissum in ancoris constiterunt. Has scaphis minoribusque navigiis compluribus immissis[1] Otacilius Crassus, qui Lissi praeerat, expugnare parabat; simul de deditione eorum agebat et incolumitatem deditis pollicebatur. Harum altera navis CCXX e legione tironum sustulerat, altera ex veterana paulo minus CC. Hic cognosci licuit, quantum esset hominibus praesidii in animi firmitudine. Tirones enim multitudine navium perterriti et salo nauseaque confecti iureiurando accepto, nihil eis nocituros hostes, se Otacilio dediderunt; qui omnes ad eum producti contra religionem iurisiurandi in

[1] immissis *suggested by me in Pitt Press edition*, 1900; submissis *MSS*.

piece of luck the south wind which had blown for
two days changed into a south-west wind.

Herein might be seen the sudden shifting of for- 27
tune. Those who had lately been in fear for themselves were now sheltered by a perfectly safe harbour;
those who had brought peril on our ships were forced
to fear peril for themselves. And so by the change
of circumstances the rough weather protected our
ships and shattered the Rhodian vessels, so that the
decked ships, numbering sixteen, were all without
exception crushed and utterly wrecked; and of the
large number of rowers and fighting men, some were
dashed on the rocks and killed, others were dragged
off by our men. All these Caesar saved and sent
back home.

Two of our ships, overtaken by night owing to the 28
slow progress of their course, not knowing what position the rest had taken, anchored opposite Lissus,
and Otacilius Crassus, who was in command of Lissus,
was preparing to capture these by sending against
them a number of row-boats and other small craft;
at the same time he was treating for the surrender of
their crews, and promising them freedom from injury
if they surrendered. One of these ships had taken
on board two hundred and twenty men of the legion
of recruits, the other rather less than two hundred
from the veteran legion. Herein might be learnt
what security men derive from strength of mind. For
the recruits, terrified by the number of the ships and
exhausted by the rough water and seasickness, after
receiving a solemn pledge that the enemy would do
them no harm, surrendered themselves to Otacilius;
and all of them, when brought to him, are most
cruelly massacred before his eyes in violation of the
sanctity of his oath. But the men of the veteran

eius conspectu crudelissime interficiuntur. At vete-
ranae legionis milites, item conflictati et tempestatis
et sentinae vitiis, neque ex pristina virtute remit-
tendum aliquid putaverunt, et tractandis condicionibus et simulatione deditionis extracto primo
noctis tempore gubernatorem in terram navem eicere
cogunt, ipsi idoneum locum nacti reliquam noctis
partem ibi confecerunt et luce prima missis ad eos
ab Otacilio equitibus, qui eam partem orae maritimae asservabant, circiter CCCC, quique eos armati ex
praesidio secuti sunt, se defenderunt et nonnullis
eorum interfectis incolumes se ad nostros receperunt.

29   Quo facto conventus civium Romanorum, qui
Lissum obtinebant, quod oppidum eis antea Caesar
attribuerat muniendumque curaverat, Antonium
recepit omnibusque rebus iuvit. Otacilius sibi timens
ex oppido fugit et ad Pompeium pervenit. Expositis omnibus copiis Antonius, quarum erat summa
veteranarum trium legionum uniusque tironum et
equitum DCCC, plerasque naves in Italiam remittit ad
reliquos milites equitesque transportandos, pontones,
quod est genus navium Gallicarum, Lissi relinquit,
hoc consilio, ut si forte Pompeius vacuam existimans
Italiam eo traiecisset exercitum, quae opinio erat
edita in vulgus, aliquam Caesar ad insequendum
facultatem haberet, nuntiosque ad eum celeriter
mittit, quibus regionibus exercitum exposuisset et
quid militum transvexisset.

30   Haec eodem fere tempore Caesar atque Pompeius

legion, though equally distressed by the discomforts of the storm and the bilge-water, considered it their duty to relax nothing of their pristine valour, and, having spun out the first part of the night by treating of terms and making a pretence at surrender, compel their helmsman to run the ship aground, and themselves finding a suitable spot, finished the rest of the night there; and at early dawn, when about four hundred horsemen, who were guarding that part of the sea-coast, and others who had followed them under arms from the garrison, were sent against them by Otacilius, they defended themselves, and after slaying some of the foe retired unhurt on our force.

After this had taken place the corporation of 29 Roman citizens who were in occupation of Lissus, a town which Caesar had previously made over to them and for the fortification of which he had arranged, admitted Antonius and assisted him in every way. Otacilius, fearing for himself, flies from the town and makes his way to Pompeius. Antonius, having disembarked all his forces, the sum of which consisted of three veteran legions and one of recruits and eight hundred cavalry, sends back most of his ships to Italy to transport the rest of his horse and foot, but leaves his pontoons, a kind of Gallic ship, at Lissus, intending that, if Pompeius, thinking Italy unguarded, should transport his army thither, as it was generally expected that he would, Caesar might have some means of going in pursuit; and he hastily sends him messages stating in what districts he had disembarked his army and what number of troops he had conveyed across.

Caesar and Pompeius become aware of this almost 30 simultaneously. For they had themselves seen the

cognoscunt. Nam praetervectas Apolloniam Dyrrachiumque naves viderant ipsi, ut iter secundum
eas terra direxerant,[1] sed quo essent eae delatae,
primus diebus ignorabant. Cognitaque re diversa sibi
ambo consilia capiunt: Caesar, ut quam primum se
cum Antonio coniungeret; Pompeius, ut venientibus in itinere se opponeret, si imprudentes ex
insidiis adoriri posset, eodemque die uterque eorum ex
castris stativis a flumine Apso exercitum educunt:
Pompeius clam et noctu, Caesar palam atque interdiu.
Sed Caesari circuitu maiore iter erat longius,
adverso flumine, ut vado transire posset; Pompeius, quia expedito itinere flumen ei transeundum non erat, magnis itineribus ad Antonium
contendit atque eum ubi appropinquare cognovit,
idoneum locum nactus ibi copias collocavit suosque
omnes in castris continuit ignesque fieri prohibuit,
quo occultior esset eius adventus. Haec ad Antonium
statim per Graecos deferuntur. Ille missis ad Caesarem nuntiis unum diem sese castris tenuit; altero
die ad eum pervenit Caesar. Cuius adventu cognito
Pompeius, ne duobus circumcluderetur exercitibus,
ex eo loco discedit omnibusque copiis ad Asparagium
Dyrrachinorum pervenit atque ibi idoneo loco castra
ponit.

31   His temporibus Scipio detrimentis quibusdam
circa montem Amanum acceptis imperatorem se
appellaverat. Quo facto civitatibus tyrannisque
magnas imperaverat pecunias, item a publicanis
suae provinciae debitam biennii pecuniam exegerat

---

[1] *The text of this sentence is doubtful, and no satisfactory interpretation of it is possible.*

ships sailing past Apollonia and Dyrrachium, as they had directed their march by land to follow them; but for the first few days they did not know whither their course had carried them. And when they had found this out they each adopted different plans, Caesar to unite himself as quickly as possible with Antonius, Pompeius to confront the approaching enemy on their march, in case he might be able to attack them unawares from an ambuscade; and on the same day they each led out their forces from their permanent camps, quitting the River Apsus, Pompeius secretly by night, Caesar openly by day. But Caesar had the longer journey up stream, with a larger circuit, to enable him to cross by a ford; Pompeius, since he had not to cross the river, his route being open, hastened by forced marches towards Antonius, and on learning of his approach, finding a suitable spot, stationed his forces there and kept all his men in camp, forbidding fires to be lighted that his arrival might be kept more secret. These facts are immediately reported to Antonius through some Greeks. He sent messengers to Caesar and kept his men one day in camp; on the next day Caesar reached him. On learning of his arrival, Pompeius, to escape being shut in by two armies, quits that spot and with all his forces arrives at Asparagium, a town of the Dyrrachians, and there pitches his camp in a suitable place.

About this time Scipio, having incurred some losses 31 near Mount Amanus, had styled himself Imperator. After doing this he had requisitioned large sums of money from the communities and the despots, and had also exacted from the tax-farmers of his province the amount owing for two years, and had

et ab eisdem insequentis anni mutuam praeceperat equitesque toti provinciae imperaverat. Quibus coactis, finitimis hostibus Parthis post se relictis, qui paulo ante M. Crassum imperatorem interfecerant et M. Bibulum in obsidione habuerant, legiones equitesque ex Syria deduxerat. Summamque in sollicitudinem ac timorem Parthici belli provincia cum venisset, ac nonnullae militum voces cum audirentur, sese, contra hostem si ducerentur, ituros, contra civem et consulem arma non laturos, deductis Pergamum atque in locupletissimas urbes in hiberna legionibus maximas largitiones fecit et confirmandorum militum causa diripiendas his civitates dedit.

32   Interim acerbissime imperatae pecuniae tota provincia exigebantur. Multa praeterea generatim ad avaritiam excogitabantur. In capita singula servorum ac liberorum tributum imponebatur; columnaria, ostiaria, frumentum, milites, arma, remiges, tormenta, vecturae imperabantur; cuius modo rei nomen reperiri poterat, hoc satis esse ad cogendas pecunias videbatur. Non solum urbibus, sed paene vicis castellisque singulis cum imperio praeficiebantur. Qui horum quid acerbissime crudelissimeque fecerat, is et vir et civis optimus habebatur. Erat plena lictorum et imperiorum provincia, differta praefectis atque exactoribus: qui praeter imperatas pecunias suo etiam privato compendio serviebant; dictitabant

borrowed in advance from the same persons the amount due for the following year, and had levied horsemen from the whole province. When these were collected, leaving in his rear the neighbouring Parthian enemy who a little before had slain the commander, M. Crassus, and had kept M. Bibulus closely invested, he had withdrawn his legions and cavalry from Syria. And as the province had fallen into a state of great anxiety and fear about a Parthian war, and remarks were heard from the soldiers that if they were being led against an enemy they would go, but that against a citizen and a consul they would not bear arms, he conducted his legions to Pergamum and the richest cities for winter quarters and bestowed on them very large bounties, and with the object of encouraging the men allowed them to plunder the towns.

Meanwhile sums of money, requisitioned with the 32 utmost harshness, were being exacted throughout the province. Many kinds of extortion, moreover, were specially devised to glut their avarice. A tribute was imposed on every head of slaves and children; pillar-taxes,[1] door-taxes, corn, soldiers, arms, rowers, engines, freightage, were requisitioned; any mode of exaction, provided a name could be found for it, was deemed a sufficient excuse for compelling contributions. Men armed with military power were set not merely over cities but almost over every hamlet and stronghold. Among these he who had acted with the greatest harshness and cruelty was accounted the best of men and the best of citizens. The province was full of lictors and military authorities, crammed with prefects and extortioners, who apart from the moneys requisitioned had an eye also to their own private gain; for they gave out that,

[1] Taxes on pillars or columns.

enim se domo patriaque expulsos omnibus necessariis egere rebus, ut honesta praescriptione rem tur-
pissimam tegerent. Accedebant ad haec gravissimae
usurae, quod in bello plerumque accidere consuevit
universis imperatis pecuniis; quibus in rebus pro-
lationem diei donationem esse dicebant. Itaque aes
alienum provinciae eo biennio multiplicatum est.
Neque minus ob eam causam civibus Romanis eius
provinciae, sed in singulos conventus singulasque
civitates certae pecuniae imperabantur, mutuasque
illas ex senatusconsulto exigi dictitabant; publicanis,
ut in Syria fecerant, insequentis anni vectigal pro-
mutuum.

33   Praeterea Ephesi a fano Dianae depositas antiquitus pecunias Scipio tolli iubebat. Certaque eius rei
die constituta cum in fanum ventum esset adhibitis
compluribus ordinis senatorii, quos advocaverat Scipio,
litterae ei redduntur a Pompeio, mare transisse cum
legionibus Caesarem: properaret ad se cum exercitu
venire omniaque posthaberet. His litteris acceptis
quos advocaverat dimittit; ipse iter in Macedoniam
parare incipit paucisque post diebus est profectus.
Haec res Ephesiae pecuniae salutem attulit.

34   Caesar Antonii exercitu coniuncto deducta Orico
legione, quam tuendae orae maritimae causa posuerat,

having been driven from home and country, they were in need of all necessaries, so that by a respectable plea they might cover up the foulest action. Added to this there was the heaviest usury, as usually happens in war, money being exacted from the whole population; and in these proceedings a postponement of the day of payment was termed a free gift. Consequently, in these two years the debt of the province was multiplied. Yet none the less on that account were fixed sums of money exacted from the Roman citizens of the province, not individually, but by separate corporations and communities, and they tried to make out that these sums were being taken as loans in accordance with a decree of the senate; from the tax-farmers they demanded the tax of the following year as an advance loan, as they had done in Syria.

Moreover, at Ephesus Scipio gave orders that sums 33 of money deposited there in former times should be removed from the temple of Diana. And a certain date having been appointed for this transaction, when they had come to the shrine and with them a number of men of the senatorial order whom Scipio had invited, a dispatch is handed him from Pompeius stating that Caesar had crossed the sea with his legions, that Scipio was to make haste to come to him with his army and to put everything else aside. On receipt of this dispatch he dismisses those whom he had invited, and himself begins to prepare for his journey into Macedonia, and a few days later he set out. This circumstance secured the safety of the money at Ephesus.

Caesar, after his junction with the army of Antonius, 34 removing from Oricum the legion which he had stationed there to protect the sea-coast, thought that

temptandas sibi provincias longiusque procedendum existimabat et, cum ad eum ex Thessalia Aetoliaque legati venissent, qui praesidio misso pollicerentur earum gentium civitates imperata facturas, L. Cassium Longinum cum legione tironum, quae appellabatur XXVII, atque equitibus CC in Thessaliam, C. Calvisium Sabinum cum cohortibus V paucisque equitibus in Aetoliam misit; maxime eos, quod erant propinquae regiones, de re frumentaria ut providerent, hortatus est. Cn. Domitium Calvinum cum legionibus duabus, XI et XII, et equitibus D in Macedoniam proficisci iussit; cuius provinciae ab ea parte, quae libera appellabatur, Menedemus, princeps earum regionum, missus legatus omnium suorum excellens studium profitebatur.

35 Ex his Calvisius primo adventu summa omnium Aetolorum receptus voluntate, praesidiis adversariorum Calydone et Naupacto eiectis, omni Aetolia potitus est. Cassius in Thessaliam cum legione pervenit. Hic cum essent factiones duae, varia voluntate civitatum utebatur: Hegesaretos, veteris homo potentiae, Pompeianis rebus studebat; Petraeus, summae nobilitatis adulescens, suis ac suorum opibus Caesarem enixe iuvabat.

36 Eodemque tempore Domitius in Macedoniam venit; et cum ad eum frequentes civitatum legationes convenire coepissent, nuntiatum est adesse Scipionem cum legionibus, magna opinione et fama omnium; nam plerumque in novitate rem fama antecedit.[1]

---

[1] in novitate fama antecedit *MSS. Various plausible corrections have been made.*

he ought to try to win over the provinces and to make a further advance. On the arrival of envoys from Thessaly and Aetolia to promise that if he sent a garrison the townships of these nations would do his bidding, he sent into Thessaly L. Cassius Longinus with the legion of recruits, called the Twenty-seventh, and two hundred horse; into Aetolia, G. Calvisius Sabinus with five cohorts and a few horsemen; and he gave them special instructions, as the districts were close at hand, to provide for the corn supply. He ordered Gn. Domitius Calvinus to go into Macedonia with two legions, the Eleventh and Twelfth, and five hundred horsemen; and in that part of this province which was called Free, Menedemus, the leading man of those districts, being sent as an envoy announced a remarkable enthusiasm on the part of all his countrymen.

Of these officers Calvisius was received on his arrival with the utmost goodwill of all the Aetolians, and having expelled the garrisons of the foe from Calydon and Naupactus gained possession of the whole of Aetolia. Cassius arrived with his legion in Thessaly; here, since there were two factions, he met with a divergence of feeling among the towns: Hegesaretos, a man of long-established influence, favoured the cause of Pompeius; Petraeus, a youth of the highest rank, energetically supported Caesar with his own and his people's resources. 35

And at the same time Domitius comes into Macedonia; and when crowded embassies from the townships had begun to gather together to meet him, the news was brought that Scipio was close at hand with his legions, arousing much expectation and rumour among the people generally; for in a novel conjuncture rumour usually outstrips truth. Scipio, lingering 36

Hic nullo in loco Macedoniae moratus magno impetu tetendit ad Domitium et, cum ab eo milia passuum xx afuisset, subito se ad Cassium Longinum in Thessaliam convertit. Hoc adeo celeriter fecit, ut simul adesse et venire nuntiaretur, et quo iter expeditius faceret, M. Favonium ad flumen Aliacmonem, quod Macedoniam a Thessalia dividit, cum cohortibus VIII praesidio impedimentis legionum reliquit castellumque ibi muniri iussit. Eodem tempore equitatus regis Cotyis ad castra Cassii advolavit, qui circum Thessaliam esse consuerat. Tum timore perterritus Cassius cognito Scipionis adventu visisque equitibus, quos Scipionis esse arbitrabatur, ad montes se convertit, qui Thessaliam cingunt, atque ex his locis Ambraciam versus iter facere coepit. At Scipionem properantem sequi litterae sunt consecutae a M. Favonio, Domitium cum legionibus adesse neque se praesidium, ubi constitutus esset, sine auxilio Scipionis tenere posse. Quibus litteris acceptis consilium Scipio iterque commutat; Cassium sequi desistit, Favonio auxilium ferre contendit. Itaque die ac nocte continuato itinere ad eum pervenit, tam opportuno tempore, ut simul Domitiani exercitus pulvis cerneretur, et primi antecursores Scipionis viderentur. Ita Cassio industria Domitii, Favonio Scipionis celeritas salutem attulit.

37 Scipio biduum castris stativis moratus ad flumen, quod inter eum et Domitii castra fluebat, Aliacmonem, tertio die prima luce exercitum vado traducit

nowhere in Macedonia, made his way to Domitius with great speed, and when about twenty miles off suddenly turned aside to Thessaly to Cassius Longinus. This he did so hastily that news of his presence and of his coming was brought simultaneously, and in order that he might march with the greater expedition he left M. Favonius at the River Aliacmon, which divides Macedonia from Thessaly, with eight cohorts to protect the baggage of the legions, and ordered a stronghold to be fortified there. At the same time the cavalry of King Cotys, which had been in the habit of frequenting the borders of Thessaly, sped to the camp of Cassius. Then Cassius, smitten with fear when he learnt of the approach of Scipio and saw the horsemen whom he supposed to be Scipio's, turned towards the mountains which enclose Thessaly, and from these parts began to direct his course towards Ambracia. But Scipio, hurrying in pursuit, was followed by letters from M. Favonius saying that Domitius was close by with his legions, and that he could not hold the post in which he had been stationed without the aid of Scipio. Receiving this dispatch, Scipio changes his purpose and his route: he ceases to follow Cassius and hastens to bear aid to Favonius. And so, continuing his march by day and night, he reached him at so opportune a moment that at the very same time the dust of the Domitian army was seen and the first advance guard of Scipio appeared in view. Thus the energy of Domitius brought safety to Cassius, and the speed of Scipio to Favonius.

Scipio, after halting for two days in his permanent 37 camp by the River Aliacmon, which flowed between him and the camp of Domitius, on the third day at early dawn takes his army across by the ford, and

et castris positis postero die mane copias ante frontem castrorum instruit. Domitius tum quoque sibi dubitandum non putavit, quin productis legionibus proelio decertaret. Sed cum esset inter bina castra campus circiter milium passuum II, Domitius castris Scipionis aciem suam subiecit; ille a vallo non discedere perseveravit. Ac tamen aegre retentis Domitianis militibus est factum, ne proelio contenderetur, et maxime, quod rivus difficilibus ripis subiectus castris Scipionis progressus nostrorum impediebat. Quorum studium alacritatemque pugnandi cum cognovisset Scipio, suspicatus fore, ut postero die aut invitus dimicare cogeretur aut magna cum infamia castris se contineret, qui magna exspectatione venisset, temere progressus turpem habuit exitum et noctu ne conclamatis quidem vasis flumen transit atque in eandem partem, ex qua venerat, redit ibique prope flumen edito natura loco castra posuit. Paucis diebus interpositis noctu insidias equitum collocavit, quo in loco superioribus fere diebus nostri pabulari consueverant; et cum cotidiana consuetudine Qu. Varus, praefectus equitum Domitii, venisset, subito illi ex insidiis consurrexerunt. Sed nostri fortiter impetum eorum tulerunt, celeriterque ad suos quisque ordines rediit, atque ultro universi in hostes impetum fecerunt; ex his circiter LXXX interfectis, reliquis in fugam coniectis, duobus amissis in castra se receperunt.

after pitching a camp, on the morning of the next day draws up his forces before the front of the camp. Then Domitius also thought it his duty not to hesitate to advance his legions and fight a pitched battle. But, though there was a plain about two miles broad between the two camps, Domitius pushed forward his line close under Scipio's camp, but Scipio persisted in not moving away from his rampart. And yet, though the troops of Domitius were with difficulty held in, a pitched battle was avoided, and mainly because a stream with difficult banks situated just under Scipio's camp hindered the advance of our men. When Scipio perceived their zeal and keenness for fighting, suspecting that on the next day he would either be compelled to fight against his will or would confine himself to his camp with great discredit after the great expectation that his coming had aroused, his rash advance came to an ignominious end. Without even the proclamation for breaking up camp, he crossed the river by night and returned to the same part from which he had come and there pitched his camp on a natural elevation near the river. After the interval of a few days, he posted a cavalry ambuscade by night in the place in which our men on previous days had been in the habit of collecting fodder; and when Q. Varus, prefect of cavalry under Domitius, had come according to his daily practice, they suddenly rose up from their ambuscade. But our men stoutly withstood their attack, and, each quickly returning to his own rank, the whole body then took the aggressive and charged the enemy. After killing about eighty of them and putting the rest to flight, they returned to the camp with the loss of two men.

38   His rebus gestis Domitius, sperans Scipionem ad pugnam elici posse, simulavit sese angustiis rei frumentariae adductum castra movere, vasisque militari more conclamatis progressus milia passuum III loco idoneo et occulto omnem exercitum equitatumque collocavit. Scipio ad sequendum paratus equitum magnam partem ad explorandum iter Domitii et cognoscendum praemisit. Qui cum essent progressi, primaeque turmae insidias intravissent, ex fremitu equorum illata suspicione ad suos se recipere coeperunt, quique hos sequebantur celerem eorum receptum conspicati restiterunt. Nostri, cognitis insidiis, ne frustra reliquos exspectarent, duas nacti turmas exceperunt (in his fuit M. Opimius, praefectus equitum), reliquos omnes aut interfecerunt aut captos ad Domitium deduxerunt.[1]

39   Deductis orae maritimae praesidiis Caesar, ut supra demonstratum est, III cohortes Orici oppidi tuendi causa reliquit isdemque custodiam navium longarum tradidit, quas ex Italia traduxerat. Huic officio oppidoque Acilius Caninus legatus praeerat. Is naves nostras interiorem in portum post oppidum reduxit et ad terram deligavit faucibusque portus navem onerariam submersam obiecit et huic alteram coniunxit; super quam turrim effectam ad ipsum introitum portus opposuit et militibus complevit tuendamque ad omnes repentinos casus tradidit.

40   Quibus cognitis rebus Cn. Pompeius filius, qui classi Aegyptiae praeerat, ad Oricum venit sub-

[1] *There is some defect in this sentence, and various attempts have been made to improve it. The simplest remedy is to omit the words* exceperunt *and* reliquos (*before* omnes).

After these events Domitius, hoping that Scipio 38
could be enticed out to fight, pretended to be shifting his camp under the stress of want of provisions,
and when the order to strike camp had been proclaimed according to military custom, he advanced
three miles and stationed his whole army and cavalry
in a suitable and secret spot. Scipio, fully prepared
for pursuit, sent forward a great part of his horse to
explore the route of Domitius and discover his position. And when they had advanced and the first
squadrons had entered the ambuscade, the neighing
of the horses having caused suspicion, they began to
retire to their own men; and those who were following them, seeing their hasty retirement, halted. Our
men, when their ambush was discovered, that they
might not have to wait in vain for the rest, caught
and cut off two squadrons. Among these was M.
Opimius, prefect of horse; all the rest of the men
they either slew or led captive to Domitius.

Having removed the garrisons from the sea-shore, 39
as explained above, Caesar left three cohorts at
Oricum to protect the town, entrusting to them the
custody of the warships which he had brought over
from Italy. The legate Acilius Caninus was placed
in charge of this duty and of the town. He withdrew our ships into the inner port behind the town,
moored them to the shore, and sank a merchant-ship
to block the mouth of the port and attached to it
another ship, on which he constructed a tower,
setting it just opposite the entrance of the harbour.
This he filled with soldiers, and gave it them to hold
against all unforeseen risks.

On learning of these proceedings the young Gn. 40
Pompeius, who was in command of the Egyptian
fleet, came to Oricum and by great efforts drew off

mersamque navim remulco multisque contendens funibus adduxit atque alteram navem, quae erat ad custodiam ab Acilio posita, pluribus aggressus navibus, in quibus ad libram[1] fecerat turres, ut ex superiore pugnans loco integrosque semper defatigatis submittens et reliquis partibus simul ex terra scalis et classe moenia oppidi temptans, uti adversariorum manus diduceret, labore et multitudine telorum nostros vicit, deiectisque defensoribus, qui omnes scaphis excepti refugerant, eam navem expugnavit, eodemque tempore ex altera parte molem tenuit naturalem obiectam, quae paene insulam oppidum effecerat, et IIII biremes subiectis scutulis impulsas vectibus in interiorem portum traduxit. Ita ex utraque parte naves longas aggressus, quae erant deligatae ad terram atque inanes, IIII ex his abduxit, reliquas incendit. Hoc confecto negotio D. Laelium ab Asiatica classe abductum reliquit, qui commeatus Bullide atque Amantia importari in oppidum prohibebat. Ipse Lissum profectus naves onerarias XXX a M. Antonio relictas intra portum aggressus omnes incendit; Lissum expugnare conatus defendentibus civibus Romanis, qui eius conventus erant, militibusque, quos praesidii causa miserat Caesar, triduum moratus paucis in oppugnatione amissis re infecta inde discessit.

41   Caesar, postquam Pompeium ad Asparagium esse

[1] ad libram *MSS., but the sense is obscure and the reading doubtful: Ciacconius* altiores.

the submerged ship with a windlass and a number of ropes; and attacking the second ship, which had been stationed by Acilius to guard it, with a number of vessels on which he had constructed towers of equal height, fighting as he was from a higher position and always sending up fresh combatants in place of the exhausted, and in other directions assailing the walls of the town at once by ladders from the land and with his fleet, so as to keep apart the forces of the foe, he thus overcame our men by sheer hard work and overwhelming showers of missiles. And having driven off the fighting men, who were all picked up by boats and escaped, he took the ship by assault, and at the same time gained possession in the other direction of the projecting natural breakwater which had almost made an island of the town, and drew across into the inner harbour four biremes, placing rollers under them and propelling them by crowbars. And so attacking from either side the warships which were empty and fastened to the shore, he drew off four of them and burned the rest. Having finished this business, he left behind D. Laelius, whom he had taken from the Asiatic fleet. This officer proceeded to prevent stores from Byllis and Amantia from being imported into the town. He himself went to Lissus and attacked thirty merchant-vessels which had been left by M. Antonius within the port and burned them all. He attempted to storm Lissus, which was defended by the Roman citizens belonging to that corporation and by the soldiers whom Caesar had sent there as a garrison, and after staying for three days and having lost a few men in the siege, he left the district without effecting anything.

Caesar, as soon as he knew that Pompeius was at 41

cognovit, eodem cum exercitu profectus expugnato in itinere oppido Parthinorum, in quo Pompeius praesidium habebat, tertio die ad Pompeium pervenit iuxtaque eum castra posuit et postridie eductis omnibus copiis acie instructa decernendi potestatem Pompeio fecit. Ubi illum suis locis se tenere animadvertit, reducto in castra exercitu aliud sibi consilium capiendum existimavit. Itaque postero die omnibus copiis magno circuitu difficili angustoque itinere Dyrrachium profectus est sperans Pompeium aut Dyrrachium compelli aut ab eo intercludi posse, quod omnem commeatum totiusque belli apparatum eo contulisset; ut accidit. Pompeius enim primo ignorans eius consilium, quod diverso ab ea regione itinere profectum videbat, angustiis rei frumentariae compulsum discessisse existimabat; postea per exploratores certior factus postero die castra movit, breviore itinere se occurrere ei posse sperans. Quod fore suspicatus Caesar militesque adhortatus, ut aequo animo laborem ferrent, parvam partem noctis itinere intermisso mane Dyrrachium venit, cum primum agmen Pompei procul cerneretur, atque ibi castra posuit.

42   Pompeius interclusus Dyrrachio, ubi propositum tenere non potuit, secundo usus consilio edito loco, qui appellatur Petra aditumque habet navibus mediocrem atque eas a quibusdam protegit ventis, castra communit. Eo partem navium longarum con-

Asparagium, set out to the same place with his army, and after storming on the way the town of the Parthini in which Pompeius had a garrison, reached Pompeius on the third day, and pitched his camp close to him, and on the following day, leading out all his forces, drew them up in battle array and gave Pompeius the chance of fighting a pitched battle. On observing that he kept in his position, he withdrew his army to the camp, considering it necessary to form a different plan. So on the next day he set out in full force for Dyrrachium, taking a wide circuit by a difficult and narrow route, in the hope that Pompeius could be either driven to Dyrrachium or cut off from it, because he had collected there all his provisions and his whole war equipment. And so it happened. For Pompeius, at first failing to understand his plan, because he saw him setting out by a route that led away from that district, thought that he had gone away because he had been compelled to do so by scarcity of food supply. Afterwards receiving information through his scouts, he shifted his camp the next day, hoping to be able to confront him by a shorter route. Caesar, suspecting that this would happen and having exhorted his men to bear their toil with an equal mind, staying his march only for a short period during the night, arrived in the morning at Dyrrachium, when for the first time the line of Pompeius was seen afar off, and there pitched his camp. [1]

Pompeius, being cut off from Dyrrachium, on failing   42 to gain his purpose adopts the next best plan and entrenches a camp on a lofty spot called Petra, which allows a moderately good approach for ships and protects them from certain winds. He gives orders for some of his warships to meet there, and for corn

[1] See map of Dyrrachium and district.

venire, frumentum commeatumque ab Asia atque omnibus regionibus, quas tenebat, comportari imperat. Caesar longius bellum ductum iri existimans et de Italicis commeatibus desperans, quod tanta diligentia omnia litora a Pompeianis tenebantur, classesque ipsius, quas hieme in Sicilia, Gallia, Italia fecerat, morabantur, in Epirum rei frumentariae causa Q. Tellium et L. Canuleium legatum misit, quodque hae regiones aberant longius, locis certis horrea constituit vecturasque frumenti finitimis civitatibus descripsit. Item Lisso Parthinisque et omnibus castellis quod esset frumenti conquiri iussit. Id erat perexiguum cum ipsius agri natura, quod sunt loca aspera ac montuosa ac plerumque frumento utuntur importato, tum quod Pompeius haec providerat et superioribus diebus praedae loco Parthinos habuerat frumentumque omne conquisitum spoliatis effossisque eorum domibus per equites comportarat.

43   Quibus rebus cognitis Caesar consilium capit ex loci natura. Erant enim circum castra Pompei permulti editi atque asperi colles. Hos primum praesidiis tenuit castellaque ibi communit. Inde, ut loci cuiusque natura ferebat, ex castello in castellum perducta munitione circumvallare Pompeium instituit, haec spectans, quod angusta re frumentaria utebatur quodque Pompeius multitudine equitum valebat, quo minore periculo undique frumentum commeatumque

and stores to be brought in from Asia and from all the districts that he held. Caesar, thinking that the war was going to be unduly prolonged, and despairing of his supplies from Italy, because all the shores were being held with such vigilance by the Pompeians, and his own fleets which he had constructed in the winter in Sicily, Gaul, and Italy were slow in coming, sent Q. Tillius and the legate L. Canuleius into Epirus in order to get provisions, and because these districts were some distance off he established granaries in certain places and apportioned and neighbouring communities their respective shares in the carriage of corn. He also gave orders that all the corn that there was should be sought and collected at Lissus, among the Parthini, and in all the fortified posts. This was of very small amount, partly from the nature of the land, because the district is rugged and hilly and the people generally use imported corn, and also because Pompeius had foreseen this and had at an earlier date treated the Parthini as spoils of war, and, hunting for all their corn by ransacking and digging up their houses, had carried it off by means of his horsemen to Petra.

On learning of these things, Caesar forms a plan to 43 suit the nature of the ground. Round Pompeius' camp there were very many lofty and rugged hills. These he first occupied with garrisons and erected strong forts on them. Then, according to the indications afforded by the nature of each locality, by drawing a line of works from fort to fort he proceeded to invest Pompeius, with these objects in view: first, that as he had a scanty supply of provisions and Pompeius had a large preponderance of cavalry, he might be able to bring in for his army corn and stores from any direction at less risk; and also that he might

exercitui supportare posset, simul, uti pabulatione Pompeium prohiberet equitatumque eius ad rem gerendam inutilem efficeret, tertio, ut auctoritatem qua ille maxime apud exteras nationes niti videbatur, minueret, cum fama per orbem terrarum percrebuisset, illum a Caesare obsideri neque audere proelio dimicare.

44   Pompeius neque a mari Dyrrachioque discedere volebat, quod omnem apparatum belli, tela, arma, tormenta ibi collocaverat frumentumque exercitui navibus supportabat, neque munitiones Caesaris prohibere poterat, nisi proelio decertare vellet; quod eo tempore statuerat non esse faciendum. Relinquebatur, ut extremam rationem belli sequens quam plurimos colles occuparet et quam latissimas regiones praesidiis teneret Caesarisque copias, quam maxime posset, distineret; idque accidit. Castellis enim XXIIII effectis XV milia passuum circuitu amplexus hoc spatio pabulabatur; multaque erant intra eum locum manu sata, quibus interim iumenta pasceret. Atque ut nostri perpetua munitione providebant, ne quo loco erumperent Pompeiani ac nostros post tergum adorirentur,[1] ita illi interiore spatio perpetuas munitiones efficiebant, ne quem locum nostri intrare atque ipsos a tergo circumvenire possent. Sed illi operibus vincebant, quod et numero militum praestabant et interiore spatio minorem circuitum habe-

---

[1] perpetuas munitiones videbant neque loco erumperent Pompeiani ac nostros post tergum adorirentur timebant *MSS.*

prevent Pompeius from foraging and might make his cavalry useless for active operations; and, thirdly, that he might diminish the moral influence on which Pompeius seemed chiefly to rely among foreign nations, when the report should have spread throughout the world that he was being beleaguered by Caesar and did not dare to fight a pitched battle.

Pompeius was unwilling to go far from the sea and Dyrrachium because he had placed there his whole war material, pikes, armour, catapults, and was bringing up, by sea, corn for his army, nor could he put a stop to Caesar's works except by choosing to fight a pitched battle, which he had decided should not be done at that time. The only remaining course was to adopt a desperate method of warfare by occupying as many hills as possible, by holding with garrisons the widest extent of land possible, and by keeping Caesar's forces as far extended as he could; and this was done. By making twenty-four redoubts he embraced a circuit of fifteen miles, and within this he foraged; and in this district there were a number of hand-sown crops with which he could meanwhile feed his animals. And just as our men by a continuous line of fortifications took measures to prevent the Pompeians from breaking out anywhere and attacking us in the rear, so the enemy made an unbroken line of defence in the interior of the space so that our men should not be able to enter any part of it and surround them from the rear. They, however, outstripped us in the work, being superior in numbers and having a shorter

44

Every conceivable emendation of this corrupt passage has been proposed. I adopt that of H. A. Koch, which at least makes sense.

bant. Quaecunque[1] erant loca Caesari capienda, etsi
prohibere Pompeius totis copiis et dimicare non
constituerat, tamen suis locis sagittarios funditoresque
mittebat, quorum magnum habebat numerum, multique ex nostris vulnerabantur, magnusque incesserat
timor sagittarum, atque omnes fere milites aut ex
coactis aut ex centonibus aut ex coriis tunicas aut
tegimenta fecerant, quibus tela vitarent.

45　　In occupandis praesidiis magna vi uterque
nitebatur: Caesar, ut quam angustissime Pompeium
contineret; Pompeius, ut quam plurimos colles quam
maximo circuitu occuparet, crebraque ob eam causam
proelia fiebant. In his cum legio Caesaris nona praesidium quoddam occupavisset et munire coepisset,
huic loco propinquum et contrarium collem Pompeius
occupavit nostrosque opere prohibere coepit et, cum
una ex parte prope aequum aditum haberet, primum
sagittariis funditoribusque circumiectis, postea levis
armaturae magna multitudine missa tormentisque
prolatis munitiones impediebat; neque erat facile
nostris uno tempore propugnare et munire. Caesar,
cum suos ex omnibus partibus vulnerari videret, recipere se iussit et loco excedere. Erat per declive
receptus. Illi autem hoc acrius instabant neque re-
gredi nostros patiebantur, quod timore adducti locum
relinquere videbantur. Dicitur eo tempore glorians
apud suos Pompeius dixisse: non recusare se, quin
nullius usus imperator existimaretur, si sine maximo

---

[1] quaecunque *Bentley*: quae cum *MSS*. *The text of the whole
passage is very uncertain.*

interior circuit to complete. Whenever Caesar had to occupy any spot, although Pompeius had decided not to try to prevent it with his whole armed force and fight a pitched battle, yet he kept sending up, in suitable positions, archers and slingers, of whom he had a great number, and many of our men were wounded. A great dread of the arrows fell on them, and to avoid the missiles nearly all the soldiers had made themselves jerkins or other protections out of felt, quilt, or hide.

In occupying positions each strove with the utmost 45 energy: Caesar to confine Pompeius within the narrowest limits, Pompeius to occupy as many hills as he could in the widest possible circuit; and for this reason frequent skirmishes took place. In one of these, when Caesar's Ninth Legion had occupied a certain post and had begun to fortify it, Pompeius occupied a hill near and opposite to it and began to hinder our men in their work; and since on one side Caesar's position admitted of an almost level approach, he first of all threw round a force of archers and slingers, and then, sending up a great multitude of light-armed men and putting forward his engines, he began to hinder the works; nor was it easy for our men at one and the same time to stand on the defensive and to fortify. Caesar, on seeing that in every direction his men were being wounded, ordered them to retire and to quit the position. The way of retreat lay down a slope. The enemy, however, pressed on all the more keenly, and did not allow our men to retire, because they appeared to be abandoning the position under the influence of fear. It was at this time that Pompeius is said to have made the boastful remark to his friends that he did not object to be considered a worthless commander if Caesar's legions should

detrimento legiones Caesaris sese recepissent inde,
quo temere essent progressae.

46   Caesar receptui suorum timens crates ad extremum tumulum contra hostem proferri et adversas
locari, intra has mediocri latitudine fossam tectis
militibus obduci iussit locumque in omnes partes
quam maxime impediri. Ipse idoneis locis fundi-
tores instruxit, ut praesidio nostris se recipientibus
essent. His rebus comparatis legionem reduci iussit.
Pompeiani hoc insolentius atque audacius nostros
premere et instare coeperunt cratesque pro munitione
obiectas propulerunt, ut fossas transcenderent.
Quod cum animadvertisset Caesar, veritus, ne non
reducti, sed reiecti viderentur, maiusque detrimentum
caperetur, a medio fere spatio suos per Antonium,
qui ei legioni praeerat, cohortatus tuba signum
dari atque in hostes impetum fieri iussit. Milites
legionis VIIII subito conspirati pila coniecerunt et ex
inferiore loco adversus clivum incitati cursu prae-
cipites Pompeianos egerunt et terga vertere coëgerunt; quibus ad recipiendum crates deiectae lon-
guriique obiecti et institutae fossae magno impedimento fuerunt. Nostri vero, qui satis habebant
sine detrimento discedere, compluribus interfectis v

---

[1] The Pompeians were storming Caesar's position, and he
was now retiring before them down the further side of the
hill. Here he made a successful stand, and finally drove the
foe back in confusion over the hill.

succeed in retiring, without the most serious loss, from the place to which they had rashly advanced.

Caesar, fearing for the retreat of his men, ordered 46 hurdles to be carried to the furthest point of the hill[1] and to be set up fronting the foe to bar their way, and within these a ditch of moderate width to be drawn athwart their path, the men being under cover, and the place to be made as difficult as possible in every direction. He himself drew up his slingers in suitable places to serve as a protection to our men in their retreat. When these arrangements were finished he ordered the legion to be withdrawn. The Pompeians then began with all the more insolence and audacity to press and close in on our men, and in order to cross the ditches overthrew the hurdles that had been set up as a defence against them. And Caesar, on observing this, fearing lest his men should appear to have been flung back rather than withdrawn and a more serious loss should be incurred, exhorted his men about midway down the slope, by the mouth of Antonius, who was in command of that legion, and ordered the signal to be given with the clarion and the enemy to be charged. The men of the Ninth with prompt and unanimous resolution hurled their pikes and, breaking into a run from the lower ground and charging up the hill, drove the Pompeians headlong and compelled them to turn their backs in flight; the overturned hurdles and the uprights planted in their way and the ditches that had been drawn across proved a great hindrance to them in their retreat. But our men, who considered it sufficient to depart without disaster, when several of the enemy had been killed and five in all of their own comrades lost, retired with

omnino suorum amissis quietissime se receperunt
pauloque citra eum locum aliis comprehensis collibus
munitiones perfecerunt.

47   Erat nova et inusitata belli ratio cum tot
castellorum numero tantoque spatio et tantis munitionibus et toto obsidionis genere, tum etiam reliquis
rebus. Nam quicumque alterum obsidere conati sunt,
perculsos atque infirmos hostes adorti aut proelio
superatos aut aliqua offensione permotos continu-
erunt, cum ipsi numero equitum militumque praestarent; causa autem obsidionis haec fere esse consuevit, ut frumento hostes prohiberent. At tum integras atque incolumes copias Caesar inferiore militum numero continebat, cum illi omnium rerum
copia abundarent; cotidie enim magnus undique
navium numerus conveniebat, quae commeatum sup-
portarent, neque ullus flare ventus poterat, quin
aliqua ex parte secundum cursum haberent. Ipse
autem consumptis omnibus longe lateque frumentis
summis erat in angustiis. Sed tamen haec singulari
patientia milites ferebant. Recordabantur enim eadem
se superiore anno in Hispania perpessos labore et
patientia maximum bellum confecisse, meminerant
ad Alesiam magnam se inopiam perpessos, multo
etiam maiorem ad Avaricum, maximarum gentium
victores discessisse. Non illi hordeum cum daretur, non legumina recusabant; pecus vero cuius
rei summa erat ex Epiro copia, magno in honore
habebant.

48   Est autem genus radicis inventum ab eis, qui

the utmost quietness and, halting a little on this side of that spot, included in their lines some other hills and completed their defensive works.

The method of warfare was new and unprece- 47 dented, both on account of the large number of redoubts, the wide space covered, the great defensive works, and the whole system of blockade, as well as in other respects. For whenever one army has attempted to blockade another, it is when they have attacked a discomfited and weakened foe, overcome in battle or demoralized by some reverse, and have thus hemmed them in, being themselves superior in number of horse and foot; while the motive of the blockade has usually been to prevent the foe from getting supplies. But on this occasion Caesar with an inferior number of men was hemming in fresh and uninjured forces, the enemy having an abundant supply of all necessaries. For every day a large number of ships was gathering from every quarter to bring up stores, nor could any wind blow without their having a favourable course from some direction. But Caesar himself was in extreme straits, all the corn far and wide having been used up. Nevertheless the men bore these hardships with exemplary patience. For they bore in mind that they had endured these same hardships the year before in Spain and by their toil and patience had concluded a very serious war. They remembered that at Alesia they had endured great privation, still greater at Avaricum, and had come off victors over very important nations. When barley was offered them they did not refuse it, or vegetables; whereas meat, of which there was a very large supply from Epirus, they held in high favour.

Some of the men who had been unemployed found 48

fuerant vacui ab operibus,[1] quod appellatur chara, quod admixtum lacte multum inopiam levabat. Id ad similitudinem panis efficiebant.[2] Eius erat magna copia. Ex hoc effectos panes, cum in colloquiis Pompeiani famem nostris obiectarent, vulgo in eos iaciebant, ut spem eorum minuerent.

49 Iamque frumenta maturescere incipiebant, atque ipsa spes inopiam sustentabat, quod celeriter se habituros copiam confidebant; crebraeque voces militum in vigiliis colloquiisque audiebantur, prius se cortice ex arboribus victuros, quam Pompeium e manibus dimissuros. Libenter etiam ex perfugis cognoscebant equos eorum tolerari, reliqua vero iumenta interisse; uti autem ipsos valetudine non bona, cum angustiis loci et odore taetro ex multitudine cadaverum et cotidianis laboribus insuetos operum, tum aquae summa inopia affectos. Omnia enim flumina atque omnes rivos, qui ad mare pertinebant, Caesar aut averterat aut magnis operibus obstruxerat, atque ut erant loca montuosa et aspera, angustias vallium[3] sublicis in terram demissis praesaepserat terramque aggesserat, ut aquam contineret. Itaque illi necessario loca sequi demissa ac palustria et puteos fodere cogebantur atque hunc laborem ad cotidiana opera addebant; qui tamen fontes a quibusdam praesidiis aberant longius et celeriter aestibus exarescebant. At Caesaris exercitus optima valetudine summaque aquae copia utebatur, tum commeatus omni genere praeter fru-

[1] vacui ab operibus *Koch*: valeribus *MSS. The passage cannot be emended with certainty.*
[2] *I retain this, though Caesar could not have written the words as they stand.*
[3] *I adopt Paul's correction of the reading of the MSS.'* montuosa et ad specus angustiae vallium has.

also a kind of root called "chara," which, when mixed with milk, greatly assuaged their need. They made this up into something resembling bread, and there was a large supply of it. When the Pompeians in conversation taunted our men with hunger they used to throw at them loaves made of this, to reduce their expectations.

Now the corn was already beginning to ripen, and 49 the mere hope served to lighten the pinch, because they were confident that they would soon have abundance; and remarks were frequently heard from the men in their talks while on sentry duty that they would feed on bark from the trees before they would let Pompeius slip from their hands. Moreover, they were glad to learn from deserters that though the cavalry horses of the enemy were being kept alive, the rest of their animals had perished, and that the men themselves were experiencing bad health, both by reason of the cramped space and the foul stench from the multitude of corpses and their daily toils, as they were unaccustomed to work, and were also troubled by an extreme scarcity of water. For all the streams and all the rivulets which ran to the sea Caesar had either diverted or blocked by great works; and as the district was hilly and rugged he had dammed the narrow defiles by sinking piles into the ground and heaping up the earth, so as to keep in the water. So the foe were necessarily compelled to keep to the low and marshy ground and to dig wells, and this labour was an addition to their daily work. These springs, however, were at a considerable distance from some of the forts and quickly dried up in the hot weather. On the other hand, Caesar's army enjoyed excellent health and an abundant supply of water, and abounded with every kind of

mentum abundabat; quibus cotidie melius succedere tempus maioremque spem maturitate frumentorum proponi videbant.

50 In novo genere belli novae ab utrisque bellandi rationes reperiebantur. Illi, cum animadvertissent ex ignibus noctu cohortes nostras ad munitiones excubare, silentio aggressi universi intra multitudinem sagittas coniciebant et se confestim ad suos recipiebant. Quibus rebus nostri usu docti haec reperiebant remedia, ut alio loco ignes facerent[1] . . .

51 Interim certior factus P. Sulla, quem discedens castris praefecerat Caesar, auxilio cohorti venit cum legionibus duabus; cuius adventu facile sunt repulsi Pompeiani. Neque vero conspectum aut impetum nostrorum tulerunt, primisque deiectis reliqui se verterunt et loco cesserunt. Sed insequentes nostros, ne longius prosequerentur, Sulla revocavit. At plerique existimant, si acrius insequi voluisset, bellum eo die potuisse finire. Cuius consilium reprehendendum non videtur. Aliae enim sunt legati partes atque imperatoris: alter omnia agere ad praescriptum, alter libere ad summam rerum consulere debet. Sulla a Caesare in castris relictus liberatis suis hoc fuit contentus neque proelio decertare voluit, quae res tamen fortasse aliquem reci-

---

[1] *We may complete the sentence by some such words as* alio excubarent, "*and bivouac in another.*" *The rest of the missing passage probably contained an account of Caesar's attempt on*

provision except grain, and for this they saw a better season daily approaching and a greater hope set before them through the ripening of the corn.

In a novel kind of warfare novel methods of 50 waging it were invented by each side. When the enemy had observed from the fires that our cohorts were lying out at night by the earthworks, silently advancing in a body they used to discharge arrows within the crowded mass and then hastily retire to their comrades. Our men, taught by experience, discovered the following remedies for these emergencies, to light fires in one place . . .

Meanwhile P. Sulla, whom Caesar at his departure 51 had put in charge of his camp, being informed of this came to the support of the cohort with two legions; and by his arrival the Pompeians were easily repulsed. In fact, they could not endure the sight or the onset of our men, and when the first of them had been overthrown the rest turned to flight and abandoned the position. But when our men followed, Sulla recalled them lest they should go too far in pursuit. Many people, however, think that if he had chosen to pursue more vigorously the war might have been finished that day. But his policy does not seem deserving of censure. For the duties of a legate and of a commander are different: the one ought to do everything under direction, the other should take measures freely in the general interest. Sulla, having been left by Caesar in charge of the camp, was contented with the liberation of his men, and did not choose to fight a pitched battle, a course which in any case admitted possibly of some reverse,

---

Dyrrachium, and of assaults made by Pompeius on Caesar's lines; cp. Appian II. 60, Dio XLI. 50, 51, *and the note in my Pitt Press edition.*

peret casum, ne imperatorias sibi partes sumpsisse
videretur. Pompeianis magnam res ad receptum
difficultatem afferebat. Nam ex iniquo progressi
loco in summo constiterant; si per declive sese reciperent, nostros ex superiore insequentes loco vere-
bantur; neque multum ad solis occasum temporis
supererat; spe enim conficiendi negotii prope in noctem rem duxerant. Ita necessario atque ex tempore capto consilio Pompeius tumulum quendam
occupavit, qui tantum aberat a nostro castello, ut
telum tormento missum adigi non posset. Hoc
consedit loco atque eum communivit omnesque ibi
copias continuit.

52   Eodem tempore duobus praeterea locis pugnatum
est: nam plura castella Pompeius pariter distinendae
manus causa temptaverat, ne ex proximis praesidiis
succurri posset. Uno loco Volcatius Tullus impetum
legionis sustinuit cohortibus tribus atque eam loco
depulit; altero Germani munitiones nostras egressi
compluribus interfectis sese ad suos incolumes
receperunt.

53   Ita uno die vi proeliis factis, tribus ad Dyrrachium,
tribus ad munitiones, cum horum omnium ratio
haberetur, ad duorum milium numero ex Pompeianis
cecidisse reperiebamus, evocatos centurionesque
complures (in eo fuit numero Valerius Flaccus,
L. filius, eius, qui praetor Asiam obtinuerat);
signaque sunt militaria sex relata. Nostri non
amplius xx omnibus sunt proeliis desiderati. Sed in

in order that he might not be thought to have taken on himself the duties of a commander. As to the Pompeians, their situation caused them great difficulty in retreating; for, having advanced from unfavourable ground, they had halted on the top: if they were to withdraw by the slope they feared the pursuit of our men from the higher ground, nor was there much time left before sunset, since in the hope of finishing the business they had prolonged the action almost till nightfall. So Pompeius, of necessity and adapting his plans to the emergency, occupied a certain hill which was so far removed from our fort that a missile discharged from a catapult could not reach it. In this place he sat down and entrenched it, and kept all his forces confined there.

At the same time there was fighting in two other 52 places besides, for Pompeius had made attempts on several redoubts with the object of keeping our force equally scattered, so that succour might not be brought from the nearest garrisons. In one place Volcatius Tullus sustained with three cohorts the attack of a legion and drove it from its position; in the other the Germans went out of our lines, and after killing a number of men retired in safety to their comrades.

Thus six battles having taken place in one day, 53 three at Dyrrachium and three at the outworks, when account was taken of them all we found that about two thousand in number of the Pompeians had fallen, and very many reservists and centurions—among them was Valerius Flaccus, son of the Lucius who had governed Asia as praetor—and that six military standards had been brought in. Of our men not more than twenty were lost in all the battles.

castello nemo fuit omnino militum, quin vulnera-
retur, quattuorque ex una cohorte centuriones oculos
amiserunt. Et cum laboris sui periculique testimo-
nium afferre vellent, milia sagittarum circiter XXX in
castellum coniecta Caesari renumeraverunt, scutoque
ad eum relato Scaevae centurionis inventa sunt in eo
foramina CXX. Quem Caesar, ut erat de se meritus
et de re publica, donatum milibus CC collaudatumque[1] ab octavis ordinibus ad primipilum se traducere
pronuntiavit (eius enim opera castellum magna ex
parte conservatum esse constabat) cohortemque
postea duplici stipendio, frumento, veste, cibariis
militaribusque donis amplissime donavit.

54 Pompeius noctu magnis additis munitionibus
reliquis diebus turres exstruxit, et in altitudinem
pedum XV effectis operibus vineis eam partem castrorum obtexit, et quinque intermissis diebus alteram
noctem subnubilam nactus obstructis omnibus castrorum portis et ad impediendum obicibus[2] obiectis
tertia inita vigilia silentio exercitum eduxit et se in
antiquas munitiones recepit.

55 Omnibus deinceps diebus Caesar exercitum in aciem
aequum in locum produxit, si Pompeius proelio decertare vellet, ut paene castris Pompei legiones subiceret; tantumque a vallo eius prima acies aberat, uti
ne telum tormento adigi posset. Pompeius autem,

---

[1] collaudatumque *Dinter:* atque *MSS. Dinter's alteration
makes sense, but is not otherwise a probable restoration of the
imperfect text.*
[2] obicibus *inserted by Meusel with unnecessary change of*
obiectis *to* adiectis.

But in the redoubt there was not a single one of the men who was not wounded, and four centurions out of one cohort lost their eyes. Wishing to produce a proof of their labour and peril, they counted out to Caesar about thirty thousand arrows which had been discharged at the redoubt, and when the shield of the centurion Scaeva was brought to him one hundred and twenty holes were found in it. For his services to himself and to the republic Caesar, having presented him with two hundred thousand sesterces and eulogized him, announced that he transferred him from the eighth cohort to the post of first centurion of the first cohort, for it was certain that the redoubt had been to a great extent preserved by his aid, and he afterwards presented the cohort in amplest measure with double pay, grain, clothing, bounties, and military gifts.

Pompeius, having added strong defences by night, 54 erected towers on the following days, and having carried his works to a height of fifteen feet, protected that part of his camp with mantlets; and after a lapse of five days, chancing on a second dark night, he blocked all the gates of the camp, setting obstacles to hinder the foe, and at the beginning of the third watch led his army out in silence and betook himself to his old entrenchments.

On every day in succession Caesar led out his 55 army to level ground in battle array so as to bring his legions almost close up to the camp of Pompeius, in case he should choose to fight a pitched battle; and his front rank was only so far from the rampart that a weapon could not be cast at it from a catapult. Pompeius, however, in order to maintain his credit

ut famam opinionemque hominum teneret, sic pro castris exercitum constituebat, ut tertia acies vallum contingeret, omnis quidem instructus exercitus telis ex vallo coniectis protegi posset.

56 Aetolia, Acarnania, Amphilochis per Cassium Longinum et Calvisium Sabinum, ut demonstravimus, receptis temptandam sibi Achaiam ac paulo longius progrediendum existimabat Caesar. Itaque eo Calenum misit eique Sabinum et Cassium cum cohortibus adiungit. Quorum cognito adventu Rutilius Lupus, qui Achaiam missus a Pompeio obtinebat, Isthmum praemunire instituit, ut Achaia Fufium prohiberet. Calenus Delphos, Thebas, Orchomenum voluntate ipsarum civitatum recepit, nonnullas urbes per vim expugnavit, reliquas civitates circummissis legationibus amicitia Caesari conciliare studebat. In his rebus fere erat Fufius occupatus.

57 Haec cum in Achaia atque apud Dyrrachium gererentur, Scipionemque in Macedoniam venisse constaret, non oblitus pristini instituti Caesar mittit ad eum A. Clodium, suum atque illius familiarem, quem ab illo traditum initio et commendatum in suorum necessariorum numero habere instituerat. Huic dat litteras mandataque ad eum; quorum haec erat summa: sese omnia de pace expertum nihil adhuc effecisse: hoc arbitrari[1] vitio factum eorum, quos esse auctores eius rei voluisset, quod sua mandata perferre

---

[1] *MSS.* nihil adhuc arbitrari. *I adopt the correction of Madvig and Meusel.*

and reputation, arranged his army in front of his camp, but in such a way that his third line rested on the rampart, while the whole army when drawn up could be protected by javelins thrown from the rampart.

Aetolia, Acarnania, and the Amphilochi having been recovered through Cassius Longinus and Calvisius Sabinus, as we have shown, Caesar thought that he ought to make an attempt on Achaea and advance a little further. And so he sent Q. Calenus thither, associating with him Sabinus and Cassius with some cohorts. On their arrival becoming known, Rutilius Lupus, who, on commission from Pompeius, was in charge of Achaea, determined to block approach to the Isthmus so as to prevent Fufius from entering Achaea. Calenus recovered Delphi, Thebes, and Orchomenus with the goodwill of the communities themselves, and took some towns by storm. The rest of the communities he endeavored to win over to friendship with Caesar by sending round embassies. Such were mainly the occupations in which Fufius was engaged.

While this was going on in Achaea and at Dyrrachium, and when it was known that Scipio had come into Macedonia, Caesar, mindful of his long-established custom, sends to him their common friend A. Clodius, who had been originally brought to his notice by an introduction from Scipio and whom he had been in the habit of regarding as one of his intimates. To him he gives a letter and instructions to carry to Scipio, of which this was the purport: that, having made every effort on behalf of peace, he thought that the fact that nothing had been done was the fault of those whom he had wished to be the prime movers in the matter, because they feared to carry his

non opportuno tempore ad Pompeium vererentur.
Scipionem ea esse auctoritate, ut non solum libere
quae probasset exponere, sed etiam ex magna parte
compellere atque errantem regere posset; praeesse
autem suo nomine exercitui, ut praeter auctoritatem
vires quoque ad coërcendum haberet. Quod si fecisset, quietem Italiae, pacem provinciarum, salutem
imperii uni omnes acceptam relaturos. Haec ad
eum mandata Clodius refert ac primis diebus, ut
videbatur, libenter auditus reliquis ad colloquium
non admittitur, castigato Scipione a Favonio, ut postea confecto bello reperiebamus, infectaque re sese
ad Caesarem recepit.

58   Caesar, quo facilius equitatum Pompeianum ad
Dyrrachium contineret et pabulatione prohiberet,
aditus duos, quos esse angustos demonstravimus,
magnis operibus praemunivit castellaque his locis
posuit. Pompeius, ubi nihil profici equitatu cognovit, paucis intermissis diebus rursus eum navibus ad
se intra munitiones recipit. Erat summa inopia
pabuli, adeo ut foliis ex arboribus strictis et teneris
harundinum radicibus contusis equos alerent (frumenta enim, quae fuerant intra munitiones sata, con-
sumpserant); cogebantur Corcyra atque Acarnania
longo interiecto navigationis spatio pabulum supportare, quodque erat eius rei minor copia, hordeo
adaugere atque his rationibus equitatum tolerare.
Sed postquam non modo hordeum pabulumque omnibus locis herbaeque desectae, sed etiam frons ex

instructions to Pompeius at an inopportune time. Scipio was a man of such authority that he could not only express with freedom what his judgment approved, but could also to a large extent compel and control one who was going astray; moreover he commanded an army in his own name, so that in addition to authority he also possessed strength to coerce. If he should do this everyone would put down to his sole credit the tranquillity of Italy, the peace of the provinces, the safety of the empire. Clodius carries these instructions to him, and though on the first few days he apparently met with a ready hearing, on subsequent days he is not admitted to a conference, because Scipio had been censured by Favonius, as we found out afterwards when the war was over; and so he returned to Caesar without having effected anything.

To keep the Pompeian cavalry more easily in check 58 at Dyrrachium and to prevent them from foraging, Caesar fortified with large works the two approaches, which, as we have shown, were narrow, and planted forts at these spots. When Pompeius found out that no advantage was gained by the cavalry, after a few days' interval he fetches them back again by sea to his own quarters within the entrenchments. There was a great scarcity of provisions, so much so that they fed their horses on leaves stripped from the trees and on the soft powdered roots of reeds, for they had used up the crops that had been sown within the entrenchments. They were gradually forced to bring up fodder from Corcyra and Acarnania, with a long sea passage intervening, and as the supply of this was deficient, to supplement it with barley and by these devices to keep their horses alive. But when not only the barley and other fodder and the herbs that had been everywhere cut down began to

arboribus deficiebat, corruptis equis macie conandum
sibi aliquid Pompeius de eruptione existimavit.

59   Erant apud Caesarem in equitum numero Allobroges duo fratres, Raucillus et Egus, Adbucilli filii,
qui principatum in civitate multis annis obtinuerat,
singulari virtute homines, quorum opera Caesar
omnibus Gallicis bellis optima fortissimaque erat
usus.   His domi ob has causas amplissimos magistratus mandaverat atque eos extra ordinem in senatum
legendos curaverat agrosque in Gallia ex hostibus
captos praemiaque rei pecuniariae magna tribuerat
locupletesque ex egentibus fecerat.   Hi propter
virtutem non solum apud Caesarem in honore erant,
sed etiam apud exercitum cari habebantur; sed freti
amicitia Caesaris et stulta ac barbara arrogantia elati
despiciebant suos stipendiumque equitum fraudabant
et praedam omnem domum avertebant.   Quibus illi
rebus permoti universi Caesarem adierunt palamque
de eorum iniuriis sunt questi et ad cetera addiderunt
falsum ab his equitum numerum deferri, quorum
stipendium averterent.

60   Caesar neque tempus illud animadversionis esse
existimans et multa virtuti eorum concedens rem
totam distulit; illos secreto castigavit, quod quaestui
equites haberent, monuitque, ut ex sua amicitia omnia
exspectarent et ex praeteritis suis officiis reliqua

fail, but even the foliage from the trees, the horses being rendered useless by emaciation, Pompeius thought that he ought to attempt something in the way of a sortie.

There were with Caesar, among his horsemen, two 59 Allobrogian brothers, Raucillus and Egus, sons of Adbucillus, who had held the chieftainship in the state for many years, men of singular valour, whose very able and valiant cooperation Caesar had enjoyed in all his Gallic wars. He had bestowed on them for these reasons offices of great dignity in their own homes, had arranged that they should be chosen on the senate out of due course, had assigned to them lands in Gaul taken from the enemy and large prizes of money, and had raised them from poverty to wealth. These men, on account of their worth, were not only held in honour by Caesar, but were also regarded with affection in the army; but, relying on Caesar's friendship and puffed up with stupid and barbarous arrogance, they began to despise their countrymen and fraudulently to appropriate the pay of the cavalry and to divert the whole of the plunder to their own homes. Deeply stirred by this conduct, the men approached Caesar in a body and openly complained of their wrong-doings, and added to their other complaints that they were in the habit of sending in a false return of the number of the cavalry in order that they might appropriate their pay.

Caesar, thinking that this was not the time for 60 punishment and overlooking much in consideration of their valour, postponed the whole matter, but privately he took the offenders to task for having made profit out of the cavalry and urged them to expect everything from his friendship, and to judge from his past good offices what they had still to hope

spererant. Magnam tamen haec res illis offensionem
et contemptionem ad omnes attulit, idque ita esse
cum ex aliorum obiectationibus tum etiam ex domes-
tico iudicio atque animi conscientia intellegebant.
Quo pudore adducti et fortasse non se liberari, sed
in aliud tempus reservari arbitrati discedere a nobis
et novam temptare fortunam novasque amicitias
experiri constituerunt. Et cum paucis collocuti
clientibus suis, quibus tantum facinus committere
audebant, primum conati sunt praefectum equitum
C. Volusenum interficere, ut postea bello confecto
cognitum est, ut cum munere aliquo perfugisse
ad Pompeium viderentur; postquam id difficilius
visum est neque facultas perficiendi dabatur, quam
maximas potuerunt pecunias mutuati, proinde ac si
suis satisfacere et fraudata restituere vellent, multis
coëmptis equis ad Pompeium transierunt cum eis,
quos sui consilii participes habebant.

61   Quos Pompeius, quod erant honesto loco nati et
instructi liberaliter magnoque comitatu et multis
iumentis venerant virique fortes habebantur et in
honore apud Caesarem fuerant, quodque novum et
praeter consuetudinem acciderat, omnia sua praesidia
circumduxit atque ostentavit. Nam ante id tempus
nemo aut miles aut eques a Caesare ad Pompeium
transierat, cum paene cotidie a Pompeio ad Caesarem
perfugerent, vulgo vero universi in Epiro atque
Aetolia conscripti milites earumque regionum omnium,

for. The occurrence, however, brought on them great obloquy and contempt in the sight of all, and they understood that this was so not merely from the reproaches of others but also from the judgment of their intimates and from their own conscience. Influenced by this sense of shame and thinking, perhaps, that they were being reserved for punishment on a future occasion rather than let off free, they determined to quit us and hazard a new fortune and make trial of new friendships. And having conferred with a few of their clients, to whom they ventured to submit such an enterprise, they first attempted to kill G. Volusenus, the prefect of horse, as was ascertained afterwards when the war was over, that they might be seen to have deserted to Pompeius with some service to show. But when this seemed rather difficult and no opportunity of carrying it out was afforded, they borrowed as large sums as possible, just as if it was their intention to satisfy their comrades and restore their defalcations, and having bought up a number of horses, they crossed over to Pompeius with those whom they had made the participators of their plans.

And as they were born in a respectable position 61 and were bountifully supplied, and had come with a great retinue and many animals, and were regarded as brave men and had been held in honour by Caesar, and as the occurrence was novel and out of the ordinary course, he conducted them round all his garrisons for purposes of display. For before that time no one, either of foot or horse, had changed sides from Caesar to Pompeius, though men were deserting almost every day from Pompeius to Caesar, and the troops levied in Epirus and Aetolia and from all the regions which were in Caesar's occupation

quae a Caesare tenebantur. Sed hi cognitis omnibus rebus, seu quid in munitionibus perfectum non erat, seu quid a peritioribus rei militaris desiderari videbatur, temporibusque rerum et spatiis locorum, custodiarum varia diligentia animadversa, prout cuiusque eorum, qui negotiis praeerant, aut natura aut studium ferebat, haec ad Pompeium omnia detulerunt.

62 Quibus ille cognitis rebus[1] eruptionisque iam ante capto consilio, ut demonstratum est, tegimenta galeis milites ex viminibus facere atque aggerem iubet comportare. His paratis rebus magnum numerum levis armaturae et sagittariorum aggeremque omnem noctu in scaphas et naves actuarias imponit et de media nocte cohortes LX ex maximis castris praesidiisque deductas ad eam partem munitionum ducit, quae pertinebant ad mare longissimeque a maximis castris Caesaris aberant. Eodem naves, quas demonstravimus, aggere et levis armaturae militibus completas, quasque ad Dyrrachium naves longas habebat, mittit et, quid a quoque fieri velit, praecipit. Ad eas munitiones Caesar Lentulum Marcellinum quaestorem cum legione VIIII positum habebat. Huic, quod valetudine minus commoda utebatur, Fulvium Postumum adiutorem submiserat.

63 Erat eo loco fossa pedum XV et vallum contra hostem in altitudinem pedum X, tantundemque eius valli agger in latitudinem patebat: ab eo in-

---

[1] rebus *omitted in MSS., inserted by me.*

were going over as a rule in mass. But these men having an acquaintance with everything, whether there was any lack of completeness in the lines of investment, or whether anything was thought lacking by men of considerable experience in warfare, and after observation of the times of occurrences and the distance between localities, and the varying watchfulness at the outposts, according to the diversities of natural temperament or zeal on the part of the several officers in charge of affairs—all these things they reported to Pompeius.

Having ascertained these facts and having already 62 planned a sortie, as we have shown, he orders his men to make protective coverings of osier for their helmets and to collect material for earthworks. When these were provided he embarks by night a large number of light-armed men and archers with all the material on board row-boats and merchant-vessels, and about midnight he leads sixty cohorts drawn from his largest camp and outposts to that part of the entrenchments which extended to the sea and was the furthest removed from Caesar's largest camp. To the same place he sends his ships, which, as we explained, had on board the material and the light-armed troops, and the warships which he had at Dyrrachium, and issues orders stating what he wishes each man to do. At these entrenchments Caesar had his quaestor Lentulus Marcellinus posted with the Ninth Legion, and as he was in unsatisfactory health, he had sent up Fulvius Postumus to assist him.

There was in that place a ditch fifteen feet wide 63 and a rampart ten feet high facing the enemy, and the earthwork of this rampart was also ten feet in breadth. And at an interval of six hundred feet

termisso spatio pedum DC alter conversus in contrariam partem erat vallus humiliore paulo munitione. Hoc enim superioribus diebus timens Caesar, ne navibus nostri circumvenirentur, duplicem eo loco fecerat vallum, ut, si ancipiti proelio dimicaretur, posset resisti. Sed operum magnitudo et continens omnium dierum labor, quod milium passuum in circuitu XVII munitiones erat complexus, perficiendi spatium non dabat. Itaque contra mare transversum vallum, qui has duas munitiones coniungeret, nondum perfecerat. Quae res nota erat Pompeio delata per Allobrogas perfugas, magnumque nostris attulerat incommodum. Nam ut ad mare duo cohortes nonae legionis excubuerant, accessere subito prima luce Pompeiani; simul navibus circumvecti milites in exteriorem vallum tela iaciebant, fossaeque aggere complebantur, et legionarii interioris munitionis defensores scalis admotis tormentis cuiusque generis telisque terrebant, magnaque multitudo sagittariorum ab utraque parte circumfundebatur.[1] Multum autem ab ictu lapidum, quod unum nostris erat telum, viminea tegimenta galeis imposita defendebant. Itaque cum omnibus rebus nostri premerentur atque aegre resisterent animadversum est vitium munitionis, quod supra demonstratum est, atque inter duos vallos, qua perfectum opus non erat, Pompeiani[2] navibus expositi

[1] *There is much uncertainty in the text of the whole of this passage, and the sense must remain obscure.*

[2] Pompeiani *Paul:* per mare *MSS., without sense.*

from this there was a second stockade facing in the other direction, with a rampart of rather lower elevation. For on the preceding days Caesar, fearing lest our men should be hemmed in by the fleet, had constructed a double stockade in this spot, so that in case of an attack on both sides it might be possible to hold out. But the magnitude of the works and the continuous toil of every day, since he had taken in entrenchments of seventeen miles circuit, did not allow opportunity of completion. And so he had not yet completed the cross stockade facing the sea to join these two lines. This fact was known to Pompeius, who had been informed of it by the Allobrogian deserters, and it had caused our men great inconvenience. For two cohorts of the Ninth Legion being on sentry duty by the sea, the Pompeians suddenly approached at early dawn; at the same time soldiers conveyed round on shipboard began to hurl javelins at the outer stockade,[1] the ditches were being filled up with earth, the Pompeian legionaries, having brought up ladders, were terrifying the defenders of the inner line with engines of every kind and missiles, and a great multitude of archers were being thrown around them on every side. But the osier coverings placed on their helmets protected them to a great extent from the blows of stones, which were the only weapon our men had. And so when our men were being hard pressed in every way and with difficulty holding their ground, the defect, mentioned above, of the line of entrenchment became observable, and between the two stockades, where the work was not yet finished, the Pompeians, disembarking, took our men in the

[1] The southern line: the *interior munitio* mentioned just after is the northern line.

in aversos nostros impetum fecerunt atque ex utraque
munitione deiectos terga vertere coëgerunt.

64   Hoc tumultu nuntiato Marcellinus cohortes
subsidio nostris laborantibus submittit ex castris;
quae fugientes conspicatae neque illos suo adventu
confirmare potuerunt neque ipsae hostium impetum
tulerunt. Itaque quodcumque addebatur subsidii, id
corruptum timore fugientium terrorem et periculum
augebat; hominum enim multitudine receptus im-
pediebatur. In eo proelio cum gravi vulnere esset
affectus aquilifer et a viribus deficeretur, conspicatus equites nostros, "hanc ego," inquit, "et vivus
multos per annos magna diligentia defendi et nunc
moriens eadem fide Caesari restituo. Nolite, obsecro,
committere, quod ante in exercitu Caesaris non
accidit, ut rei militaris dedecus admittatur, incolu-
memque ad eum deferte." Hoc casu aquila conser-
vatur omnibus primae cohortis centurionibus interfectis praeter principem priorem.

65   Iamque Pompeiani magna caede nostrorum castris
Marcellini appropinquabant non mediocri terrore
illato reliquis cohortibus, et M. Antonius, qui proximum locum praesidiorum tenebat, ea re nuntiata
cum cohortibus XII descendens ex loco superiore
cernebatur. Cuius adventus Pompeianos compressit
nostrosque firmavit, ut se ex maximo timore colli-
gerent. Neque multo post Caesar significatione per
castella fumo facta, ut erat superioris temporis consuetudo, deductis quibusdam cohortibus ex praesidiis

rear on both sides and, dislodging them from each line, compelled them to take to flight.

On the announcement of this sudden attack Marcellinus sends up some cohorts from the camp to the support of our suffering troops. And these, seeing them fleeing, could not strengthen them by their coming and themselves failed to sustain the onset of the enemy. And so every additional reinforcement that was sent up was demoralized by the fright of the fugitives and increased the terror and the peril; for retreat was hindered by the multitude of men. An eagle-bearer who had been seriously wounded in this battle and whose strength was now failing, seeing our horsemen, exclaimed: "This eagle in my life I defended with great care for many years, and now, dying, I restore it to Caesar with the same loyalty. Do not, I beseech, suffer a military disgrace to take place, which has never happened before in Caesar's army, and convey it to him in safety." By this chance the eagle was preserved, though all the centurions of the first cohort were slain except the senior centurion of the second maniple.

Already the Pompeians, after great slaughter of our men, were approaching the camp of Marcellinus, causing no slight terror in the rest of the cohorts, when M. Antonius, who held the nearest position among the outposts, after receiving the news was seen coming down with twelve cohorts from the higher ground. His arrival checked the Pompeians and encouraged our men, so that they recovered themselves from their extreme fear. And not long after Caesar, signalling by smoke from one redoubt to another, according to his previous custom, brought down some cohorts from the garrisons and came to

eodem venit. Qui cognito detrimento cum animadvertisset Pompeium extra munitiones egressum,
castra secundum mare munire,[1] ut libere pabulari
posset nec minus aditum navibus haberet, commutata
ratione belli, quoniam propositum non tenuerat,
castra iuxta Pompeium munire iussit.

66   Qua perfecta munitione animadversum est a specu-
latoribus Caesaris, cohortes quasdam, quod instar
legionis videretur, esse post silvam et in vetera castra
duci. Castrorum sic situs erat. Superioribus diebus
nona Caesaris legio, cum se obiecisset Pompeianis
copiis atque opere, ut demonstravimus, circum-
muniret, castra eo loco posuit. Haec silvam
quandam contingebant neque longius a mari passibus CCC aberant. Post mutato consilio quibusdam de
causis Caesar paulo ultra eum locum castra transtulit,
paucisque intermissis diebus eadem Pompeius occupaverat et, quod eo loco plures erat legiones habi-
turus, relicto interiore vallo maiorem adiecerat munitionem. Ita minora castra inclusa maioribus cas-
telli atque arcis locum obtinebant. Item ab angulo
castrorum sinistro munitionem ad flumen perduxerat
circiter passus CCCC, quo liberius a periculo milites
aquarentur. Sed is quoque mutato consilio quibusdam de causis, quas commemorari necesse non est,
eo loco excesserat. Ita complures dies inania[2]
manserant castra; munitiones quidem omnes inte-
grae erant.

[1] munire *added by Köchly, not in MSS.*
[2] inania *not in MSS., added by Madvig.*

the same place. And having learnt of the loss sustained, on observing that Pompeius had gone out of his lines and was entrenching a camp near the sea so as to be able to get fodder freely and to have none the less a way of approach for his ships, he changed his tactics, since he had failed to gain his purpose, and ordered his men to entrench a camp close to Pompeius.

When this entrenchment was finished it was 66 noticed by Caesar's scouts that certain cohorts, enough to seem equivalent to a legion, were behind the wood[1] and were being led to the old camp. The position of the camp was this: on the preceding days Caesar's Ninth Legion, after it had confronted the Pompeian forces and was investing them (as we have shown) with earthworks, encamped in that spot. This camp bordered on a wood and was not more than three hundred paces from the sea. Afterwards changing his plans for certain reasons, Caesar transferred his camp a little beyond that spot, and after a few days' interval Pompeius had occupied the same camp, and as he was likely to have several legions in that place he had abandoned the inner rampart and had added a larger entrenchment. So the smaller camp included in a larger one took the place of a redoubt and citadel. Also from the left corner of his camp he had drawn a line of entrenchments to the river, about four hundred paces long, in order that his men might get water with more freedom from risk. But he, too, changing his plan for certain reasons which it is not necessary to mention, had quitted that place. So for many days the camp had remained empty; as for the earthworks, they were all intact.

[1] A wood near the coast and between the River Lesnikia and Caesar's lines.

67 Eo signa legionis illata speculatores Caesari renuntiarunt. Hoc idem visum ex superioribus quibusdam castellis confirmaverunt. Is locus aberat a novis Pompei castris circiter passus quingentos. Hanc legionem sperans Caesar se opprimere posse et cupiens eius diei detrimentum sarcire, reliquit in opere cohortes duas, quae speciem munitionis[a] praeberent; ipse diverso itinere quam potuit occultissime reliquas cohortes, numero XXXIII, in quibus erat legio nona multis amissis centurionibus deminutoque militum numero, ad legionem Pompei castraque minora duplici acie eduxit. Neque eum prima opinio fefellit. Nam et pervenit prius, quam Pompeius sentire posset, et tametsi erant munitiones castrorum magnae, tamen sinistro cornu, ubi erat ipse, celeriter aggressus Pompeianos ex vallo deturbavit. Erat obiectus portis ericius. Hic paulisper est pugnatum, cum irrumpere nostri conarentur, illi castra defenderent, fortissime Tito Pulione, cuius opera proditum exercitum C. Antoni demonstravimus, eo loco propugnante. Sed tamen nostri virtute vicerunt excisoque ericio primo in maiora castra, post etiam in castellum, quod erat inclusum maioribus castris, irruperunt, quo pulsa legio sese receperat, et nonnullos ibi repugnantes interfecerunt.

[a] munitionis *MSS.*: munientium *Meusel.*

[1] Referring back to *eo* in the first line of this chapter, indicating the enlarged camp, described in ch. 66, near the River Lesnikia.

[2] The camp entrenched by Pompeius on the spot where he had broken through Caesar's lines, as described in ch. 65.

The scouts reported to Caesar that the standards of the legion had been borne thither. They assured him that the same thing had been seen from some of the higher redoubts. This place[1] was about five hundred paces from the new camp[2] of Pompeius. Caesar, hoping to be able to crush this legion and anxious to repair the loss of that day, left two cohorts at the work to give an appearance of fortifying. Himself taking a divergent route in the utmost secrecy, he led out in double line towards Pompeius' legion and the smaller camp[3] the remaining cohorts, numbering thirty-three, among which was the Ninth Legion, which had suffered the loss of many centurions and a diminution of the rank and file. Nor did his original idea fail him. For he arrived before Pompeius could be aware of it, and though the defences of the camp were large, yet by attacking quickly with the left wing, where he himself was, he drove the Pompeians from the rampart. Beams studded with spikes barred the gates. Here there was fighting for a while, our men attempting to break in, the others defending their camp, Titus Pulio, by whose aid we have said that the army of G. Antonius was betrayed, leading the fighting with the utmost bravery at that spot. Nevertheless our men won by their endurance, and cutting down the beams burst first into the larger camp, then also into the fort which was included within the larger camp, whither the legion when routed had retired for shelter. There they slew a few men who continued the struggle.

[3] The old interior portion of the enlarged camp near the Lesnikia. In ch. 66 this smaller portion is said to have served as a *castellum*, and it is so styled at the end of the present chapter.

68   Sed fortuna, quae plurimum potest cum in reliquis
rebus tum praecipue in bello, parvis momentis
magnas rerum commutationes efficit; ut tum accidit.
Munitionem, quam pertinere a castris ad flumen
supra demonstravimus, dextri Caesaris cornu cohortes ignorantia loci sunt secutae, cum portam
quaererent castrorumque eam munitionem esse arbitrarentur.   Quod cum esset animadversum con-
iunctam esse flumini, prorutis munitionibus defen-
dente nullo transcenderunt, omnisque noster equitatus eas cohortes est secutus.

69   Interim Pompeius hac satis longa interiecta mora
et re nuntiata v legiones ab opere deductas subsidio suis duxit, eodemque tempore equitatus eius
nostris equitibus appropinquabat, et acies instructa
a nostris, qui castra occupaverant, cernebatur, omniaque sunt subito mutata. Legio Pompeiana celeris
spe subsidii confirmata ab decumana porta resistere
conabatur atque ultro in nostros impetum faciebat.
Equitatus Caesaris, quod angusto itinere per aggeres
ascendebat, receptui suo timens initium fugae faciebat. Dextrum cornu, quod erat a sinistro seclusum,
terrore equitum animadverso, ne intra munitionem
opprimeretur, ea parte, quam proruerat, sese recipiebat, ac plerique ex his, ne in angustias inciderent,
ex x pedum munitione se in fossas praecipitabant,
primisque oppressis reliqui per horum corpora
salutem sibi atque exitum pariebant. Sinistro cornu

But fortune, which has great influence in affairs   68
generally and especially in war, produces by a slight
disturbance of balance important changes in human
affairs; and so it happened then.   The cohorts
of Caesar's right wing in their ignorance of the
locality followed up the entrenchment which, as
we have explained above, extended from the camp
to the river, looking for the gate, and supposing that
these lines were a part of the camp.   And when
they observed that they only served to connect the
camp with the river they threw down the defences,
no one opposing them, and crossed over, and our
whole cavalry followed the cohorts.

Meanwhile, a fairly long interval of time had   69
elapsed, and the news having reached Pompeius,
he withdrew five legions from their work and led
them to the relief of his men; and at the same
time his cavalry approached our horsemen, and his
serried ranks came into the view of our men who
had occupied the camp.   At once everything was
changed.   The Pompeian legion, encouraged by the
hope of speedy succour, attempted resistance by the
decuman gate, and taking the aggressive began to
attack our men.   Caesar's cavalry, fearing for its
retreat, as it was mounting by a narrow track over
the earthworks, began to flee.   The right wing, cut
off from the left, observing the panic among the
cavalry, to avoid being overwhelmed within the defences began to withdraw by the part of the rampart
which it had levelled; and many of these men, fearing that they might get involved in the cramped
space, flung themselves from the ten-foot rampart
into the fosses, and when the first were crushed
the rest tried to attain safety and a way of escape over
their bodies.   On the left wing the soldiers, seeing

milites, cum ex vallo Pompeium adesse et suos
fugere cernerent, veriti, ne angustiis intercluderentur, cum extra et intus hostem haberent, eodem,
quo venerant, receptu sibi consulebant, omniaque
erant tumultus, timoris, fugae plena, adeo ut, cum
Caesar signa fugientium manu prenderet et consistere iuberet, alii admissis equis eodem cursu
confugerent, alii metu[1] etiam signa dimitterent,
neque quisquam omnino consisteret.

70   His tantis malis haec subsidia succurrebant, quo
minus omnis deleretur exercitus, quod Pompeius
insidias timens, credo, quod haec praeter spem
acciderant eius, qui paulo ante ex castris fugientes
suos conspexerat, munitionibus appropinquare aliquamdiu non audebat, equitesque eius angustis
spatiis atque his ab Caesaris militibus occupatis ad
insequendum tardabantur. Ita parvae res magnum
in utramque partem momentum habuerunt. Munitiones enim a castris ad flumen perductae expugnatis iam castris Pompei prope iam[2] expeditam
Caesaris victoriam interpellaverunt, eadem res
celeritate insequentium tardata nostris salutem
attulit.

71   Duobus his unius diei proeliis Caesar desideravit
milites DCCCCLX et notos equites Romanos Tuticanum
Gallum, senatoris filium, C. Fleginatem Placentia,
A. Granium Puteolis, M. Sacrativirum Capua, tribunos militum[3] et centuriones XXXII; sed horum
omnium pars magna in fossis munitionibusque et
fluminis ripis oppressa suorum in terrore ac fuga sine

---

[1] metu *Dinter:* ex metu MSS. *There may be further corruption in this passage.*
[2] prope iam *Voss:* propriam MSS.
[3] *A numeral giving the number of tribunes slain has probably
dropped out.*

294

from the rampart the approach of Pompeius and the flight of their own men, fearing that they might be cut off in the narrow space, as they had the enemy both inside and outside the camp, took counsel for themselves, retreating by the way by which they had come; and every place was full of disorder, panic, and flight, so much so that when Caesar grasped the standards of the fugitives and bade them halt, some without slackening speed fled at full gallop, others in their fear even let go their colours, nor did a single one of them halt.

The only relief that came to mitigate these great 70 disasters, preventing the destruction of the whole army, was the fact that Pompeius, fearing, I suppose, an ambuscade, since these events had happened contrary to his expectation, for a little while before he had seen his men fleeing from the camp, did not venture for a long time to approach the lines, and his horsemen were hindered in their pursuit by the narrowness of the passages, especially as they were occupied by Caesar's troops. So have small events often turned the scale of fortune for good or evil. For the lines which were drawn from the camp to the river interrupted the victory of Caesar, which when once Pompeius' camp had been stormed was all but assured, and the same circumstance by checking the speed of the pursuers brought safety to our men.

In these two battles in one day Caesar lost nine 71 hundred and sixty men and some well-known Roman knights—Tuticanus the Gaul, son of a senator, G. Fleginas of Placentia, A. Granius of Puteoli, M. Sacrativir of Capua—and thirty-two military tribunes and centurions; but the majority of these were overwhelmed at the ditches and lines of investment and river-banks in the panic and flight of

ullo vulnere interiit; signaque sunt militaria amissa
XXXII. Pompeius eo proelio imperator est appellatus. Hoc nomen obtinuit atque ita se postea
salutari passus est, sed neque in litteris scribere est
solitus, neque in fascibus insignia laureae praetulit. [1]
At Labienus, cum ab eo impetravisset, ut sibi
captivos tradi iuberet, omnes productos ostentationis, ut videbatur, causa, quo maior perfugae
fides haberetur, commilitones appellans et magna
verborum contumelia interrogans, solerentne veterani milites fugere, in omnium conspectu interfecit.

72   His rebus tantum fiduciae ac spiritus Pompeianis
accessit, ut non de ratione belli cogitarent, sed vicisse
iam viderentur. Non illi paucitatem nostrorum militum, non iniquitatem loci atque angustias praeoccupatis castris et ancipitem terrorem intra extraque
munitiones, non abscisum in duas partes exercitum,
cum altera alteri auxilium ferre non posset, causae
fuisse cogitabant. Non ad haec addebant non concursu acri facto, non proelio dimicatum, sibique ipsos
multitudine atque angustiis maius attulisse detrimentum, quam ab hoste accepissent. Non denique
communes belli casus recordabantur, quam parvulae
saepe causae vel falsae suspicionis vel terroris repentini vel obiectae religionis magna detrimenta intulissent, quotiens vel ducis vitio vel culpa tribuni in

---

[1] *This sentence is imperfect in the MSS. I have adopted what
seems a reasonable correction.*

their comrades and perished without any wound; and thirty-two military standards were lost. In this battle Pompeius received the appellation of Imperator. To this title he adhered and afterwards allowed himself to be saluted as such, but he was never wont to use the ascription in his dispatches, nor did he display the insignia of the laurel on his fasces. But Labienus, having induced Pompeius to order the captives to be handed over to him, brought them all out, apparently for the sake of display, to increase his own credit as a traitor, and, styling them "comrades" and asking them with much insolence of language whether veterans were in the habit of running away, killed them in the sight of all.

By these successes the Pompeians gained so much 72 confidence and spirit that instead of forming a plan of campaign they regarded themselves as having already conquered. They did not reflect that the cause of their success had been the small number of our troops, the unfavourable conditions of the site and the narrow space, when they had forestalled us in the occupation of the camp; the twofold panic, within and without the fortifications; the severance of the army into two parts, one being unable to bear aid to the other. They did not consider further that they had not fought in a sharp encounter or in a pitched battle, and that our men had brought a greater loss upon themselves by their numbers and the confined space than they had suffered from the enemy. Finally, they did not recollect the common chances of warfare, how often trifling causes, originating in a false suspicion, a sudden alarm, or a religious scruple, have entailed great disasters, whensoever a mistake has been made in an army through the incapacity of a general or the fault of a

exercitu esset offensum; sed, proinde ac si virtute vicissent, neque ulla commutatio rerum posset accidere, per orbem terrarum fama ac litteris victoriam eius diei concelebrabant.

73   Caesar a superioribus consiliis depulsus omnem sibi commutandam belli rationem existimavit. Itaque uno tempore praesidiis omnibus deductis et oppugnatione dimissa coactoque in unum locum exercitu contionem apud milites habuit hortatusque est, ne ea, quae accidissent, graviter ferrent neve his rebus terrerentur multisque secundis proeliis unum adversum et id mediocre opponerent. Habendam fortunae gratiam, quod Italiam sine aliquo vulnere cepissent, quod duas Hispanias bellicosissimorum hominum peritissimis atque exercitatissimis ducibus pacavissent, quod finitimas frumentariasque provincias in potestatem redegissent; denique recordari debere, qua felicitate inter medias hostium classes oppletis non solum portibus, sed etiam litoribus omnes incolumes essent transportati. Si non omnia caderent secunda, fortunam esse industria sublevandam. Quod esset acceptum detrimenti, cuiusvis potius quam suae culpae debere tribui. Locum se aequum ad dimicandum dedisse, potitum esse hostium castris, expulisse ac superasse pugnantes. Sed sive ipsorum perturbatio sive error aliquis sive etiam fortuna partam iam praesentemque victoriam interpellavisset, dandam omnibus operam, ut acceptum incommodum virtute sarciretur. Quod si esset factum, futurum, uti ad

tribune; but just as if their victory were due to their valour and no change of fortune could occur, by reports and dispatches they proceeded to celebrate throughout the world the victory of that day.

Caesar, driven from his former plans, came to the 73 conclusion that he must alter his whole method of campaign. And so simultaneously withdrawing all his garrisons, abandoning the siege, and gathering all his army together, he delivered an harangue before his troops and exhorted them not to take to heart what had happened nor to be terrified by these events and set one reverse, and that a slight one, against many successful battles. They should be grateful to fortune that they had captured Italy without a disaster of some kind; that they had pacified the two Spains, the home of most warlike races, with generals of the utmost skill and experience; that they had brought under their own control the neighbouring corn-supplying provinces; finally, they should remember with what good fortune they had all been transported in safety through the midst of the enemy's fleets when not only the harbours but even the shores were crowded with their foes. If everything did not fall out favourably, they must assist fortune by their own energy. The loss that had been sustained should be attributed to the fault of anyone rather than himself. He had given them a favourable situation for fighting, he had gained possession of the enemy's camp, he had expelled and overcome them in fight. But whether it was their own nervousness or some blunder, or even a chance of fortune that had interrupted a victory already won and within their hands, they must all exert themselves to repair by their valour the damage they had sustained. If this were done, the

Gergoviam contigisset, ut detrimentum in bonum verteret, atque qui ante dimicare timuissent, ultro se proelio offerrent.

74 Hac habita contione nonnullos signiferos ignominia notavit ac loco movit. Exercitui quidem omni tantus incessit ex incommodo dolor tantumque studium infamiae sarciendae, ut nemo aut tribuni aut centurionis imperium desideraret, et sibi quisque etiam poenae loco graviores imponeret labores, simulque omnes arderent cupiditate pugnandi, cum superioris etiam ordinis nonnulli ratione permoti manendum eo loco et rem proelio committendam existimarent. Contra ea Caesar neque satis militibus perterritis confidebat spatiumque interponendum ad recreandos animos putabat, et relictis munitionibus magnopere rei frumentariae timebat.

75 Itaque nulla interposita mora sauciorum modo et aegrorum habita ratione impedimenta omnia silentio prima nocte ex castris Apolloniam praemisit. Haec conquiescere ante iter confectum vetuit. His una legio missa praesidio est. His explicitis rebus duas in castris legiones retinuit, reliquas de quarta vigilia compluribus portis eductas eodem itinere praemisit parvoque spatio intermisso, ut et militare institutum servaretur, et quam serissime eius profectio cognosceretur conclamari iussit statimque egressus et novissimum agmen consecutus celeriter ex conspectu castrorum discessit. Neque vero Pompeius cognito consilio eius moram ullam ad insequendum intulit;

300

result would be that the loss would be turned to advantage, as had happened at Gergovia, and those who had previously feared to fight would voluntarily offer themselves for battle.

After delivering this harangue he publicly dis- 74 graced and degraded some standard-bearers. The army, as a whole, was seized with such remorse as a result of the disaster, and such eagerness to repair the discredit, that no one waited for the commands of tribune or centurion, and each man imposed even heavier tasks on himself by way of penalty, and all were alike inflamed by an eager desire for fighting, while some even of higher rank, moved by reflection, thought that they ought to remain on the spot and entrust the issue to a pitched battle. On the other hand, Caesar had not sufficient confidence in his panic-stricken troops and thought that an interval should be allowed to restore their spirits; and if he abandoned his lines he was in great fear for his corn supply.

And so, with only such delay as attention to the 75 sick and wounded required, he quietly sent on all his baggage-train from the camp at nightfall to Apollonia and forbade it to stop for rest till the journey was finished, and one legion was sent to protect it. Having arranged these matters, he kept back two legions in camp and led out the rest at the fourth watch by several gates and sent them on by the same route; and after a short interval he ordered the signal to be given in order that the military custom might be observed and that his departure might be known as late as possible; and at once marching out and following the rearguard, he quickly departed out of sight of the camp. Nor, on the other hand, did Pompeius, when he learnt of his design, allow any delay in pursuit, but with the same object in

sed eodem spectans, si itinere impeditos perterritos
deprehendere posset, exercitum e castris eduxit
equitatumque praemisit ad novissimum agmen de-
morandum, neque consequi potuit, quod multum
expedito itinere antecesserat Caesar. Sed cum
ventum esset ad flumen Genusum, quod ripis erat
impeditis, consecutus equitatus novissimos proelio
detinebat. Huic suos Caesar equites opposuit expe-
ditosque antesignanos admiscuit CCCC; qui tantum
profecerunt, ut equestri proelio commisso pellerent
omnes compluresque interficerent ipsique incolumes
se ad agmen reciperent.

76   Confecto iusto itinere eius diei Caesar traductoque
exercitu flumen Genusum veteribus suis in castris
contra Asparagium consedit militesque omnes intra
vallum continuit equitatumque per causam pabulandi
emissum confestim decumana porta in castra se
recipere iussit. Simili ratione Pompeius confecto eius diei itinere in suis veteribus castris ad
Asparagium consedit. Eius milites, quod ab opere
integris munitionibus vacabant, alii lignandi pabu-
landique causa longius progrediebantur, alii, quod
subito consilium profectionis ceperant magna parte
impedimentorum et sarcinarum relicta, ad haec
repetenda invitati propinquitate superiorum castrorum, depositis in contubernio armis, vallum
relinquebant. Quibus ad sequendum impeditis
Caesar, quod fore providerat, meridiano fere tempore
signo profectionis dato exercitum educit duplicatoque

view, hoping to overtake the foe in the confusion and alarm of a difficult march, led his army from the camp and sent forward his horse to delay the rearguard, but was unable to overtake them, because Caesar, being in light marching order, had gone far ahead. But when they reached the River Genusus, with its difficult banks, the cavalry following up engaged and hindered the rearguard. Caesar opposed his own horsemen to them, mixing with them four hundred light-armed front-rank men, who gained such success that, engaging in a cavalry skirmish, they repelled them all, slaying many, and withdrew unhurt to the main body.

Having completed his full march for that day, 76 and having taken his army across the River Genusus, Caesar established himself in his old camp over against Asparagium and kept all his men within the rampart of the camp, and ordered his cavalry, which had been sent out under the pretence of foraging, to return to camp at once by the decuman gate. In the same way Pompeius, having finished his day's march, sat down in his old camp at Asparagium. Of his soldiers, who were free from work owing to the fortifications being intact, some were going to a distance for the purpose of getting wood and fodder; others, who had left behind a great part of their baggage-train and accoutrements, when they suddenly formed the design of setting out, being induced by the propinquity of their last camp to fetch them back, had deposited their arms in their quarters and were leaving the ramparts. As they were thus hindered from pursuing, Caesar, having foreseen that this would happen, gave the signal for departure, and about noon led out his army, and doing a double march this

eius diei itinere VIII milia passuum ex eo loco procedit;
quod facere Pompeius discessu militum non potuit.

77   Postero die Caesar similiter praemissis prima nocte
impedimentis de quarta vigilia ipse egreditur, ut, si
qua esset imposita dimicandi necessitas, subitum
casum expedito exercitu subiret. Hoc idem reliquis
fecit diebus. Quibus rebus perfectum est, ut altissimis fluminibus atque impeditissimis itineribus
nullum acciperet incommodum. Pompeius primi
diei mora illata et reliquorum dierum frustra labore
suscepto, cum se magnis itineribus extenderet et
praegressos consequi cuperet, quarto die finem
sequendi fecit atque alius sibi consilium capiendum
existimavit.

78   Caesari ad saucios deponendos, stipendium exercitui dandum, socios confirmandos, praesidium
urbibus relinquendum necesse erat adire Apolloniam.
Sed his rebus tantum temporis tribuit, quantum
erat properanti necesse; timens Domitio, ne adventu
Pompei praeoccuparetur, ad eum omni celeritate
et studio incitatus ferebatur. Totius autem rei consilium his rationibus explicabat, ut, si Pompeius
eodem contenderet, abductum illum a mari atque
ab eis copiis, quas Dyrrachii comparaverat, abstractum[1]
pari condicione belli secum decertare cogeret; si in
Italiam transiret, coniuncto exercitu cum Domitio
per Illyricum Italiae subsidio proficisceretur; si

[1] MSS. *have* frumento ac commeatu *before* abstractum.
I follow Schneider and others in omitting the words.

day, he advanced about eight miles from this place. This Pompeius was unable to do owing to the dispersal of his men.

On the next day Caesar, having in the same way 77 sent on his baggage-train at nightfall, himself marched out at the fourth watch, so that if any necessity for fighting should be laid on him he might meet the sudden emergency with a lightly equipped force. He did the same thing on the following days. By which means it resulted that, notwithstanding the very deep streams and the extremely difficult routes, he sustained no damage. For Pompeius, after the delay caused on the first day and the toil undertaken to no purpose on the subsequent days, pressing forward as he did by forced marches in his eagerness to overtake the troops in front of him, ended his pursuit on the fourth day and concluded that he must adopt a different plan.

It was necessary for Caesar to go to Apollonia for 78 the purpose of depositing his wounded, paying his army, encouraging his allies, and leaving garrisons for the towns. But to these measures he assigned only so much time as the hurry of his movements allowed. Fearing for Domitius, lest he should be taken unawares by the arrival of Pompeius, Caesar hastened to him with all speed and urgent endeavour. Now he was evolving his general plan of campaign with various contingencies in view: if Pompeius should hurry to the same place he would compel him, when drawn away from the sea and separated from the stores that he had gathered at Dyrrachium, to fight with him under equal conditions of warfare; if he should cross into Italy he would join his army with that of Domitius and set out through Illyricum to succour Italy; if Pompeius

Apolloniam Oricumque oppugnare et se omni maritima ora excludere conaretur, obsesso Scipione
necessario illum suis auxilium ferre cogeret. Itaque
praemissis nuntiis ad Cn. Domitium Caesar ei scripsit
et, quid fieri vellet, ostendit, praesidioque Apolloniae
cohortibus IIII, Lissi I, III Orici relictis, quique erant
ex vulneribus aegri depositis, per Epirum atque Atha-
maniam iter facere coepit. Pompeius quoque de
Caesaris consilio coniectura iudicans ad Scipionem
properandum sibi existimabat: si Caesar iter illo
haberet, ut subsidium Scipioni ferret; si ab ora
maritima Oricoque discedere nollet, quod legiones
equitatumque ex Italia exspectaret, ipse ut omnibus
copiis Domitium aggrederetur.

79   His de causis uterque eorum celeritati studebat,
et suis ut esset auxilio, et ad opprimendos adversarios ne occasioni temporis deesset. Sed Caesarem
Apollonia a directo itinere averterat; Pompeius
per Candaviam iter in Macedoniam expeditum
habebat. Accessit etiam ex improviso aliud incommodum, quod Domitius, qui dies complures
castris Scipionis castra collata habuisset, rei frumentariae causa ab eo discesserat et Heracliam,
quae est subiecta Candaviae,[1] iter fecerat, ut ipsa
fortuna illum obicere Pompeio videretur. Haec
ad id tempus Caesar ignorabat. Simul a Pompeio litteris per omnes provincias civitatesque dimissis proelio ad Dyrrachium facto latius inflatius-
que multo, quam res erat gesta, fama percrebuerat,
pulsum fugere Caesarem paene omnibus copiis

---

[1] *The words* quae est subiecta Candaviae, *though found in all
the MSS., should probably be omitted.*

should attempt to besiege Apollonia and Oricum and
to exclude him from the whole coast, he would
blockade Scipio, and so compel Pompeius of necessity to take aid to his own people. And so Caesar
sent on messengers and wrote to Gn. Domitius explaining what he wanted done; and leaving a garrison
of four cohorts at Apollonia, one at Lissus, and three at
Oricum, and depositing at various places those who
were suffering from wounds, he began his march
through Epirus and Athamania. Pompeius also,
forming a conjecture as to Caesar's plans, thought
it his duty to hasten to Scipio, so that if Caesar was
marching thither he should go to the aid of Scipio,
but if Caesar did not choose to leave the coast and
the district of Oricum, waiting for his legions and
cavalry from Italy, he should himself attack Domitius
in full force.

For these reasons each of them aimed at celerity 79
of movement, both to succour his own allies, and not
to miss the opportunity that any moment might afford
of crushing his adversaries. But Apollonia had turned
Caesar aside from the direct route, and Pompeius was
marching in light equipment through Candavia into
Macedonia. Another unforeseen difficulty also arose in
the fact that Domitius, whose camp had been pitched
over against that of Scipio for several days, had moved
away from him for foraging purposes and had marched
to Heraclia, which lies close under Candavia, so that
fortune itself seemed to expose him to the attack of
Pompeius. Of this, however, Caesar was till then
ignorant. At the same time, letters having been sent
by Pompeius through all the provinces and communities after the battle of Dyrrachium, couched in a more
exaggerated and inflated style than the facts war-
ranted, a report had spread abroad that Caesar had

amissis; haec itinera infesta reddiderat, haec civitates nonnullas ab eius amicitia avertebat. Quibus accidit rebus, ut pluribus dimissi itineribus a Caesare ad Domitium et a Domitio ad Caesarem nulla ratione iter conficere possent. Sed Allobroges, Raucilli atque Egi familiares, quos perfugisse ad Pompeium demonstravimus, conspicati in itinere exploratores Domitii, seu pristina sua consuetudine, quod una in Gallia bella gesserant, seu gloria elati cuncta, ut erant acta, exposuerunt et Caesaris profectionem et adventum Pompei docuerunt. A quibus Domitius certior factus vix IIII horarum spatio antecedens hostium beneficio periculum vitavit et ad Aeginium, quod est oppidum obiectum[1] Thessaliae, Caesari venienti occurrit.

80   Coniuncto exercitu Caesar Gomphos pervenit, quod est oppidum primum Thessaliae venientibus ab Epiro; quae gens paucis ante mensibus ultro ad Caesarem legatos miserat, ut suis omnibus facultatibus uteretur, praesidiumque ab eo militum petierat. Sed eo fama iam praecurrerat, quam supra docuimus, de proelio Dyrrachino, quod multis auxerat partibus. Itaque Androsthenes, praetor Thessaliae, cum se victoriae Pompei comitem esse mallet quam socium Caesaris in rebus adversis, omnem ex agris multitudinem servorum ac liberorum in oppidum cogit portasque praecludit et ad Scipionem Pompeiumque nuntios mittit, ut sibi subsidio veniant: se confidere

----

[1] oppidum obiectum *Meusel*: obiectum oppositumque *MSS*.

been beaten and was in flight with the loss of nearly all his forces. This rumour had made the routes full of danger, and was drawing off some of the communities from their friendship with him. In consequence of this it happened that persons sent by various routes from Caesar to Domitius and from Domitius to Caesar could by no means finish their journey. But the Allobroges, friends of Raucillus and Egus, who, as we have explained, had deserted to Pompeius, having seen on the route some scouts of Domitius, either by reason of their old intimacy because they had waged war together in Gaul, or in the elation of vainglory, set before them everything that had happened, and told them of the departure of Caesar and the arrival of Pompeius. Domitius, who was scarcely four hours ahead, receiving this information from them, escaped his peril thanks to the foe, and met Caesar on his way to Aeginium, a town which lies over against Thessaly.

With his army thus united Caesar arrived at 80 Gomphi, the first town in Thessaly as one comes from Epirus: a few months before, the people had voluntarily sent envoys to Caesar bidding him use all their resources, and had asked him for a garrison of troops. But the rumour which we have mentioned above about the battle at Dyrrachium, which it had considerably exaggerated, had already outstripped him. And so Androsthenes, governor of Thessaly, preferring to share the victory of Pompeius rather than be associated with Caesar in adversity, compels the whole multitude of slaves and freedmen to come from the fields to the town, shuts the gates, and sends messengers to Scipio and Pompeius asking them to come to his aid, saying that he has confidence in the defences of the town if succour is

munitionibus oppidi, si celeriter succurratur; longinquam oppugnationem sustinere non posse. Scipio
discessu exercituum ab Dyrrachio cognito Larisam
legiones adduxerat; Pompeius nondum Thessaliae
appropinquabat. Caesar castris munitis scalas musculosque ad repentinam oppugnationem fieri et crates
parari iussit. Quibus rebus effectis cohortatus milites
docuit, quantum usum haberet ad sublevandam omnium rerum inopiam potiri oppido pleno atque opulento, simul reliquis civitatibus huius urbis exemplo
inferre terrorem et id fieri celeriter, priusquam auxilia
concurrerent. Itaque usus singulari militum studio
eodem, quo venerat, die post horam nonam oppidum
altissimis moenibus oppugnare aggressus ante solis
occasum expugnavit et ad diripiendum militibus concessit statimque ab oppido castra movit et Metropolim venit, sic ut nuntios expugnati oppidi famamque
antecederet.

81   Metropolitae primum eodem usi consilio isdem
permoti rumoribus portas clauserunt murosque armatis compleverunt; sed postea casu civitatis Gomphensis cognito ex captivis, quos Caesar ad murum
producendos curaverat, portas aperuerunt. Quibus
diligentissime conservatis collata fortuna Metropolitum cum casu Gomphensium nulla Thessaliae fuit
civitas praeter Larisaeos, qui magnis exercitibus
Scipionis tenebantur, quin Caesari parerent atque

brought quickly, but that he cannot hold out against a long siege. Scipio, having learnt of the departure of the armies from Dyrrachium, had brought his legions to Larisa. Pompeius was not yet near Thessaly. Caesar, having made an entrenched camp, ordered ladders and mantlets for a hasty siege to be made and hurdles to be got ready. When these measures had been taken he exhorted his troops and explained to them how useful it would be for the purpose of alleviating the general scarcity to get possession of a well-filled and opulent town, and at the same time to strike terror into the remaining communities by the example of this town, and that this should be done quickly before reinforcements could come together. And so, experiencing the utmost zeal on the part of his troops, he began to besiege the town, which had very high walls, on the very day of his arrival after the ninth hour, and took it by storm before sunset, and gave it over to his men for plunder. He then immediately moved his camp away from the town and came to Metropolis so quickly as to outstrip all news and rumour of the storming of the town.

The Metropolitans, at first following the same 81 policy, influenced by the same rumours as the others, closed their gates and manned their walls with armed men; but afterwards learning from captives, whom Caesar had directed to be produced before the walls, of the fall of the town of Gomphi, they opened their gates. The inhabitants were most carefully preserved from harm, and when their fortune was compared with the fate of the men of Gomphi there was no state of Thessaly, with the exception of the Larisaeans, who were held in check by the large armies of Scipio, that did not obey Caesar and

311

imperata facerent. Ille idoneum locum in agris nactus, qua prope iam matura frumenta erant, ibi adventum exspectare Pompei eoque omnem belli rationem conferre constituit.

82 Pompeius paucis post diebus in Thessaliam pervenit contionatusque apud cunctum exercitum suis agit gratias, Scipionis milites cohortatur, ut parta iam victoria praedae ac praemiorum velint esse participes, receptisque omnibus in una castra legionibus suum cum Scipione honorem partitur classicumque apud eum cani et alterum illi iubet praetorium tendi. Auctis copiis Pompei duobusque magnis exercitibus coniunctis pristina omnium confirmatur opinio, et spes victoriae augetur, adeo ut, quicquid intercederet temporis, id morari reditum in Italiam videretur, et si quando quid Pompeius tardius aut consideratius faceret, unius esse negotium diei, sed illum delectari imperio et consulares praetoriosque servorum habere numero dicerent. Iamque inter se palam de praemiis[1] ac de sacerdotiis contendebant in annosque consulatum definiebant, alii domos bonaque eorum, qui in castris erant Caesaris, petebant; magnaque inter eos in consilio fuit controversia, oporteretne Lucili Hirri, quod is a Pompeio ad Parthos missus esset, proximis comitiis praetoriis absentis rationem haberi, cum eius necessarii fidem implorarent Pompei, praestaret, quod proficiscenti recepisset, ne per eius auctoritatem deceptus videretur, reliqui, in labore

[1] praemiis *MSS.:* imperiis *Paul:* provinciis *Kraffert:* praeturis *Markland.*

submit to his authority. Finding a suitable place in the country district where the crops were now nearly ripe, he determined there to await the arrival of Pompeius and to transfer thither all his military operations.

Pompeius reached Thessaly a few days later, and, haranguing his whole army, thanks his own men and exhorts those of Scipio to consent to share the plunder and prizes of war when once the victory is won, and after getting all the legions into one camp, he shares his official dignity with Scipio and gives orders that the bugle should be sounded before him and a second pavilion erected for his headquarters. By this accession to the forces of Pompeius and the joining of two large armies into one, the old confidence of the troops is confirmed and their hope of victory increased, so that the interval that separated them from battle seemed merely a postponement of their return to Italy; and whenever any action of Pompeius showed some degree of slowness and deliberation, they declared it was only a single day's task, but that he was making the most of his imperial command and treating men of consular and praetorian rank as though they were slaves. Already they openly contended for rewards and priesthoods and apportioned the consulship for successive years, while others clamoured for the houses and property of those who were in Caesar's camp; and it was hotly argued in their discussions whether Lucilius Hirrus, who had been sent by Pompeius to the Parthians, might be allowed to compete in absence at the ensuing election of praetors, his friends imploring Pompeius to keep his word and fulfil the promise he made him at his departure, that people might not think that Hirrus had trusted his authority in vain; the rest objecting to one man's getting the advantage

pari ac periculo ne unus omnes antecederet, recusarent.

83 Iam de sacerdotio Caesaris Domitius, Scipio Spintherque Lentulus cotidianis contentionibus ad gravissimas verborum contumelias palam descenderunt, cum Lentulus aetatis honorem ostentaret, Domitius urbanam gratiam dignitatemque iactaret, Scipio affinitate Pompei confideret. Postulavit etiam L. Afranium proditionis exercitus Acutius Rufus apud Pompeium, quod gestum in Hispania diceret. Et L. Domitius in consilio dixit placere sibi bello confecto ternas tabellas dari ad iudicandum eis, qui ordinis essent senatorii belloque una cum ipsis interfuissent, sententiasque de singulis ferrent, qui Romae remansissent quique intra praesidia Pompei fuissent neque operam in re militari praestitissent: unam fore tabellam, qui liberandos omni periculo censerent; alteram, qui capitis damnarent; tertiam, qui pecunia multarent. Postremo omnes aut de honoribus suis aut de praemiis pecuniae aut de persequendis inimicitiis agebant nec, quibus rationibus superare possent, sed, quemadmodum uti victoria deberent, cogitabant.

84 Re frumentaria praeparata confirmatisque militibus et satis longo spatio temporis a Dyrrachinis proeliis intermisso, quo satis perspectum habere militum animum videretur, temptandum Caesar existimavit,

over all the others, when the labour and the danger had been shared equally.

Already Domitius, Scipio, and Lentulus Spinther, 83 in daily rivalry for the priesthood of Caesar, publicly condescended to the gravest insolence of speech, Lentulus parading the distinction of age, Domitius boasting of his urban influence and dignity, Scipio expressing confidence in his kinship with Pompeius. Acutius Rufus also arraigned L. Afranius before Pompeius on a charge of betraying the army, which he said had been done in Spain. And L. Domitius said, in a council of war, that it was his view that, when the war was over, there should be given to those who belonged to the senatorial order and had taken part with themselves in the war three tablets apiece for the purpose of recording their vote, and that votes should be given separately about those who had remained at Rome and those who had been in Pompeius' garrisons but had not offered their services in the field: one tablet, they said, would be for those who should decide that such persons should be exempted from all peril, the second for those who should condemn them to loss of civil status, the third for those who should mulct them in a fine. In a word, all were agitating about honours for themselves, or about prizes of money, or about the prosecution of their private quarrels, nor were their reflections concerned with the means by which they could gain the upper hand, but with the way in which they ought to use their victory.

When he had arranged for his corn supply and 84 had encouraged his soldiers and had allowed a sufficient time to elapse after the battles of Dyrrachium to admit of his feeling assured of the temper of his troops, Caesar thought it right to find out what

CAESAR

quidnam Pompeius propositi aut voluntatis ad dimicandum haberet. Itaque exercitum ex castris
eduxit aciemque instruxit, primum suis locis pauloque a castris Pompei longius, continentibus vero
diebus, ut progrederetur a castris suis collibusque
Pompeianis aciem subiceret. Quae res in dies
confirmatiorem eius exercitum efficiebat. Superius
tamen institutum in equitibus, quod demonstravimus,
servabat, ut, quoniam numero multis partibus esset
inferior, adulescentes atque expeditos ex antesignanis
electis[1] ad pernicitatem armis inter equites proe-
liari iuberet, qui cotidiana consuetudine usum quoque eius generis proeliorum perciperent. His erat
rebus effectum, ut equitum mille etiam apertioribus
locis VII milium Pompeianorum impetum, cum adesset
usus, sustinere auderent neque magnopere eorum
multitudine terrerentur. Namque etiam per eos
dies proelium secundum equestre fecit atque unum
Allobrogem ex duobus, quos perfugisse ad Pompeium supra docuimus, cum quibusdam interfecit.

85   Pompeius, qui castra in colle habebat, ad in-
fimas radices montis aciem instruebat semper, ut
videbatur, exspectans, si iniquis locis Caesar se
subiceret. Caesar nulla ratione ad pugnam elici
posse Pompeium existimans hanc sibi commodissi-
mam belli rationem iudicavit, uti castra ex eo loco
moveret semperque esset in itineribus, haec spectans, ut movendis castris pluribusque adeundis locis

[1] electis milites *MSS.*: electos mutatis *Madvig.*

316

purpose or what disposition for fighting Pompeius had. And so he led his army out of the camp and drew up his lines, first of all in a position favourable to himself and some little distance from the camp of Pompeius, [1] but on subsequent days advancing away from his own camp and pushing his line up to the foot of the hills held by the Pompeians. This action made his army day by day more confident. But in the case of his cavalry he retained his previous custom which we have explained above: since they were many times inferior in number, he gave orders that lightly equipped youths from among the first-rank men, with arms selected with a view to fleetness, should go into battle among the cavalry, so that by daily practice they might win experience in this kind of fighting also. The result of these measures was that one thousand horsemen, even in the more open ground, ventured, with the experience they had gained, to sustain the attack of seven thousand Pompeian horse, and were not greatly terrified by their numbers. For even on those days he fought a successful cavalry skirmish and killed among some others one of the two Allobrogians who, as we explained above, had deserted to Pompeius.

Pompeius, who had his camp on the hill, kept 85 drawing up his line on the lowest spurs of the mountain, apparently always waiting to see whether Caesar would approach close up to the unfavourable ground. Caesar, thinking that Pompeius could by no means be enticed out to a battle, judged that his most convenient plan of campaign was to move his camp from that place, and to be always on the march, with the view of getting his supplies more conveniently by moving camp and visiting various

[1] See plan of the battle of Pharsalus.

commodiore re frumentaria uteretur, simulque in
itinere ut aliquam occasionem dimicandi nancisceretur
et insolitum ad laborem Pompei exercitum cotidianis
itineribus defatigaret. His constitutis rebus, signo
iam profectionis dato tabernaculisque detensis animadversum est paulo ante extra cotidianam consuetudinem longius a vallo esse aciem Pompei progres-
sam, ut non iniquo loco posse dimicari videretur.
Tum Caesar apud suos, cum iam esset agmen in
portis, "differendum est" inquit, "iter in praesentia
nobis et de proelio cogitandum, sicut semper depo-
poscimus; animo simus ad dimicandum parati: non
facile occasionem postea reperiemus"; confestimque
expeditas copias educit.

86   Pompeius quoque, ut postea cognitum est, suorum
omnium hortatu statuerat proelio decertare. Namque
etiam in consilio superioribus diebus dixerat,
priusquam concurrerent acies, fore uti exercitus
Caesaris pelleretur. Id cum essent plerique admirati,
"scio me," inquit, "paene incredibilem rem polliceri;
sed rationem consilii mei accipite, quo firmiore animo
in proelium prodeatis. Persuasi equitibus nostris
(idque mihi facturos confirmaverunt), ut, cum propius
sit accessum, dextrum Caesaris cornu ab latere aperto
aggrederentur et circumventa ab tergo acie prius
perturbatum exercitum pellerent, quam a nobis telum
in hostem iaceretur. Ita sine periculo legionum et
paene sine vulnere bellum conficiemus. Id autem
difficile non est, cum tantum equitatu valeamus."

318

places, and at the same time of meeting with some opportunity of fighting on the route, and of wearing out the army of Pompeius, which was unaccustomed to hard work, by daily marches. After making these arrangements, when the signal for starting had now been given and the tents had been unstretched, it was noticed that a little while before, contrary to its daily custom, Pompeius' line had advanced somewhat further from the rampart, so that it seemed possible for a battle to be fought in no disadvantageous position. Then Caesar, addressing his men, when his force was just at the gates, said: "We must put off our march for the present and think of giving battle, as we have always demanded. Let us be prepared in heart for a conflict; we shall not easily hereafter find an opportunity." At once he leads out his troops in light order.

Pompeius, too, as was found out afterwards, had **86** determined, with the general encouragement of his men, to fight a pitched battle. For he had gone so far as to assert in the council of war on previous days that Caesar's army would be repulsed before the lines met. When several had expressed their surprise at this: "I know," he said, "that I am promising a thing almost incredible, but listen to the nature of my plan that you may go forth to battle with a stouter heart. I have induced my cavalry —and they have assured me that they will do it—as soon as the two armies have drawn nearer, to attack Caesar's right wing on his open flank, and by surrounding his column from the rear to drive his army in confused rout before a weapon is cast at the foe by us. So we shall finish the war without imperilling the legions and almost without a wound. And this is not difficult, considering that we are so strong in cavalry."

CAESAR

Simul denuntiavit, ut essent animo parati in posterum
et, quoniam fieret dimicandi potestas, ut saepe rogi-
tavissent, ne suam neu[1] reliquorum opinionem fal-
lerent.

87   Hunc Labienus excepit et, cum Caesaris copias
despiceret, Pompei consilium summis laudibus efferret,
"noli," inquit, "existimare, Pompei, hunc esse exercitum, qui Galliam Germaniamque devicerit. Omnibus
interfui proeliis neque temere incognitam rem
pronuntio. Perexigua pars illius exercitus superest;
magna pars deperiit, quod accidere tot proeliis fuit
necesse, multos autumni pestilentia in Italia con-
sumpsit, multi domum discesserunt, multi sunt
relicti in continenti. An non audistis ex eis, qui
per causam valetudinis remanserunt, cohortes esse
Brundisi factas? Hae copiae, quas videtis, ex dilectibus horum annorum in citeriore Gallia sunt refectae,
et plerique sunt ex coloniis Transpadanis. Ac tamen
quod fuit roboris duobus proeliis Dyrrachinis interiit."
Haec cum dixisset, iuravit se nisi victorem in castra
non reversurum reliquosque, ut idem facerent,
hortatus est. Hoc laudans Pompeius idem iuravit;
nec vero ex reliquis fuit quisquam, qui iurare
dubitaret. Haec cum facta sunt in consilio, magna
spe et laetitia omnium discessum est; ac iam animo
victoriam praecipiebant, quod de re tanta et a tam
perito imperatore nihil frustra confirmari videbatur.

[1] ne suam neu *Landgraf:* ne usu manu *MSS.*

320

At the same time he urged upon them that they should be strong in spirit for the coming day, and since they had now the opportunity for fighting which they had often demanded, they should not disappoint either his expectation or that of the rest.

Labienus followed him. Depreciating Caesar's 87 forces and extolling to the utmost the strategy of Pompeius, he said: "Do not suppose, Pompeius, that this is the army that subdued Gaul and Germany. I was present at all the battles and do not rashly pronounce on a matter of which I am ignorant. A very small part of that army survives; a great part of it has perished—a necessary result of so many battles; autumnal pestilence has destroyed many in Italy; many have departed home; many have been left on the mainland. Have you not heard that cohorts have been composed at Brundisium of those who remained behind on the pretence of ill-health? These forces which you see have been made up from the levies of these last few years in hither Gaul, and most of them come from the Transpadane colonies. And nevertheless all the flower of them has fallen in the two Dyrrachian battles." Having said this, he swore that he would not return to the camp except as conqueror and exhorted the rest to do the same. Pompeius, commending this, took the same oath, nor was there any one of the rest who hesitated to swear. Such were their proceedings at this council, and they departed with general rejoicing and high expectation. And already in their thoughts they were anticipating the victory, because it did not seem likely that they should receive groundless encouragement on so important a matter and from so experienced a commander.

88 Caesar, cum Pompei castris appropinquasset, ad
hunc modum aciem eius instructam animadvertit.
Erant in sinistro cornu legiones duae traditae a Caesare
initio dissensionis ex senatusconsulto; quarum una
prima, altera tertia appellabatur. In eo loco ipse
erat Pompeius. Mediam aciem Scipio cum legionibus Syriacis tenebat. Ciliciensis legio coniuncta cum
cohortibus Hispanis, quas traductas ab Afranio docuimus, in dextro cornu erant collocatae. Has firmis-
simas se habere Pompeius existimabat. Reliquas
inter aciem mediam cornuaque interiecerat numero-
que cohortes CX expleverat. Haec erant milia XLV,
evocatorum circiter duo, quae ex beneficiariis
superiorum exercituum ad eum convenerant; quae
tota acie disperserat. Reliquas cohortes VII castris
propinquisque castellis praesidio disposuerat. Dextrum cornu eius rivus quidam impeditis ripis
muniebat; quam ob causam cunctum equitatum,
sagittarios funditoresque omnes sinistro cornu obie-
cerat.

89 Caesar superius institutum servans decimam
legionem in dextro cornu, nonam in sinistro collocaverat, tametsi erat Dyrrachinis proeliis vehementer attenuata, et huic sic adiunxit octavam, ut
paene unam ex duabus efficeret, atque alteram
alteri praesidio esse iusserat. Cohortes in acie
LXXX constitutas habebat, quae summa erat milium
XXII; cohortes VII[1] castris praesidio reliquerat.

[1] *MSS.* II, *but it is generally agreed that* VII *is required.*

Caesar, having approached the camp of Pompeius, **88** observed that his line was drawn up as follows: On the left wing were the two legions which had been handed over by Caesar at the beginning of the civil strife by decree of the senate, one of which was called the First, the other the Third. At that place was Pompeius himself. Scipio occupied the middle of the line with the Syrian legions. The Cilician legion, united with the Spanish cohorts, which, as we explained, had been brought over by Afranius, was stationed on the right wing. These legions Pompeius regarded as the strongest under his command. The rest he had interposed between the centre and the wings and had made up the number of one hundred and ten cohorts. These forces amounted to forty-five thousand men, and about two thousand reserves who had come to him from the beneficiaries[1] of his former armies; and these he had distributed throughout the whole force. Seven remaining cohorts he had placed on garrison duty in the camp and the neighbouring forts. A stream with difficult banks protected his right wing; for which reason he had stationed his whole cavalry and all his archers and slingers opposite the enemy on the left wing.

Caesar, observing his previous custom, had posted **89** his Tenth Legion on the right wing, and his Ninth on the left, though it had been seriously attenuated by the Dyrrachian battles. To this legion he added the Eighth, so that he almost made the two into one, having given orders that the one should support the other. He had eighty cohorts posted in his lines, making a total of twenty-two thousand men; seven cohorts he had left as a protection for the camp.

[1] Soldiers of various grades who had owed their advancement to the personal interest of the general: *cp.* I. 75.

Sinistro cornu Antonium, dextro P. Sullam, media
acie Cn. Domitium praeposuerat. Ipse contra Pompeium constitit. Simul his rebus animadversis, quas
demonstravimus, timens, ne a multitudine equitum
dextrum cornu circumveniretur, celeriter ex tertia
acie singulas cohortes detraxit atque ex his quartam
instituit equitatuique opposuit et, quid fieri vellet,
ostendit monuitque eius diei victoriam in earum
cohortium virtute constare. Simul tertiae aciei
totique exercitui[1] imperavit, ne iniussu suo con-
curreret: se, cum id fieri vellet, vexillo signum
daturum.

90   Exercitum cum militari more ad pugnam cohorta-
retur suaque in eum perpetui temporis officia prae-
dicaret, imprimis commemoravit: testibus se militibus uti posse, quanto studio pacem petisset; quae
per Vatinium in colloquiis, quae per Aulum Clodium
cum Scipione egisset, quibus modis ad Oricum cum
Libone de mittendis legatis contendisset. Neque
se umquam abuti militum sanguine neque rem
publicam alterutro exercitu privare voluisse. Hac
habita oratione exposcentibus militibus et studio
pugnae ardentibus tuba signum dedit.

91   Erat C. Crastinus evocatus in exercitu Caesaris,
qui superiore anno apud eum primum pilum in
legione x duxerat, vir singulari virtute. Hic signo
dato, "sequimini me," inquit, "manipulares mei
qui fuistis, et vestro imperatori quam constituistis

---

[1] *There is probably some corruption in the MSS. here.*

He had placed Antonius in command on the left wing, P. Sulla on the right, and Gn. Domitius in the centre. He himself confronted Pompeius. At the same time, having noticed the arrangements mentioned above, fearing lest his right wing should be surrounded by the multitude of cavalry; he hastily withdrew individual cohorts from the third line and out of these constructed a fourth line, stationing it opposite the cavalry, explaining what his object was and reminding them that the day's victory depended on the valour of these cohorts. At the same time he commanded the third line and the whole army not to join battle without orders from himself, saying that when he wished this to be done he would give the signal with a flag.

When, according to the custom of war, he was 90 exhorting his army to battle, and setting forth his unbroken record of kindness to his men, he particularly reminded them that he could call his troops to witness with what zeal he had sought peace, what negotiations he had conducted through Vatinius in conferences and through Aulus Clodius with Scipio, how at Oricum he had urged Libo about the sending of envoys. He had never, he said, wished to squander the blood of his soldiers or to deprive the republic of either of its armies. After delivering this speech, the soldiers clamouring for action and burning with zeal for the fight, he gave the signal with a trumpet.

There was in Caesar's army a reservist, G. Crastinus, 91 who in the previous year had served under him as first centurion in the Tenth Legion, a man of remarkable valour. On the signal being given: "Follow me," said he, "you who have been my comrades, and give your commander your wonted loyal service.

operam date. Unum hoc proelium superest; quo confecto et ille suam dignitatem et nos nostram libertatem recuperabimus." Simul respiciens Caesarem, "faciam," inquit, "hodie, imperator, ut aut vivo mihi aut mortuo gratias agas." Haec cum dixisset, primus ex dextro cornu procucurrit, atque eum electi milites circiter CXX voluntarii eiusdem cohortis[1] sunt prosecuti.

92   Inter duas acies tantum erat relictum spatii, ut satis esset ad concursum utriusque exercitus. Sed Pompeius suis praedixerat, ut Caesaris impetum exciperent neve se loco moverent aciemque eius distrahi paterentur; idque admonitu C. Triarii fecisse dicebatur, ut primus incursus visque militum infringeretur aciesque distenderetur, atque in suis ordinibus dispositi dispersos adorirentur; leviusque casura pila sperabat in loco retentis militibus, quam si ipsi immissis telis occurrissent, simul fore, ut duplicato cursu Caesaris milites exanimarentur et lassitudine conficerentur. Quod nobis quidem nulla ratione factum a Pompeio videtur, propterea quod est quaedam animi incitatio atque alacritas naturaliter innata omnibus, quae studio pugnae incenditur; hanc non reprimere, sed augere imperatores debent; neque frustra antiquitus institutum est, ut signa undique concinerent clamoremque universi tollerent; quibus rebus et hostes terreri et suos incitari existimaverunt.

93   Sed nostri milites dato signo cum infestis pilis

[1] centuriae *MSS., which must be wrong. I suggest* cohortis.

326

This one battle alone remains; when it is over he will recover his dignity and we our liberty." At the same time, looking at Caesar, he says: "To-day, General, I will give you occasion to thank me alive or dead." Having said this, he ran forward first from the right wing, and about one hundred and twenty picked men of the same cohort, serving as volunteers, followed him.

Between the two lines there was only as much 92 space left as was necessary for the charge of each army. But Pompeius had previously ordered his men to await Caesar's attack without moving from their position, and to allow his line to fall into disorder. He is said to have done this on the advice of G. Triarius, in order that the first charge and impetus of the troops might be broken and their line spread out, and that so the Pompeians marshalled in their proper ranks might attack a scattered foe. He hoped, too, that the javelins would fall with less effect if the men were kept in their place than if they themselves discharged their javelins and advanced; also that by having a double distance to run Caesar's soldiers would be breathless and overdone with fatigue. Now this seems to us to have been an irrational act on the part of Pompeius, because there is a certain keenness of spirit and impetuosity implanted by nature in all men which is kindled by the ardour of battle. This feeling it is the duty of commanders not to repress but to foster, nor was it without good reason that the custom was instituted of old that signals should sound in every direction and the whole body of men raise a shout, by which means they thought that the enemy were terrified and their own men stimulated.

But when our men, on the giving of the signal, had 93

procucurrissent atque animum advertissent non concurri a Pompeianis, usu periti ac superioribus pugnis exercitati sua sponte cursum represserunt et ad medium fere spatium constiterunt, ne consumptis viribus appropinquarent, parvoque intermisso temporis spatio ac rursus renovato cursu pila miserunt celeriterque, ut erat praeceptum a Caesare, gladios strinxerunt. Neque vero Pompeiani huic rei defuerunt. Nam et tela missa exceperunt et impetum legionum tulerunt et ordines suos servarunt pilisque missis ad gladios redierunt. Eodem tempore equites ab sinistro Pompei cornu, ut erat imperatum, universi procucurrerunt, omnisque multitudo sagittariorum se profudit. Quorum impetum noster equitatus non tulit, sed paulatim loco motus cessit, equitesque Pompei hoc acrius instare et se turmatim explicare aciemque nostram a latere aperto circumire coeperunt. Quod ubi Caesar animadvertit, quartae aciei, quam instituerat sex cohortium, dedit signum. Illi celeriter procucurrerunt infestisque signis tanta vi in Pompei equites impetum fecerunt, ut eorum nemo consisteret, omnesque conversi non solum loco excederent, sed protinus incitati fuga montes altissimos peterent. Quibus submotis omnes sagittarii funditoresque destituti inermes sine praesidio interfecti sunt. Eodem impetu cohortes sinistrum cornu pugnantibus etiam tum ac resistentibus in acie Pompeianis circumierunt eosque a tergo sunt adorti.

94   Eodem tempore tertiam aciem Caesar, quae quieta

run forward with javelins levelled and had observed that the Pompeians were not advancing against them, profiting by the experience they had gained in former battles, they spontaneously checked their speed and halted in about the middle of the space, so that they might not approach the foe with their vigour exhausted; and after a brief interval, again renewing their rapid advance, they discharged their javelins and quickly drew their swords, according to Caesar's directions. Nor indeed did the Pompeians fail to meet the emergency. For they parried the shower of missiles and withstood the attack of the legions without breaking their ranks, and after discharging their javelins had recourse to their swords. At the same time the horse on Pompeius' left wing, according to orders, charged in a body, and the whole multitude of archers poured forth. Our cavalry, failing to withstand their attack, gradually quitted their position and retired. Pompeius' cavalry pressed forward all the more eagerly, and deploying by squadrons began to surround our lines on their exposed flank. Caesar, observing it, gave the signal to his fourth line, which he had composed of six cohorts. These advanced rapidly and with colours flying attacked Pompeius' horse with such fury that not one of them stood his ground, and all, wheeling round, not only quitted the position but forthwith in hurried flight made for the highest hills. When these were dislodged all the archers and slingers, left defenceless, without support, were slain. With the same onslaught the cohorts surrounded the left wing, the Pompeians still fighting and continuing their resistance in their lines, and attacked them in the rear.

At the same time Caesar ordered the third line, 94 which had been undisturbed and up to that time had

fuerat et se ad id tempus loco tenuerat, procurrere iussit. Ita cum recentes atque integri defessis successissent, alii autem a tergo adorirentur, sustinere Pompeiani non potuerunt, atque universi terga verterunt. Neque vero Caesarem fefellit, quin ab eis cohortibus, quae contra equitatum in quarta acie collocatae essent, initium victoriae oriretur, ut ipse in cohortandis militibus pronuntiaverat. Ab his enim primum equitatus est pulsus, ab isdem factae caedes sagittariorum ac funditorum, ab isdem acies Pompeiana a sinistra parte circumita atque initium fugae factum.[1] Sed Pompeius, ut equitatum suum pulsum vidit atque eam partem, cui maxime confidebat, perterritam animadvertit, aliis quoque diffisus acie excessit protinusque se in castra equo contulit et eis centurionibus, quos in statione ad praetoriam portam posuerat, clare, ut milites exaudirent, "tuemini," inquit, "castra et defendite diligenter, si quid durius acciderit. Ego reliquas portas circumeo et castrorum praesidia confirmo." Haec cum dixisset, se in praetorium contulit summae rei diffidens et tamen eventum exspectans.

95   Caesar Pompeianis ex fuga intra vallum compulsis nullum spatium perterritis dari oportere existimans milites cohortatus est, ut beneficio fortunae uterentur castraque oppugnarent. Qui, etsi magno aestu fatigati (nam ad meridiem res erat perducta), tamen ad omnem laborem animo parati imperio paruerunt. Castra a cohortibus, quae ibi praesidio erant relictae, industrie defendebantur, multo etiam acrius a Thracibus barbarisque auxiliis. Nam qui acie

[1] *Bentley was very likely right in proposing to omit the whole of this passage from* Neque vero Caesarem (§§ 3–4).

retained its position, to advance. So, as they had come up fresh and vigorous in place of the exhausted troops, while others were attacking in the rear, the Pompeians could not hold their ground and turned to flight in mass. Nor was Caesar wrong in thinking that the victory would originate with those cohorts which had been posted opposite the cavalry in the fourth line, as he had himself stated in exhorting his troops; for it was by them that the cavalry was first repulsed, by them that the archers and slingers were slaughtered, by them that the Pompeian force was surrounded on the left and the rout first started. But Pompeius, when he saw his cavalry beaten back and that part of his force in which he had most confidence panic-stricken, mistrusting the rest also, left the field and straightway rode off to the camp. To the centurions whom he had placed on duty at the praetorian gate he exclaimed in a loud voice that the troops might hear: "Protect the camp and defend it carefully if anything goes amiss. I am going round the other gates and encouraging the guards of the camp." Having said this, he betook himself to the general's headquarters, mistrusting his fortunes and yet waiting to see the issue.

When the Pompeians were driven in flight within   95 the rampart, Caesar, thinking that no respite should be given them in their terror, urged his men to take advantage of the kindness of fortune and attack the camp. And though fatigued by the great heat, for the action had been prolonged till noon, they never-theless obeyed his command, with a spirit ready for every toil. The camp was being zealously defended by the cohorts which had been left there on guard, and much more keenly still by the Thracians and barbaric auxiliaries. For the soldiers who had fled

refugerant milites, et animo perterriti et lassitudine
confecti, missis plerique armis signisque militaribus,
magis de reliqua fuga quam de castrorum defensione
cogitabant. Neque vero diutius, qui in vallo constiterant, multitudinem telorum sustinere potuerunt,
sed confecti vulneribus locum reliquerunt, protinusque
omnes ducibus usi centurionibus tribunisque militum
in altissimos montes, qui ad castra pertinebant,
confugerunt.

96   In castris Pompei videre licuit trichilas structas,
magnum argenti pondus expositum, recentibus
caespitibus tabernacula constrata, Lucii etiam
Lentuli et nonnullorum tabernacula protecta edera,
multaque praeterea, quae nimiam luxuriam et victoriae fiduciam designarent, ut facile existimari posset nihil eos de eventu eius diei timuisse, qui non
necessarias conquirerent voluptates. At hi miserrimo
ac patientissimo exercitui Caesaris luxuriam obiciebant, cui semper omnia ad necessarium usum de-
fuissent. Pompeius, iam cum intra vallum nostri
versarentur, equum nactus, detractis insignibus imperatoris, decumana porta se ex castris eiecit protinusque equo citato Larisam contendit. Neque ibi
constitit, sed eadem celeritate, paucos suos ex fuga
nactus, nocturno itinere non intermisso, comitatu
equitum xxx ad mare pervenit navemque frumentariam conscendit, saepe, ut dicebatur, querens
tantum se opinionem fefellisse, ut, a quo genere

from the battlefield, panic-stricken in spirit and exhausted by fatigue, many of them having thrown away their arms and their military standards, were thinking more of further flight than of the defence of the camp. Nor could those who had planted themselves on the rampart stand up any longer against the multitude of javelins, but, worn out by wounds, quitted their position, and forthwith all, following the guidance of centurions and military tribunes, fled for refuge to some very lofty hills that stretched up to the camp.

In the camp of Pompeius one might see bowers 96 constructed, a great weight of silver plate set out, soldiers' huts laid with freshly cut turf, and those of Lucius Lentulus and some others covered over with ivy, and many other indications of excessive luxury and confidence of victory, so that it could easily be supposed that they had felt no fear about the issue of the day, inasmuch as they sought out unnecessary indulgences. Yet these men kept taunting Caesar's most wretched and long-suffering army with luxurious indulgence, though it had always lacked every article of necessary use. When our men were now circulating within the rampart, Pompeius, procuring a horse and tearing off his insignia as Imperator, flung himself out of the camp by the decuman gate and, putting spurs to his horse, hurried straight off to Larisa. Nor did he halt there, but, coming across a few of his men in flight, with undiminished speed, not stopping his course at night, arrives at the sea with a retinue of thirty horsemen and embarks on board a corn-ship, often complaining, as it was said, that his expectations had been so utterly falsified that it almost seemed as if he had been betrayed, the flight having originated with that particular

hominum victoriam sperasset, ab eo initio fugae facto
paene proditus videretur.

97   Caesar castris potitus a militibus contendit, ne in
praeda occupati reliqui negotii gerendi facultatem
dimitterent. Qua re impetrata montem opere circummunire instituit. Pompeiani, quod is mons erat
sine aqua, diffisi ei loco relicto monte universi
iugis eius Larisam versus se recipere coeperunt.
Qua re animadversa Caesar copias suas divisit par-
temque legionum in castris Pompei remanere iussit,
partem in sua castra remisit, IIII secum legiones
duxit commodioreque itinere Pompeianis occurrere
coepit et progressus milia passuum VI aciem instruxit. Qua re animadversa Pompeiani in quodam
monte constiterunt. Hunc montem flumen subllue-
bat. Caesar milites cohortatus, etsi totius diei continenti labore erant confecti noxque iam suberat, tamen munitione flumen a monte seclusit, ne noctu
aquari Pompeiani possent. Quo perfecto opere illi
de deditione missis legatis agere coeperunt. Pauci
ordinis senatorii, qui se cum eis coniunxerant, nocte
fuga salutem petiverunt.

98   Caesar prima luce omnes eos, qui in monte consederant, ex superioribus locis in planiciem descendere atque arma proicere iussit. Quod ubi sine
recusatione fecerunt passisque palmis proiecti ad
terram flentes ab eo salutem petiverunt, consolatus
consurgere iussit et pauca apud eos de lenitate sua
locutus, quo minore essent timore, omnes conservavit

part of his force from which he had hoped for the victory.

Caesar, having got possession of the camp, urgently 97 demands of his men not to let slip an opportunity of completing their task through absorption in plunder. Having gained his object, he begins to surround the hill with earthworks. The Pompeians, as the hill had no water supply, distrusting the position, began to withdraw in mass by its ridges towards Larisa. Caesar, observing this, divided his forces and ordered a part of the legions to remain in Pompeius' camp, and sent back part to his own camp; four legions he took with him and began to advance against the Pompeians by a more convenient route, and when he had proceeded four miles drew up his line. On observing this the Pompeians halted on a certain hill. The foot of this was washed by the river. Caesar exhorted his troops, and then, although they were worn out by the continuous toil of a whole day, and night was now coming on, nevertheless cut off the river from the hill by a line of fortification, so that the Pompeians might be unable to get water at night. When this work was concluded the enemy sent a deputation and began to treat of surrender. A few men of the senatorial order who had joined them sought safety in flight at nightfall.

At early dawn Caesar ordered all those who had 98 taken up their position on the hill to come down from the higher ground to the plain and to throw down their arms. When they did this without demur and, flinging themselves on the ground in tears, with outstretched hands begged him for safety, he consoled them and bade them rise, and addressing a few words to them about his own lenity to lessen their fears, preserved them all safe and commended them

militibusque suis commendavit, ne qui eorum violaretur, neu quid sui desiderarent. Hac adhibita diligentia ex castris sibi legiones alias occurrere et eas, quas secum duxerat, in vicem requiescere atque in castra reverti iussit eodemque die Larisam pervenit.

99 In eo proelio non amplius CC milites desideravit, sed centuriones, fortes viros, circiter XXX amisit. Interfectus est etiam fortissime pugnans Crastinus, cuius mentionem supra fecimus, gladio in os adversum coniecto. Neque id fuit falsum, quod ille in pugnam proficiscens dixerat. Sic enim Caesar existimabat, eo proelio excellentissimam virtutem Crastini fuisse, optimeque eum de se meritum iudicabat. Ex Pompeiano exercitu circiter milia XV cecidisse videbantur, sed in deditionem venerunt amplius milia XXIIII (namque etiam cohortes, quae praesidio in castellis fuerant, sese Sullae dediderunt), multi praeterea in finitimas civitates refugerunt; signaque militaria ex proelio ad Caesarem sunt relata CLXXX et aquilae VIIII. L. Domitius ex castris in montem refugiens, cum vires eum lassitudine defecissent, ab equitibus est interfectus.

100 Eodem tempore D. Laelius cum classe ad Brundisium venit eademque ratione, qua factum a Libone antea demonstravimus, insulam obiectam portui Brundisino tenuit. Similiter Vatinius, qui Brundisio praeerat, tectis instructisque scaphis elicuit naves Laelianas atque ex his longius productam unam quinqueremem et minores duas in angustiis portus

336

to his soldiers, urging that none of them should be injured and that they should not find any of their property missing. After this exercise of care he ordered the other legions to come from the camp and join him, and those which had been under his command to take rest in their turn and to return to the camp, and on the same day he arrived at Larisa.

In this battle he lost not more than two hundred 99 from the ranks, but about thirty brave centurions. Also Crastinus, whom we have mentioned above, was slain by a sword-stroke in his face while fighting with the utmost bravery. Nor did the remark which he had made when starting out for the fight prove false, for Caesar was of opinion that the valour of Crastinus in that battle had been most remarkable, and judged that he had rendered him a great service. Of the Pompeian army about fifteen thousand appeared to have fallen, but more than twenty-four thousand surrendered, for even the cohorts which had been on garrison duty in the forts surrendered to Sulla; many besides fled to the neighbouring communities. There were brought to Caesar from the battle one hundred and eighty military standards and nine eagles. L. Domitius in his flight from the camp to the mountain was slain by the cavalry, his strength having failed him from fatigue.

At the same time D. Laelius reached Brundisium 100 with the fleet and occupied the island lying over against the Brundisian port, as we have shown that Libo did previously. In the same way Vatinius, who was in charge of Brundisium, having covered over with a deck and carefully equipped some rowing-boats, enticed out the ships of Laelius and captured in the narrows of the harbour one quinquereme which had been brought out too far and two smaller

cepit, itemque per equites dispositos aqua prohibere classiarios instituit. Sed Laelius tempore anni commodiore usus ad navigandum onerariis navibus Corcyra Dyrrachioque aquam suis supportabat, neque a proposito deterrebatur neque ante proelium in Thessalia factum cognitum aut ignominia amissarum navium aut necessariarum rerum inopia ex portu insulaque expelli potuit.

101 Isdem fere temporibus C. Cassius cum classe Syrorum et Phoenicum et Cilicum in Siciliam venit, et cum esset Caesaris classis divisa in duas partes, dimidiae parti praeesset P. Sulpicius praetor ad Vibonem,[1] dimidiae M. Pomponius ad Messanam, prius Cassius ad Messanam navibus advolavit, quam Pomponius de eius adventu cognosceret, perturbatumque eum nactus nullis custodiis neque ordinibus certis, magno vento et secundo completas onerarias naves taeda et pice et stupa reliquisque rebus, quae sunt ad incendia,[2] in Pomponianam classem immisit atque omnes naves incendit xxxv, e quibus erant xx constratae. Tantusque eo facto timor incessit, ut, cum esset legio praesidio Messanae, vix oppidum defenderetur, et nisi eo ipso tempore quidam nuntii de Caesaris victoria per dispositos equites essent allati, existimabant plerique futurum fuisse, uti amitteretur. Sed opportunissime nuntiis allatis oppidum est defensum; Cassiusque ad Sulpicianam inde classem profectus est Vibonem, applicatisque nostris ad terram navibus pari atque antea ratione Cassius secundum nactus ventum onerarias naves praeparatas ad incendium immisit,[3] et flamma ab

---

[1] Vibonem ad fretum *MSS.*: ad Vibonem *Forchhammer.*

[2] ad incendia *MSS. I have suggested* ad incendia idoneae.

[3] *The text of this sentence is in great disorder. I have adopted various plausible corrections.*

ones, and also by placing pickets of cavalry here and there took measures to prevent the sailors from getting water. But Laelius, finding the time of year more suitable for navigation, brought up supplies of water for his men from Corcyra and Dyrrachium in merchant-vessels, and, until news was brought of the battle fought in Thessaly, he was not deterred from his purpose, nor could he be driven to leave the port and the island either by the disgrace of losing his ships or by the want of necessaries.

About the same time G. Cassius came to Sicily 101 with the Syrian, Phoenician, and Cilician fleets, and as Caesar's fleet was divided into two parts, the praetor P. Sulpicius at Vibo being in command of one half, and M. Pomponius at Messana of the other, Cassius hurried with his ships to Messana before Pomponius could learn of his approach, and finding him in a state of disorganization, with no surveillance and no fixed order of battle, with the aid of a strong and favourable wind he sent against the fleet of Pomponius some merchant-ships loaded with pine, pitch, tow, and other combustibles and burnt all thirty-five ships, of which twenty were decked. Such terror was caused by this action that, though there was a legion on guard at Messana, the town was scarcely defended, and had not some news of Caesar's victory been brought, just at that time, by relays of horsemen, many were of opinion that it would have been lost. But news having most opportunely arrived, the town was defended. Cassius departed thence to Vibo to the Sulpician fleet, and our ships having been moored to the shore in the same way as before, Cassius, with the advantage of a favourable wind, sent down some merchant-vessels prepared for burning, and the fleet having caught

utroque cornu comprensa naves sunt combustae
quinque. Cumque ignis magnitudine venti latius
serperet, milites, qui ex veteribus legionibus erant
relicti praesidio navibus ex numero aegrorum, ignominiam non tulerunt, sed sua sponte naves con-
scenderunt et a terra solverunt impetuque facto in
Cassianam classem quinqueremes duas, in quarum
altera erat Cassius, ceperunt; sed Cassius exceptus
scapha refugit; praeterea duae sunt depressae
triremes. Neque multo post de proelio facto in
Thessalia cognitum est, ut ipsis Pompeianis fides
fieret; nam ante id tempus fingi a legatis amicisque
Caesaris arbitrabantur. Quibus rebus cognitis ex
his locis Cassius cum classe discessit.

102   Caesar omnibus rebus relictis persequendum sibi
Pompeium existimavit, quascumque in partes se ex
fuga recepisset, ne rursus copias comparare alias et
bellum renovare posset, et quantumcumque itineris
equitatu efficere poterat, cotidie progrediebatur
legionemque unam minoribus itineribus subsequi
iussit. Erat edictum Pompei nomine Amphipoli
propositum, uti omnes eius provinciae iuniores,
Graeci civesque Romani, iurandi causa convenirent.
Sed utrum avertendae suspicionis causa Pompeius
proposuisset, ut quam diutissime longioris fugae
consilium occultaret, an ut novis dilectibus, si nemo
premeret, Macedoniam tenere conaretur, existimari
non poterat. Ipse ad ancoram unam noctem constitit et vocatis ad se Amphipoli hospitibus et pecunia

fire on each wing, five ships were consumed. And when the fire, through the greatness of the wind, spread more widely, some soldiers on the sick list, who had been left from the veteran legions to guard the ships, could not brook the ignominy, but of their own accord boarded the ships and let loose from the land; and making an attack on the Cassian fleet, they captured two quinqueremes, in one of which was Cassius himself, but he was taken off by a boat and escaped; besides this two triremes were sunk. And not long after news arrived of the battle fought in Thessaly, the result being that the Pompeians themselves believed it, for up to that time they thought it was an invention of Caesar's envoys and friends. So these events having become known, Cassius departed with his fleet from this district.

Caesar thought it right to put aside everything 102 else and follow Pompeius, into whatever parts he should have betaken himself in his flight, that he might not be able again to collect other forces and to renew the war: he advanced every day as great a distance as he could cover with his cavalry, and ordered one legion to follow by shorter marches. An edict had been issued at Amphipolis in the name of Pompeius that all the youths of that province, whether Greeks or Roman citizens, should assemble to take the oath. But no opinion could be formed whether Pompeius had proposed this to avert suspicion, in order that he might keep his purpose of a distant flight concealed as long as possible, or that with the new levies he might attempt to hold Macedonia, if no one checked him. He himself stopped there one night at anchor, and after inviting his friends at Amphipolis to a conference and collecting money for necessary expenses,

ad necessarios sumptus corrogata, cognito Caesaris adventu, ex eo loco discessit et Mytilenas paucis diebus venit. Biduum tempestate retentus navibusque aliis additis actuariis in Ciliciam atque inde Cyprum pervenit. Ibi cognoscit consensu omnium Antiochensium civiumque Romanorum, qui illic negotiarentur, arma capta[1] esse excludendi sui causa nuntiosque dimissos ad eos, qui se ex fuga in finitimas civitates recepisse dicerentur, ne Antiochiam adirent: id si fecissent, magno eorum capitis periculo futurum. Idem hoc L. Lentulo, qui superiore anno consul fuerat, et P. Lentulo consulari ac nonnullis aliis acciderat Rhodi; qui cum ex fuga Pompeium sequerentur atque in insulam venissent, oppido ac portu recepti non erant missisque ad eos nuntiis, ut ex his locis discederent contra voluntatem suam naves solverant. Iamque de Caesaris adventu fama ad civitates perferebatur.

103 Quibus cognitis rebus Pompeius deposito adeundae Syriae consilio pecunia societatis sublata et a quibusdam privatis sumpta et aeris magno pondere ad militarem usum in naves imposito duobusque milibus hominum armatis, partim quos ex familiis societatum delegerat, partim a negotiatoribus coëgerat, quosque ex suis quisque ad hanc rem idoneos existimabat, Pelusium pervenit. Ibi casu rex erat Ptolomaeus, puer aetate, magnis copiis cum sorore Cleopatra bellum gerens, quam paucis ante mensibus per suos

---

[1] arma capta *Forchhammer:* arcem (*or* aram) captam *MSS.*

on receiving news of Caesar's approach he quitted that place and in a few days arrived at Mytilenae. Detained there for two days by rough weather, after adding to his fleet other small craft he came to Cilicia and thence to Cyprus. There he learns that, by the consent of all the people of Antioch and of the Roman citizens engaged in business there, arms had been taken up for the purpose of excluding him, and that messages had been sent to those who were said to have betaken themselves in flight to the neighbouring townships bidding them not to go to Antioch. If they did so, they were told, it would be at great peril of their lives. The same thing had happened at Rhodes to L. Lentulus, who had been consul the previous year, to P. Lentulus, an ex-consul, and to some others, who, when they were following Pompeius in flight and had come to the island, had not been allowed admittance in the town and the harbour, and on messages being sent to them to quit these parts, had weighed anchor contrary to their intention. And already a report of Caesar's approach was being conveyed to the communities.

Ascertaining these facts, Pompeius gave up his 103 idea of visiting Syria, took the funds belonging to the association of tax-farmers, borrowed money from certain private persons, and deposited on shipboard a great weight of bronze coinage for the use of the soldiers; and having armed two thousand men, partly those whom he had selected from the households of the tax-farmers, partly those whom he had requisitioned from the merchants and those of their own men whom each owner judged to be fit for the purpose, arrived at Pelusium. There by chance was King Ptolomaeus, a boy in years, waging war with large forces against his sister Cleopatra, whom a few

propinquos atque amicos regno expulerat; castraque
Cleopatrae non longo spatio ab eius castris distabant.
Ad eum Pompeius misit, ut pro hospitio atque amicitia
patris Alexandria reciperetur atque illius opibus in
calamitate tegeretur. Sed qui ab eo missi erant, confecto legationis officio liberius cum militibus regis
colloqui coeperunt eosque hortari, ut suum officium
Pompeio praestarent, neve eius fortunam despicerent.
In hoc erant numero complures Pompei milites, quos
ex eius exercitu acceptos in Syria Gabinius Alexandriam traduxerat belloque confecto apud Ptolomaeum,
patrem pueri, reliquerat.

104   His tum cognitis rebus amici regis, qui propter
aetatem eius in procuratione erant regni, sive timore
adducti, ut postea praedicabant, sollicitato exercitu
regio ne Pompeius Alexandriam Aegyptumque occuparet, sive despecta eius fortuna, ut plerumque in
calamitate ex amicis inimici exsistunt, his, qui erant
ab eo missi, palam liberaliter responderunt eumque
ad regem venire iusserunt; ipsi clam consilio inito
Achillam, praefectum regium, singulari hominem
audacia, et L. Septimium, tribunum militum, ad
interficiendum Pompeium miserunt. Ab his liberaliter
ipse appellatus et quadam notitia Septimii productus,
quod bello praedonum apud eum ordinem duxerat,
naviculam parvulam conscendit cum paucis suis:
ibi ab Achilla et Septimio interficitur. Item L.
Lentulus comprehenditur ab rege et in custodia
necatur.

months before he had expelled from the throne by the help of his relations and friends. The camp of Cleopatra was not far distant from his camp. To him Pompeius sent begging to be received in Alexandria and supported in his calamity by the king's resources, in remembrance of the hospitality and friendship that he had shown his father. But his messengers, having fulfilled the duty of their embassy, began to converse more freely with the king's soldiers and to exhort them to show their dutiful loyalty to Pompeius, and not to despise his fortunes. In the number of these men were very many soldiers of Pompeius, whom Gabinius had taken over from his army in Syria and had transported to Alexandria, and on the conclusion of the war had left them with Ptolomaeus, the youth's father.

Then, on learning of these proceedings, the king's 104 friends, who, on account of his youth, were in charge of the kingdom, whether moved by fear, as they afterwards gave out, lest Pompeius should seize on Alexandria and Egypt after tampering with the royal army, or because they despised his fortunes, according to the common rule that in misfortune friends become enemies, gave in public a generous reply to his messengers and bade him visit the king, but themselves formed a secret plot, and sent Achillas, the king's prefect, a man of singular audacity, and L. Septimius, a military tribune, to assassinate Pompeius. And he, being courteously addressed by them and being lured forth by some previous knowledge of Septimius, because he had been a centurion under him in the pirate war, embarked in a little boat with a few of his friends, and is thereupon assassinated by Achillas and Septimius. L. Lentulus is also arrested by the king and slain in prison.

CAESAR

105   Caesar, cum in Asiam venisset, reperiebat T. Ampium conatum esse pecunias tollere Epheso ex fano Dianae eiusque rei causa senatores omnes ex provincia evocasse, ut his testibus in summa pecuniae uteretur, sed interpellatum adventu Caesaris profugisse. Ita duobus temporibus Ephesiae pecuniae Caesar auxilium tulit. Item constabat Elide in templo Minervae repetitis atque enumeratis diebus, quo die proelium secundum Caesar fecisset, simulacrum Victoriae, quod ante ipsam Minervam collocatum esset et ante ad simulacrum Minervae spectavisset, ad valvas se templi limenque convertisse. Eodemque die Antiochiae in Syria bis tantus exercitus clamor et signorum sonus exauditus est, ut in muris armata civitas discurreret. Hoc idem Ptolomaide accidit. Pergami in occultis ac reconditis templi, quo praeter sacerdotes adire fas non est, quae Graeci ἄδυτα appellant, tympana sonuerunt. Item Trallibus in templo Victoriae, ubi Caesaris statuam consecraverant, palma per eos dies inter coagmenta lapidum ex pavimento exstitisse ostendebatur.

106   Caesar paucos dies in Asia moratus, cum audisset Pompeium Cypri visum, coniectans eum in Aegyptum iter habere propter necessitudines regni reliquasque eius loci opportunitates cum legione una, quam se ex Thessalia sequi iusserat, et altera, quam ex Achaia a

On Caesar's arrival in Asia he found that T.   105
Ampius had attempted to remove sums of money
from Ephesus from the temple of Diana, and that with
this object he had summoned all the senators from
the province, that he might employ them as witnesses
in reference to the amount of the sum, but that he
had fled when interrupted by Caesar's arrival. So
on two occasions Caesar saved the Ephesian funds.
Also it was established, by going back and calcu-
lating the dates, that at Elis in the temple of
Minerva, on the very day on which Caesar had
fought his successful battle, the image of Victory,
which had been placed in front of Minerva herself
and had previously looked towards the image of
Minerva, had turned itself towards the folding-doors
and threshold of the temple. And on the same day
at Antioch in Syria so great a clamour of a host and
a noise of trumpetings had twice been heard that
the body of citizens rushed about in arms on the
walls. The same thing happened at Ptolomais. At
Pergamum in the secret and concealed parts of the
temple, whither no one but the priests is allowed to
approach, which the Greeks call ἄδυτα, there was
a sound of drums. Also at Tralles in the temple of
Victory, where they had dedicated a statue of Caesar,
a palm was pointed out as having grown up during
those days from the pavement between the joints
of the stones.

When Caesar, after lingering a few days in Asia,   106
had heard that Pompeius had been seen in Cyprus,
conjecturing that he was on his way to Egypt
because of his ties with the kingdom and the further
advantages of the place, he went to Alexandria with
one legion which he had ordered to follow him from
Thessaly and another which he had summoned

347

Q. Fufio legato evocaverat, equitibusque DCCC et navibus longis Rhodiis X et Asiaticis paucis Alexandriam pervenit. In his erant legionibus hominum milia tria CC; reliqui vulneribus ex proeliis et labore ac magnitudine itineris confecti consequi non potuerant. Sed Caesar confisus fama rerum gestarum infirmis auxiliis proficisci non dubitaverat, aeque omnem sibi locum tutum fore existimans. Alexandriae de Pompei morte cognoscit atque ibi primum e nave egrediens clamorem militum audit, quos rex in oppido praesidii causa reliquerat, et concursum ad se fieri videt, quod fasces anteferrentur. In hoc omnis multitudo maiestatem regiam minui praedicabat. Hoc sedato tumultu crebrae continuis diebus ex concursu multitudinis concitationes fiebant, compluresque milites huius[1] urbis omnibus partibus interficiebantur.

107   Quibus rebus animadversis legiones sibi alias ex Asia adduci iussit, quas ex Pompeianis militibus confecerat. Ipse enim necessario etesiis tenebatur, qui navigantibus Alexandria flant[2] adversissimi venti. Interim controversias regum ad populum Romanum et ad se, quod esset consul, pertinere existimans atque eo magis officio suo convenire, quod superiore consulatu cum patre Ptolomaeo et lege et senatusconsulto societas erat facta, ostendit sibi placere regem Ptolomaeum atque eius sororem Cleopatram exercitus, quos haberent, dimittere et de

[1] huius MSS.: in viis Madvig.
[2] flant Paul: fiunt MSS.

348

out of Achaea from his legate Q. Fufius, and also with eight hundred horse and with ten warships from Rhodes and a few from Asia. In these legions there were about three thousand two hundred men; the rest, worn out by wounds received in battle and by their toil and the severity of their march, had been quite unable to follow. But Caesar, trusting in the report of his exploits, had not hesitated to advance with weak supports, thinking that every place would be equally safe for him. At Alexandria he learns of the death of Pompeius, and there immediately on landing he hears the shouting of the soldiers whom the king had left in the town on garrison duty and sees them hurrying to meet him, because the fasces were being carried in front of him. Hereby the whole multitude asserted that the royal authority was being infringed. When this tumult was appeased frequent disturbances took place on successive days from the gathering of the multitude, and many soldiers were killed in all parts of this town.

Observing these events, he ordered other legions 107 which he had made up out of the Pompeian troops to be brought him from Asia. For he was himself compulsorily detained by the etesian winds, which blow directly counter to those sailing from Alexandria. Meanwhile, thinking that the controversies of the princes affected the Roman people and himself as consul, and concerned his functions all the more because in his previous consulship an alliance had been formed with the elder Ptolomaeus both by legislative enactment and by decree of the senate, he declares that it is his pleasure that King Ptolomaeus and his sister Cleopatra should disband the armies that they controlled, and should settle their

controversiis iure apud se potius quam inter se armis
disceptare.

108   Erat in procuratione regni propter aetatem pueri
nutricius eius, eunuchus nomine Pothinus. Is primum inter suos queri atque indignari coepit regem
ad causam dicendam evocari; deinde adiutores quosdam consilii sui nactus ex regis amicis exercitum a
Pelusio clam Alexandriam evocavit atque eundem
Achillam, cuius supra meminimus, omnibus copiis
praefecit. Hunc incitatum suis et regis inflatum[1]
pollicitationibus, quae fieri vellet, litteris nuntiisque
edocuit. In testamento Ptolomaei patris heredes
erant scripti ex duobus filiis maior et ex duabus
filiabus ea, quae aetate antecedebat. Haec uti fierent,
per omnes deos perque foedera, quae Romae fecisset,
eodem testamento Ptolomaeus populum Romanum
obtestabatur. Tabulae testamenti unae per legatos
eius Romam erant allatae, ut in aerario ponerentur
(hic[2] cum propter publicas occupationes poni non
potuissent, apud Pompeium sunt depositae), alterae
eodem exemplo relictae atque obsignatae Alexandriae proferebantur.

109   De his rebus cum ageretur apud Caesarem,
isque maxime vellet pro communi amico atque
arbitro controversias regum componere, subito exercitus regius equitatusque omnis venire Alexandriam
nuntiatur. Caesaris copiae nequaquam erant tantae,
ut eis, extra oppidum si esset dimicandum, confideret. Relinquebatur, ut se suis locis oppido teneret

---

[1] *Probably either* incitatum *or* inflatum *should be omitted.*
[2] hic *Paul:* haec *or* hae *MSS.*

disputes by process of law before himself rather than by armed force between themselves.

On account of the king's youth his tutor, a eunuch named Pothinus, was in charge of the kingdom. He at first began to complain among his friends and express his indignation that the king should be summoned to plead his cause; then, finding certain persons among the king's friends to abet his plot, he secretly summoned the army from Pelusium to Alexandria and put the same Achillas, whom we have mentioned above, in command of all the forces. This man, puffed up as he was by his own and the king's promises, he urged to action, and informed him by letter and messenger what he wished to be done. In the will of their father Ptolemaeus the elder of the two sons and the elder of the two daughters were inscribed as heirs. In the same will Ptolemaeus adjured the Roman people in the name of all the gods and of the treaties which he had made at Rome to carry out these provisions. One copy of the will had been taken to Rome by his envoys to be placed in the treasury, but had been deposited with Pompeius because it had not been possible to place it there owing to the embarrassments of the state; a second duplicate copy was left sealed for production at Alexandria. 108

When these matters were being dealt with by Caesar, and he was particularly desirous of settling the disputes of the princes as a common friend and arbitrator, word is suddenly brought that the royal army and all the cavalry are on their way to Alexandria. Caesar's forces were by no means so large that he could trust them if he had to fight outside the town. It remained that he should keep in his own position in the town and learn the intentions of 109

consiliumque Achillae cognosceret. Milites tamen omnes in armis esse iussit regemque hortatus est, ut ex suis necessariis, quos haberet maximae auctoritatis, legatos ad Achillam mitteret et, quid esset suae voluntatis, ostenderet. A quo missi Dioscorides et Serapion, qui ambo legati Romae fuerant magnamque apud patrem Ptolomaeum auctoritatem habuerant, ad Achillam pervenerunt. Quos ille, cum in conspectum eius venissent, priusquam audiret aut, cuius rei causa missi essent, cognosceret, corripi atque interfici iussit; quorum alter accepto vulnere occupatus per suos pro occiso sublatus, alter interfectus est. Quo facto regem ut in sua potestate haberet, Caesar efficit, magnam regium nomen apud suos auctoritatem habere existimans et ut potius privato paucorum et latronum quam regio consilio susceptum bellum videretur.

110 Erant cum Achilla eae copiae, ut neque numero neque genere hominum neque usu rei militaris contemnendae viderentur. Milia enim XX in armis habebat. Haec constabant ex Gabinianis militibus qui iam in consuetudinem Alexandrinae vitae ac licentiae venerant et nomen disciplinamque populi Romani dedidicerant uxoresque duxerant, ex quibus plerique liberos habebant. Huc accedebant collecti ex praedonibus latronibusque Syriae Ciliciaque provinciae finitimarumque regionum. Multi praeterea capitis damnati exulesque convenerant; fugitivis omnibus nostris certus erat Alexandriae receptus certaque vitae condicio, ut dato nomine militum

Achillas. But he ordered all his men to stand by their arms, and exhorted the king to send to Achillas those of his friends whom he judged to be of chief authority and to explain what his intentions were. Accordingly Dioscorides and Serapion, who had both been envoys at Rome and had possessed great influence with his father Ptolemaeus, were commissioned by the king and came to Achillas. And when they had come into his presence, before hearing them or learning for what reason they had been sent he ordered them to be arrested and killed. And one of them, having received a wound, was promptly snatched away by his friends and carried off for dead; the other was slain. After this deed Caesar manages to bring the king under his own control, because he thinks that the king's title had great weight with his subjects, and in order to make it apparent that the war had been undertaken on the private initiative of a small clique and a set of brigands rather than on that of the king.

The forces with Achillas were not such as to seem 110 contemptible in respect of number or grade of men or experience in warfare. For he had twenty thousand men under arms. These consisted of soldiers of Gabinius who had habituated themselves to Alexandrian life and licence and had unlearnt the name and discipline of the Roman people and married wives by whom very many of them had children. To them were added men collected from among the freebooters and brigands of Syria and the province of Cilicia and the neighbouring regions; also many condemned criminals and exiles had joined them. All our own fugitive slaves had a sure place of refuge at Alexandria, and assurance of their lives on the condition of giving in their names and being on the army roll; and if any one of them was

essent numero; quorum si quis a domino prehen-
deretur, consensu militum eripiebatur, qui vim
suorum, quod in simili culpa versabantur, ipsi pro suo
periculo defendebant. Hi regum amicos ad mortem
deposcere, hi bona locupletum diripere, stipendii
augendi causa regis domum obsidere, regno expellere
alios, alios arcessere vetere quodam Alexandrini
exercitus instituto consuerant. Erant praeterea
equitum milia duo. Inveteraverant hi omnes compluribus Alexandriae bellis; Ptolomaeum patrem in
regnum reduxerant, Bibuli filios duos interfecerant,
bella cum Aegyptiis gesserant. Hunc usum rei
militaris habebant.

111   His copiis fidens Achillas paucitatemque militum
Caesaris despiciens occupabat Alexandriam praeter
eam oppidi partem, quam Caesar cum militibus
tenebat, primo impetu domum eius irrumpere conatus;
sed Caesar dispositis per vias cohortibus impetum eius
sustinuit. Eodemque tempore pugnatum est ad
portum, ac longe maximam ea res attulit dimica-
tionem. Simul enim diductis copiis pluribus viis
pugnabatur, et magna multitudine naves longas occupare hostes conabantur; quarum erant L auxilio
missae ad Pompeium proelioque in Thessalia facto
domum redierant, quadriremes omnes et quinqueremes aptae instructaeque omnibus rebus ad navigandum, praeter has XXII, quae praesidii causa
Alexandriae esse consuerant, constratae omnes; quas
si occupavissent, classe Caesari erepta portum ac

arrested by his owner he would be rescued by the common consent of the soldiery, who repelled violence done to their comrades as a peril to their own selves, since they were all alike involved in similar guilt. These men had been in the habit of demanding for execution the friends of the princes, of plundering the property of the rich, of besetting the king's palace to secure an increase of pay, of driving one man from the throne and summoning another to fill it, after an ancient custom of the Alexandrian army. There were besides two thousand cavalry. All these had grown old in the numerous wars at Alexandria, had restored the elder Ptolomaeus to the throne, had killed the two sons of Bibulus, had waged war with the Egyptians. Such was their experience in warfare.

Achillas, trusting in these forces and despising the small number of Caesar's troops, was trying to occupy Alexandria, except that part of the town which Caesar held with his troops, though at the first assault he had endeavoured to burst into his house; but Caesar, placing cohorts about the streets, held his attack in check. And at the same time a battle was fought at the port, and this affair produced by far the most serious fighting. For at one and the same time a battle was going on with scattered forces in several streets and the enemy were attempting in great numbers to seize the warships, of which fifty had been sent to the support of Pompeius and had returned home after the battle in Thessaly, all of them quadriremes and quinqueremes fitted and equipped with everything necessary for navigation, and, besides these, twenty-two which had usually been on duty at Alexandria, all of them decked. And if they had seized these, by robbing Caesar of

111

mare totum in sua potestate haberent, commeatu
auxiliisque Caesarem prohiberent. Itaque tanta est
contentione actum, quanta agi debuit, cum illi celerem in ea re victoriam, hi salutem suam consistere
viderent. Sed rem obtinuit Caesar omnesque eas naves
et reliquas, quae erant in navalibus, incendit, quod
tam late tueri parva manu non poterat, confestimque
ad Pharum navibus milites exposuit.

112   Pharus est in insula turris magna altitudine,
mirificis operibus exstructa; quae nomen ab insula
accepit. Haec insula obiecta Alexandriae portum
efficit; sed a superioribus regibus in longitudinem
passuum DCCC in mare iactis molibus angusto itinere
ut ponte cum oppido coniungitur. In hac sunt insula
domicilia Aegyptiorum et vicus oppidi magnitudine;
quaeque ibi naves imprudentia aut tempestate paulum
suo cursu decesserunt, has more praedonum diripere
consuerunt. Eis autem invitis, a quibus Pharus
tenetur, non potest esse propter angustias navibus
introitus in portum. Hoc tum veritus Caesar, hostibus in pugna occupatis, militibus expositis Pharum
prehendit atque ibi praesidium posuit. Quibus est
rebus effectum, uti tuto frumentum auxiliaque
navibus ad eum supportari possent. Dimisit enim
circum omnes propinquas provincias atque inde
auxilia evocavit. Reliquis oppidi partibus sic est
pugnatum, ut aequo proelio discederetur et neutri

his fleet they would have the harbour and the whole seaboard in their control and would shut off Caesar from supplies and reinforcements. Consequently the struggle was fought with the intense eagerness that was bound to occur when the one side saw a speedy victory, the other their own safety, depending on the event. But Caesar gained his purpose. He burnt all those ships and the rest that were in the docks, because he could not protect so wide an extent with his small force, and at once he embarked his men and landed them on Pharos.

On the island there is a tower called Pharos, of great height, a work of wonderful construction, which took its name from the island. This island, lying over against Alexandria, makes a harbour, but it is connected with the town by a narrow roadway like a bridge, piers nine hundred feet in length having been thrown out seawards by former kings. On this island there are dwelling-houses of Egyptians and a settlement the size of a town, and any ships that went a little out of their course there through carelessness or rough weather they were in the habit of plundering like pirates. Moreover, on account of the narrowness of the passage there can be no entry for ships into the harbour without the consent of those who are in occupation of Pharos. Caesar, now fearing such difficulty, landed his troops when the enemy was occupied in fighting, and seized Pharos and placed a garrison on it. The result of these measures was that corn and reinforcements could be safely conveyed to him on shipboard. For he sent messengers to all the neighbouring provinces and summoned reinforcements from them. In the remaining parts of the town the result of the fighting was that they separated after an indecisive engagement and neither

112

pellerentur (id efficiebant angustiae loci), paucisque
utrimque interfectis Caesar loca maxime necessaria
complexus noctu praemuniit. In eo tractu oppidi
pars erat regiae exigua, in quam ipse habitandi causa
initio erat inductus, et theatrum coniunctum domui
quod arcis tenebat locum aditusque habebat ad
portum et ad reliqua navalia. Has munitiones inse-
quentibus auxit diebus, ut pro muro obiectas haberet
neu dimicare invitus cogeretur. Interim filia minor
Ptolomaei regis vacuam possessionem regni sperans
ad Achillam sese ex regia traiecit unaque bellum
administrare coepit. Sed celeriter est inter eos de
principatu controversia orta; quae res apud milites
largitiones auxit; magnis enim iacturis sibi quisque
eorum animos conciliabat. Haec dum apud hostes
geruntur, Pothinus, nutricius pueri et procurator
regni in parte Caesaris,[1] cum ad Achillam nuntios
mitteret hortareturque, ne negotio desisteret neve
animo deficeret, indicatis deprehensisque internuntiis a Caesare est interfectus. Haec initia belli
Alexandrini fuerunt.

[1] *It is probable that the words* nutricius . . . Caesaris *should
be omitted.*

side was beaten, the reason of this being the narrowness of the space; and a few men having been slain on both sides, Caesar drew a cordon round the most necessary positions and strengthened the defences by night. In this region of the town there was a small part of the palace to which he had been at first conducted for his personal residence, and a theatre was attached to the house which took the place of a citadel, and had approaches to the port and to the other docks. These defences he increased on subsequent days so that they might take the place of a wall as a barrier against the foe, and that he might not be obliged to fight against his will. Meanwhile the younger daughter of King Ptolomaeus, hoping to have the vacated tenure of the throne, removed herself from the palace to join Achillas, and began to conduct the war with him. But there quickly arose a controversy between them about the leadership, an event which increased the bounties to the soldiers, for each strove separately to win their favour by large sacrifices. While this was going on among the enemy, Pothinus, the young king's tutor and controller of the kingdom, in Caesar's part of the town, while sending messengers to Achillas and exhorting him not to slacken in the business nor to fail in spirit, was slain by Caesar, his messengers having been informed against and arrested. This was the beginning of the Alexandrian war.

INDEX OF PERSONS AND PLACES

C. = Caesar; P. = Pompeius; cos. = consul or consulship.

The numbers, where they do not indicate dates, refer to the pages of the translation.

361

INDEX

Amanus (mons), mountain range between Cilicia and Syria, 239

Ambracia, district of Epirus N. of the sinus Ambracicus (Gulf of Arta), 247

Amphilochi, people of Amphilochia, between Epirus and Acarnania, E. of Gulf of Arta, 275

Amphipolis, town near the mouth of the Strymon (Kara-su) in Macedonia, 341

Ampius Balbus, T., an adherent of P., 347

Anas, river, now Guadiana, which separates S. Portugal from Spain, 57

Ancona, Ancone, town on the Adriatic coast of Italy, 19

Androsthenes, a Greek, acting as governor of Thessaly under Roman control, 309

Anquillaria, town near the River Bagrada and Cape Bon in Africa, about 20 miles from Clupea, 159

Antiochia, Antioch in Syria on the Orontes, 343

Antiochus, ruler of Commagene district in N.E. Syria, 201

Antonius, M., the famous triumvir with Octavian and Lepidus in 43. His brother G. Antonius was one of C.'s legates, 209

Apollonia, now Polina, town in Illyricum near the Adriatic, S. of Dyrrachium, 203

Apsus, now the Ergent, river of Illyricum, entering sea N. of Apollonia, 215

Apulia, district of S. Italy bordering on the Adriatic, 23

Aquitani, people of Aquitania, district of S.W. Gaul between the Garonne and the Pyrenees, 59

Arelate, now Arles, on the Rhone 55

Ariminum, now Rimini, on the Adriatic coast of N. Italy, 15

Ariobarzanes, king of Cappadocia

in Asia Minor, adherent of P., 201

Arretium, now Arezzo, about 40 miles S.E. of Florence, 19

Asculum, now Ascoli, town of Italy on the Tronto in the Marches, 25

Asia, the Roman province of Asia comprising the N.W. portion of Asia Minor, 9

Asparagium, town on the Genusus in Illyricum, S. of Dyrrachium, 239

Athamania, district in S.E. Epirus near border of Thessaly, 307

Athenae, Athens, 199

Attius: (i) Titus Attius Labienus, an able and trusted officer in C.'s army in Gaul, who deserted to P. at the beginning of the Civil War, 25; (ii) P. Attius Varus, propraetor of Africa 52, one of P.'s officers, 21; (iii) Q. Attius Varus, cavalry officer under C., 249; (iv) A. Attius, a Pelignian, serving under P., 27

Ausetani, a coast tribe dwelling on S. slope of Pyrenees, 83

Auster, S. wind, 233

Auximum, now Osimo, town 11 miles S. of Ancona, 21

Avaricum, now Bourges, chief town of the Bituriges, a Gallic tribe, 265

BAGRADA, now Medjerdah, river in Roman province of Africa, flowing into Gulf of Tunis, 161

Balbus, L. Cornelius, native of Gades, on friendly terms with P. and C., 225

Belica (porta), gate of Bêl or Baal, one of the gates of Utica, 161

Bessi, a Thracian tribe S. of Philippopolis, 203

Bibulus, M. Calpurnius, cos. with C. 59, commanded P.'s fleet in Adriatic, died after battle at Dyrrachium, 203

INDEX

Bithynia, district of N.W. Asia Minor near the Bosporus, 199

Boeotia, district of Greece above Attica, chief town Thebes, 201

Britannia, Britain, invaded by C. without much success in 55, 54: 77

Brundisium, now Brindisi, then as now the chief port of embarkation from Italy to Greece, 37

Bruttii, people of Bruttium, district of S. Italy below Lucania, 47

Brutus, D. Junius, in command of C.'s fleet at Massilia, afterwards one of the conspirators who murdered C. in 44, put to death by Antonius in 43, 55

Buthrotum, now Butrinto, town on mainland opposite Corcyra (Corfu), 217

Byllis, town in Illyricum on the River Aous (Voyussa), 252

CAECILIUS: (i) L. Caecilius Rufus, a senator on side of P., 35; (ii) L. Caecilius Metellus, tribune 49, also partisan of P., 51; (iii) T. Caecilius, centurion in P.'s army, 69

Caelius Rufus, M., praetor 49, socialistic reformer, 225

Caesar, see Iulius

Calagurritani, people of Calagurris, now perhaps Loarre, about 80 miles N.W. of Lerida, 83

Calenus, Q. Fufius, cos. 47, one of C.'s legates, 121

Calidius, M., candidate for cos. 50, partisan of C., 5

Calydon, town in Aetolia near entrance to Gulf of Corinth, 245

Camerinum, now Camerino, town in the Umbrian Apennines E. of Perugia, 25

Candavia, district of Illyricum W. of Lake Lychnitis, now Lake Ochrida in Albania, 211

Caninius Rebilus, G., one of C.'s legates, 41

Cantabri, a warlike tribe on N. coast of Spain, 57

Canuleius, L., one of C.'s legates, 257

Canusium, now Canosa, town in Apulia on the Aufidius (Ofanto), 37

Capitolium, the Roman Capitol, 13

Capua, town of Campania in Italy, about 3 miles from the present Capua, 19

Caralitani, people of Caralis, now Cagliari, in Sardinia, 47

Carmonenses, people of Carmo, now Carmone, in Andalusia, N.E. of Seville, 153

Casilinum, town on the Volturnus, near Capua, 227

Cassius, three brothers: (i) Q. Cassius Longinus, tribune 49, adherent of C., 5; (ii) G. Cassius Longinus, also tribune 49, adherent of P., 203; (iii) L. Cassius Longinus, fought on C.'s side, 245

Castra Cornelia, an old military station on a promontory near Utica established by Scipio Africanus in Second Punic War, 161

Castulonensis saltus, part of the Sierra Morena in Castile, N. of the Guadalquivir, 57

Cato, M. Porcius, whose suicide at Utica in 46 gained him the title of Uticensis, the well-known political opponent of Caesar, 7

Celtiberia, district occupied by a mixed race of Celts and Iberians, nearly equivalent to the provinces of Guadalajara and Cuenca, 57

Ceraunia (saxa), or Acroceraunia, rocky promontory in Epirus (Albania) forming the Bay of Avlona, 203

Cilicia, district of Asia Minor between the Taurus range and the sea, chief town Tarsus, 201

INDEX

364

INDEX

Delotarus, tetrarch of Galatia in Asia Minor, adherent of P., 201

Delphi, the seat of the famous oracle in Phocis in N. Greece, 275

Diana, goddess in Roman mythology, identified with Greek Artemis, 243

Dioscorides, an influential Greek in service of King Ptolomaeus, 353

Domitius: (i) L. Domitius Ahenobarbus, cos. 54, strong opponent of C., killed in 48, 11; (ii) Gn. Domitius Calvinus, cos. 53, commanded centre of C.'s army at Pharsalus, 245; (iii) Gn. Domitius, cavalry officer under Curio, 189

Domnilaus, chieftain from Galatia, adherent of P., 201

Dyrrachium, now Durazzo in Albania, the Greek port of embarkation for Italy, 39

EGUS, son of Adbucillus, chieftain of the Allobroges, 279

Elis, town in Elis, district in W. of Peloponnese, 347

Ephesus, capital of Roman province of Asia, famed for temple of Artemis (Diana), 243

Epirus, district of Greece facing Corcyra (Corfu), 201

FABIUS, G., one of C.'s legates, 55. There was a Pelignian named Fabius, a centurion of low grade, serving under Curio, 179

Fanum, now Fano, near Pisaurum, on the Adriatic coast of Italy, 19

Favonius, M., one of P.'s legates, 247

Firmum, now Fermo, town in Picenum on the Adriatic coast of Italy, 25

Fleginas, G., Roman knight from Placentia, adherent of C., 295

Frentani, Italian tribe bordering the Adriatic, S. of the Marrucini

and N. of the Larinates, in the modern Abruzzo, 37

Fulginius, Q., centurion in C.'s army, 69

Fulvius, Postumus, officer in C.'s army, 283

GABINIUS, A., cos. 58, fought in various Eastern campaigns, 201

Gades, Cadiz, 149

Gallia, Gaul, roughly corresponding to modern France, but Gallia Narbonensis is the Roman province roughly corresponding to Provence, and Gallia Cisalpina is Italy Gn. of the Po, 15

Gallonius, G., Roman knight, officer of P., 149

Genusus, now Schkumbe, river in Illyricum debouching between the Apsus and Dyrrachium, 303

Gergovia, town of Gaul on left bank of Allier a few miles S. of Clermont Ferrand, 301

Germania, the part of modern Germany that borders on the Rhine. C. had conquered this district during his Gallic campaigns, 15

Gomphi, now Palaeo-Episkopi on W. border of Thessaly, lying under the Pindus range, 309

Gracchi, the famous brothers Tiberius and Galus Gracchus, of the gens Sempronia, tribunes 133 and 121 respectively, popular reformers, both killed in civil strife, 15

Granius, A., Roman knight from Puteoli, serving under C., 295

HADRUMETUM, now Susa, town on E. coast of Tunis, 159

Hegesaretus, influential Thessalian, adherent of P., 245

Helvii, Gallic tribe, occupying what is now the department of Ardèche, 55

365

INDEX

Heraclia, town of Macedonia near the modern Monastir and Lake Ochrida, 307

Hercules, god of Roman mythology, who had a well-known temple near Gades (Cadiz), 149

Hiberus, River Ebro in N.E. Spain, 83

Hirrus, G. Lucilius, one of the tribunes of 53, partisan of P., 25

Hispalis, now Seville, on the Guadalquivir, 149

Hispania, Spain, divided into two provinces, Hispania Ulterior and Hispania Citerior, the former comprising Portugal and W. Spain, bounded roughly by a line drawn S.E. from Bragança to Almeria Bay; the latter Spain E. of a line drawn roughly from Oviedo to Almeria Bay, 33

IACETANI, tribe on coast of Spain N. of River Ebro, 83

Igilium, now Giglio, small island off coast of Tuscany, 53

Iguvium, now Gubbio, town in the Umbrian Apennines, 21

Ilerda, now Lerida, town in N.E. Spain, centre of campaign of 49, 57

Illurgavonenses, Spanish coast tribe S. of the Ebro, 83

Issa, now Lissa, island off the coast of Illyricum, 207

Isthmus, the isthmus of Corinth, 275

Italica, town on the bank of the Guadalquivir a few miles N. of Seville, 149

Iuba, king of Numidia, ally of P., killed at Thapsus 46, 11

Iulius. The chief representative of the gens Iulia is G. Julius Caesar, founder of the Romana Empire. Others are L. Julius Caesar, 15, a distant connexion, whose father was one of C.'s legates, and Sex.

Julius Caesar, also a relative, afterwards governor of Syria in 47, 155; the lex Iulia, an agrarian law, was passed by C. in his cos. 59, 23

LACEDAEMON, Sparta, 201

Laelius, D., naval officer under P., 203

Larinates, Italian tribe S.E. of the Frentani, between the River Biferno and Fortore, 37

Larisa, chief town of Thessaly on the Peneus, 311

Latinae feriae, the annual Latin festival, lasting 4 days, celebrated by C. in December 49, 199

Lentulus, see Cornelius.

Leptitani, people of Leptis minor on N. coast of Africa, 183

Liburnae (naves), Liburnian galleys, particular kind of light swift warship, named from Liburnia, a district of Illyricum, 207

Longinus, see Cassius.

Longus, G. Considius, one of P.'s officers, 159

Lucani, people of Lucania, district of S. Italy, N. of the Bruttii, 47

Lucceius, L., adherent of P., 221

Luceria, now Lucera, in N. of Apulia, 37

Lucilius Hirrus, G., tribune 53, partisan of P., 25

Lucretius, Q., Roman senator who died at Sulmo, which he held for P., 27. Another Q. Lucretius Vespillo served in P.'s fleet, 205

Lusitania, part of Hispania Ulterior, comprising Portugal S. of Oporto and a portion of W. Spain, 57

MACEDONIA, Roman province N. of Thessaly, E. of Lake Ochrida. The W. portion of it was known as Macedonia libera, 201

Magius, N., chief engineer to P., 37

INDEX

Manlius Torquatus, L., praetor 49, partisan of P., 37

Marcelius: (i) G. Claudius Marcellus, cos. 49, 11; (ii) his brother M. Claudius Marcelius, cos. 51, both adherents of P., 3

Marrucini, Italian tribe between Corfinium (Pentima in the Abruzzo) and the Adriatic, 37

Marsi, tribe in Central Italy E. of Rome round Lake Fucinus, 25

Massilia, Marseille, 53

Mauritania, land of the Mauri or Moors, N. coast of Africa from the Atlantic to Numidia, 11

Menedemus, a Greek, chief of Macedonia libera, 245

Messana, Messina, 127

Metellus, see Caecilius

Metropolis, now Palaeo-Kastro, town about 15 miles S.E. of Gomphi in Thessaly, 311

Milo, T. Annius, tribune 57, banished for murder of Clodius 52, 227

Minerva, goddess of Roman mythology, 347

Minucius Rufus, in command of Asiatic ships in P.'s fleet, 205

Murcus, L. Statius, one of C.'s legates, 217

Mytilenae, chief town of the island of Lesbos, 343

NARBO, Narbonne, chief town of Gallia Narbonensis, 57

Nasidius, L., Roman knight, naval officer under P., 127

Naupactus, now Lepanto, town in Aetolia at entrance to Gulf of Corinth, 245

Neapolis, Naples, 227

Noricum, country between the Danube and the Alps, chief town Noreia, now Neumarkt in Carinthia, 29

Numidae, people of Numidia, part of Roman province of Africa, 161

Nymphaeum, town on bay of Medua in Illyricum, near Lissus, 283

OCTAVIUS, M., commanded ships in P.'s fleet, 203

Octogesa, probably now Mequinenza on left bank of Ebro and on the right of the Segre, in the angle formed by their junction, 87

Opimius, M., officer in P.'s army, 251

Orchomenus, town in Boeotia in N. Greece, 275

Oricum, Palaeo-Kastro, at S. extremity of Bay of Avlona, separated from Adriatic by Acroceraunian promontory, 205

Oscenses, people of Osca, now Huesca, about 60 miles N.W. of Lerida, 83

Otacilius, Crassus, adherent of P., 235

PALAESTE, town on Acroceraunian promontory in Epirus, 205

Parthi, the Parthians, a powerful and aggressive Eastern nation with whom the Romans waged constant war, 241

Parthini, a tribe dwelling N. of Dyrrachium with chief town Parthus, 211

Pedius, Q., relation of C., cos. 43, 229

Peligni, Italian tribe E. of the Marsi and Lake Fucinus, 25

Pelusium, town at the mouth of one of the branches of the Nile, about 20 miles S.E. of Port Said, 343

Pergamum, now Bergama, town of Mysia in Asia Minor on the Caicus, 241

Petra, now Sasso Bianco, a rocky height on Illyrian coast S. of Dyrrachium, 255

367

INDEX

Petraeus, a young Thessalian of influence, adherent of C., 245

Petreius, M., legate of P. in Spain, defeated at Thapsus 46 and committed suicide, 57

Pharus, island off Alexandria with famous lighthouse also called Pharus, 357

Philippus, L. Marcius, cos. 56, second husband of Atia, mother of Augustus; his son of the same name was tribune in 49, 11

Phoenice, Phoenicia, district on coast of Syria with chief towns Tyre and Sidon, 199

Picenum, district of Italy lying between the Apennines and the Adriatic, 21

Pisaurum, now Pisaro, town on the Adriatic coast of Italy, 19

Piso Caesoninus, L. Calpurnius, cos. 58. His daughter Calpurnia became Caesar's wife in 59, 11

Placentia, now Piacenza, Roman colony on the Padus (Po), 295

Plancus, L. Munatius, one of C.'s legates, cos. 42, 61

Plotius, M., officer in P.'s army, 225

Pompeius: (i) Gn. Pompeius Magnus, born 106, murdered after battle of Pharsalus 48; (ii) his son Gn. Pompeius commanded a division of the fleet under Bibulus, killed at Munda 45, 201. The lex Pompeia de ambitu was passed by Pompeius in his cos. 52 to check bribery at elections, 197

Pomponius, M., commanded detachment of C.'s fleet, 339

Pontus, district of Asia Minor bordering on the Pontus Euxinus, 199

Pothinus, tutor of the young king Ptolomaeus and controller of the kingdom during his minority, 351

Ptolomaeus, king of Egypt, 12th of his dynasty, aged 13, son of

Ptolomaeus Auletes, joint sovereign with his sister Cleopatra, 343

Ptolomais, town in Phoenice, now Akka or Acre, 347

Puleio, T., centurion in C.'s army, 291

Pupius, L., centurion in P.'s army, 21

Puteoli, now Pozzuoli, town in Campania near Naples, 295

Pyrenaei (saltus), Pyrenean passes: there were two well-known routes over the Pyrenees between Narbo and N.E. Spain, 57

RAUCILLUS, son of Adbucillus, chieftain of the Allobroges, 279

Ravenna, town of Gallia Cisalpina in N. Italy, on the Adriatic, 11

Rebilus, see Caninius

Rhascypolis, Macedonian cavalry officer under P., 201

Rhodanus, Rhone, 125

Rhodus, Rhodes, island and town, 343

Roscius Fabatus, L., praetor 49, one of C.'s legates, 7

Rubrius, L., captured at Corfinium, 35

Rufus, cognomen of a number of Romans, see Acutius, Caecilius, Caelius, Sulpicius, Vibullius, cp. William Rufus; Marcius Rufus, quaestor under Curio, 159

Ruteni, Gallic tribe occupying what is now the department of Aveyron, chief town Segodunum, now Rodez, 75

Rutilius Lupus, P., praetor 49, partisan of P., 37

SABINUS, G. Calvisius, one of C.'s legates, 245

Saburra, one of King Juba's generals, 183

Sacrativir, M., Roman knight from Capua, adherent of C., 295

INDEX

Sadala, son of Cotys, the Thracian ruler, joined P., 201

Sallyes, or Salluvii, a Gallic tribe N. of Marseille, 55

Salonae, town near Spalato in Dalmatia, 207

Sardinia, with Corsica, constituted a Roman province, 47

Sason, now Sasino, small island N. of Acroceraunian promontory, 205

Saturninus, L. Apuleius, tribune 100, proposer of agrarian law in democratic interest, killed the same year by senatorial troops, 15

Saxa, L. Decidius, officer in C.'s army, 93

Scaeva, centurion in C.'s army, 273

Scipio, Q. Caecilius Metellus Pius, cos. with P. the latter half of 52. P. married his daughter Cornelia after Julia's death, 3

Scribonius: (i) G. Scribonius Curio, a brilliant and dissolute young Roman, tribune 50, whose adherence was bought by C.; he died in battle near Utica, 21; (ii) L. Scribonius Libo, naval officer under P., engaged in peace negotiations; his sister Scribonia was second wife of Augustus, 41

Septimius, L., military tribune, who with Achillas murdered P., 345

Serapion, influential Greek in the service of Ptolomaeus, 353

Sertorius, G., Roman officer who possessed great influence in Spain and headed a formidable revolt finally quelled by P. in 80, 35

Servilius Vatia Isauricus, P., cos. with C. in 48; his father, cos. 79, gained title of Isauricus by his victories over the Isaurians, 197

Sicilia, Sicily, Roman province from which Rome drew much of its corn supply, 39

Sicoris, now Segre, a tributary of the Ebro, 59

Staberius, L., adherent of P., 213

Sulla, *see* Cornelius

Sulmonenses, people of Sulmo, Ovid's birthplace, among the Peligni, 27

Sulpicius: (i) P. Sulpicius Rufus, one of C.'s legates, 103; (ii) Ser Sulpicius, Roman senator in suite of King Juba, 193

Syria, Roman province established by P. in 63, capital Antioch, 9

Tarcondarius Castor, officer from Galatia or Gallograecia in P.'s army, 201

Tarracina, now Terracina, formerly called Anxur, on coast of Latium, 37

Tarraco, now Tarragona, in Spain, 101

Taurois, fortified post near Marseille, 129

Terentius: (i) M. Terentius Varro, famed for his erudition and voluminous writings, propraetor of Hispania Ulterior in 49, friend of P. and C., 57; (ii) A. Terentius Varro Murena, partisan of P., 223

Thebae, Thebes, chief town of Boeotia, 275

Theophanes, Greek of Miletus, a writer, and adherent of P., 221

Thermus, Q. Minucius, propraetor of Asia 52–50, 21

Thessalia, Thessaly, part of Roman province of Macedonia but with some degree of autonomy, chief town Larisa, 201

Thracia, Thrace, between the Danube and the Aegean, 201

Thurii, town of the Bruttii in S. Italy, on the Mediterranean coast somewhere near the modern Belvedere, 229

Tiburtius, L., adherent of C., 225

369

INDEX

Tillius, Q., adherent of C., 257

Torquatus, *see* Manlius

Tralles, town in Asia Minor N. of the Maeander (Mindere) in the vilayet of Smyrna, 347

Transpadanae coloniae, Roman colonies N. of the Padus (Po), 321

Trebonius, G., one of C.'s legates. As tribune 55 he proposed the lex Trebonia which prolonged C.'s provincial administration of Gaul for a second period of 5 years, 55

Triarius, *see* Valerius

Tubero, L. Aelius, nominated governor of Africa 49, 47

Tuticanus, Gaul and Roman knight, son of a Roman senator, 295

UTICA, chief town of the Roman province of Africa at the mouth of the River Bagrada, 49

VALERIUS: (i) Q. Valerius, one of C.'s legates, 47; (ii) L. Valerius Flaccus, praetor 63, governor of the province of Asia 48, 271; (iii) P. Valerius Flaccus, son of the former, killed at Dyrrachium,

271; (iv) G. Valerius Triarius, officer in P.'s army, 203

Varro, *see* Terentius

Varus, *see* Attius

Varus, Sex Quintilius, quaestor, captured by C. at Corfinium, 35

Varus, now Var, river in Gallia Narbonensis debouching a few miles W. of Nice, 121

Vatinius, P., one of C.'s legates, 223

Vettones, Spanish tribe settled between the Douro and the Gaudiana, covering the province of Salamanca, 57

Vibius Curius, cavalry officer under C., 37

Vibo, now Bivona, town on W. coast of Bruttium in Italy near Monteleone, 339

Vibullius Rufus, L., officer of P. employed in peace negotiations, 25

Volcae Arecomici, Gallic tribe on Gulf of Lyons, with chief town Nemausus (Nimes), 55

Volcatius Tullus, G., one of C.'s officers, 271

Volusenus Quadratus, G., cavalry officer under C., 281

370

MAPS

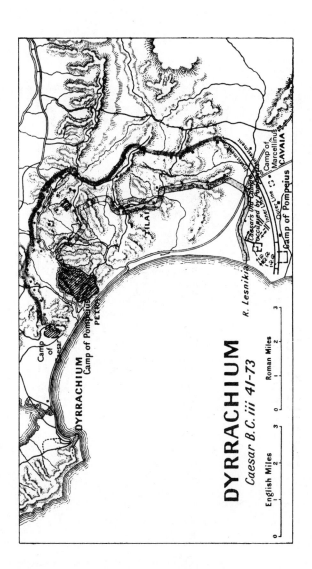

DYRRACHIUM

Caesar B.C. iii 41–73

Camp of
Caesar

DYRRACHIUM

Camp of Pompeius
PETRA

R. Lesnikia

Camp of
Marcellinus

Camp of Pompeius

CAVAIA

Caesar's inner line
blockaded by Pompeius

Outer line

Winter line

English Miles

Roman Miles

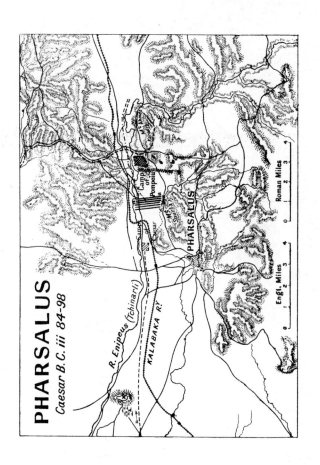

PHARSALUS
Caesar B.C. iii 84-98

R. Enipeus (Tchinarli)

KALABAKA R.

Camp of Caesar

Camp of Pompeius

M. 133

M. 190

PHARSALUS

Roman Miles
0   1   2   3   4

Engl. Miles
0   1   2   3   4

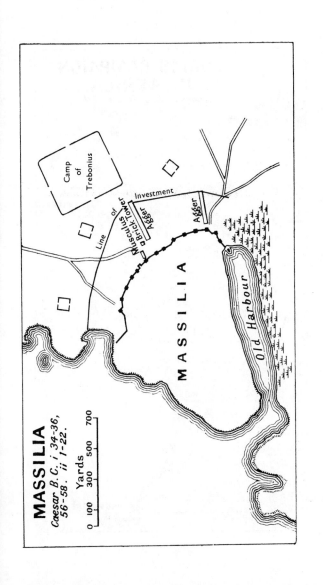

MASSILIA

Caesar B.C. i 34-36,
56-58. ii 1-22.

Yards

0   100   300   500   700

Camp
of
Trebonius

Line of Investment

Musculus or
Brick Tower

Agger

Agger

MASSILIA

Old Harbour

CURIOS CAMPAIGN
IN AFRICA
Caesar B.C. ii 23-44

Apollinis Promontorium

Mercurii Promontorium (C. Bon)

UTICA

ANQUILLARIA?

Castra Cornelia

GULF of TUNIS

R. Bagrada

Herculis Promontorium

CLUPEA

TUNIS

CARTHAGE

HADRUMETUM

English Miles
0   5   10   15   20

Roman Miles
0   5   10   15   20   25

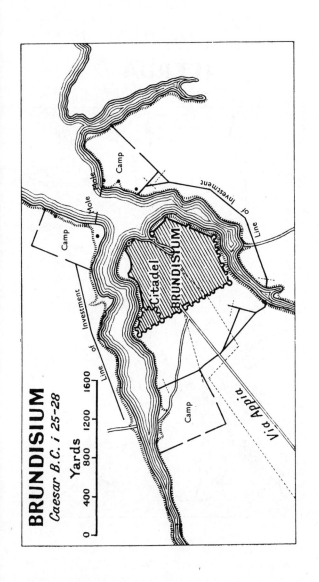

BRUNDISIUM

Caesar B.C. i 25–28

Yards

0   400   800   1200   1600

Line of Investment

Camp

Hole

Camp

Citadel

BRUNDISIUM

Line of Investment

Camp

Via Appia

ILERDA

Caesar B. C. i 38-64

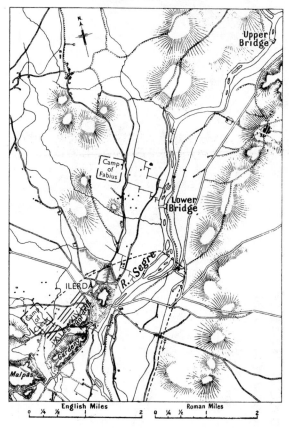

English Miles
0 ¼ ½ 1 2

Roman Miles
0 ¼ ½ 1 2